I, Audrey

All About Audrey I

I, Audrey

by George Logan

I, Audrey

All about Audrey I

by

George Logan

ISBN: 9798618026185

Big Aud Books

39 Avenue de Verdun
87210 Le Dorat
France

Dedication

To all those depicted within.

Principally, to Nicky, Connie, Wilma,

Dorothy, Shirley, Angie, Elaine.

And to my family, in recognition of their inexhaustible

patience and support, despite the trials I imposed on them

'And then there's Audrey, lovely Audrey;
If life were tawdry and impoverished as before
She might not like me, she might not want me.
Without my plant, she might not love me any more.'

Little Shop of Horrors
© Howard Ashman 1982

Contents

Introduction

September 2015

Any attempt to recreate, recapture or relive the past is a problematic exercise. Memories elude one, dates recalled refuse to coincide, whole aeons seem to vanish into the void. I have done my best, but have certainly had to extrapolate occasionally. Luckily, one of the persons who shared that time with me is still around, and between us we have been able to cudgel out the order of events.

Kind people have said on a few occasions, "You should write a book", when, after rather too many glasses of wine, I have recounted some slightly *risqué* incident from my distant past; an incident which I hope will at least amuse. Maybe they are just being generous. Perhaps, behind my back, I am considered as much of a bore as John X. or Tom Y.

Be that as it may, I have come round to thinking that some memories of that distant era ought to be preserved. Why? For historical reasons, maybe; for my own satisfaction, and as a kind of personal voyage into the past, certainly; and of course, for anyone who may be interested enough to read them. They tell of a period now completely gone, and in danger of being forgotten entirely. Gay life—indeed life itself—has changed beyond recognition since 1962, when I first trotted up Glasgow's Hope Street *en route* to adventure.

But human beings, I am convinced, have not fundamentally altered. And maybe a few of the scary feelings of confusion and exclusion I experienced in my early years will resonate with some young person of the current generation. If they do, perhaps my memoirs will serve some purpose beyond self-indulgent rambling; possibly they will help to reassure whomever it may be that You Are Not Alone. A reassurance I personally longed for, and eventually found.

I appreciate that this book may initially be a slightly confusing read; stories and anecdotes concerning a group of men, some of whom are referred to regularly, but not always, in female terms. Bear with me, please, that's the way it was, and you get used to it in time. It took me a wee while, myself.

It may be difficult for a young gay man today to believe that there was ever a time when the sub-culture—or at least the part of it I

1

inhabited—aped so slavishly the mores and attitudes of the so-called 'straight' majority; when gay couples were made up of 'husbands' and 'wives', and the 'wives' were frequently and unthinkingly addressed and referred to by their peers in the feminine. Such a social structure belongs, surely, in a museum, along with the feudal system, the doctrine of Papal Infallibility and the dinosaurs?

Perhaps it does. But museums are meant to be visited. Consider this an instructive and, hopefully, an agreeable history lesson.

Discovering one is gay, and dealing with the consequences is, I am convinced, never easy, despite the progress that has been made. But it is hopefully less fraught in the twenty-first century than it was when an ill-considered move might result in a police record or even a prison sentence. It is surely more straightforward. I am not certain that it is as much fun, or as heart-stoppingly exciting as it was in those far off days.

Or is that just nostalgia? Very possibly.

I recently had occasion to revisit Glasgow. I have not lived there for more than fifty years, and the few returns I have made have been either work-related—'Hinge and Bracket' toured extensively north of the border—or, in later years, to attend family funerals. But this trip was rather different.

I had been invited to take part in a television documentary whose remit was to examine the splendours and miseries of growing up gay in Scotland before the decriminalisation of homosexual activity between consenting adults. Effectively, the very subject this book deals with. The idea was irresistible.

It was an interesting experience. Much, I found, has changed; other things have not. In some areas the very layout of the streets as I knew them has altered; the geography is different; quite a few of the landmarks I remember have disappeared. But Central Station is still there, and the surrounding quarter is much as it was.

And one thing that is unchanged is the character of the Scottish people. Wry, kindly, humorous, friendly and infinitely helpful. I had forgotten how wonderful they are. That had somehow slipped to the back of my mind. I was delighted to be reminded that these are still 'my ain folk'.

I decided not to show my face in any of the gay hangouts in the city, of which there is now a considerable number. The haunts that I knew are long gone, of course. And gay society is still, just as it was in my glory days, the preserve of the young and desirable. I had no wish to appear in their midst like a spectre at the feast, an ancient monument, a relic of an age long gone. No, I leave these gatherings with pleasure (and maybe a little relief) to those who can benefit from them, just as I did so very long ago.

Every incident in this book happened just as it is related, although the order of events may not always precisely reflect the reality. Partly due to imperfect memory, and partly in the interests of effect—life isn't always as well-constructed as one might wish. But everything took place as I have described it, and every character existed and behaved as I have indicated. And sometimes they behaved far worse.

So here it is, the story of the making of Audrey, and her early adventures in a world that was, it now seems, eternally amusing, often exciting, occasionally terrifying, but never dull. The world of my youth.

A certain amount of discretion has been invoked. To pursue the museum analogy, I know where the mummies are stored. So, just in case some of the friends (and enemies) pictured within are still alive, a few names have been changed to protect the guilty. The innocent, naturally, have nothing to worry about.

The cast list is extensive, and since some of the actors play more than one rôle, I thought it might be helpful to list them at the end of the book.

I have no more to say. Let the rest speak for itself

Welcome to the séance. Make yourself comfortable, sit down at the table, turn down the lights, everyone join hands. It's time to consult the spirits.

It's time to raise the dead.

1. Don't Treat Me Like a Child

Now just because I'm in my teens
And I still go to school.
Don't think that I dream childish dreams,
I'm nobody's fool.
Helen Shapiro, 1961

1944–1951

I am George Logan.

Born on the seventh of July, nineteen-forty-four, the seventh day of the seventh month. And, according to my mother, at the seventh hour.

However, a later perusal of my birth certificate revealed that I was born at seven in the evening, which is officially the nineteenth hour. And since not just single, but double summer time was in force in 1944, during the war years, really at the seventeenth hour.

Well, there's one more lucky seven in there.

My birth certificate also disclosed the surprising information that my parents, George Logan, son of George and Sarah Logan, and Georgina Logan, *née* Rae, were married in November 1943, rather less than a decent nine months prior to my birth; and at eight and a half pounds, I don't suppose I was premature.

To fully appreciate why I call this 'surprising', you would have to have known my mother, ever the model of propriety and respectability. To this day I find it difficult to credit that she yielded prior to the nuptials. Of course, it is quite likely, given the one month shortfall, that she didn't know at the time that I was imminent. Not that that changes anything.

My mother liked to tell the story of how, when she was pregnant, she visited a 'spaewife', or fortune teller. The inquirer was expected to take along an egg—uncooked—and the divinatrix would reveal the future by cracking the egg and examining its contents.

The oracle reported that the child she was expecting would be a boy, and that this boy would become a healer.

As I grew up into my twenties, this outcome seemed less and less likely.

But it is well known that oracles speak in riddles. A healer is also a doctor. And I would, indeed, become a doctor of sorts.

Distinctly middle-class, my family; well, the Logan side of it, anyway. The Raes were from a rather lower social rung, definitely working-class, although highly respectable members of that order; with

5

one notable exception. My mother's mother, Granny Rae, another Georgina.

Granny Rae, originally from Northern Ireland, was not *entirely* respectable. She was a bit flighty, liked a drink rather more than the next person, and, despite her lack of means, knew how to enjoy herself. When my sister Jennifer and I were parked on her, as we were from time to time, we saw an altogether different side of life, and we revelled in our grandmother's lively, devil-may-care attitude. She allowed us both to do pretty much as we pleased when she was charged with looking after us, and was quite happy to lie shamelessly (particularly to my mother, who strongly disapproved of Granny's shenanigans) to avoid criticism of her free and easy lifestyle.

I suspect that that's where I got some of my more bohemian qualities from.

My mother had three brothers and one sister. Two of my uncles on that side of the family, Joseph and Sandy, offer an interesting study in contrasts.

Uncle Sandy had married a German girl while on army service near the end of the Second War. When you consider that we had been on opposite sides for six years, and that many of my compatriots died in that same struggle, it says something remarkable about the Scots that my Aunt Kitty, or Käthe, never encountered the least prejudice or discrimination after she moved to our country. On the contrary, she told me, she settled in painlessly, and was readily accepted as an honorary Scot. I think the general attitude was that she couldn't help being born a Kraut, and it was not her fault if her fellow-countrymen were a bit thick, and daft enough to take on the might of the Highland Light Infantry.

Uncle Joseph, on the other hand, had committed the unpardonable sin—he had married a Catholic. Though he produced four daughters, we didn't tend to see a great deal of that side of the family. I don't think Granny Georgina, staunch Protestant and enthusiastic supporter of the Orange Walk, ever really forgave him.

Better Hitler than the Pope, it appears.

My father was born in 1902, so he was forty-two years old when I arrived. I was told later that it was a great relief for his mother, Granny Sarah Logan, to finally see him settled. All four of his siblings had been married for years.

That business taken care of, Granny Logan turned up her toes and died a few months before I arrived.

I have always assumed that it was from her side of the family that our artistic propensities originated. In addition to myself and my sister, four of our cousins made a career of one sort or another in the theatre.

Going further back in search of the source, my paternal grandfather and great-grandfather were in the wines and spirits business—both died in their thirties from causes alcoholic. So Granny Sarah Logan was, I presume, the vehicle for the transmission of the thespian impulse.

As my father married late in life, all these theatrical cousins were considerably older than were my sister and I. I remember one of them, Margo Henderson, twenty years our senior, insisting that we not refer to her as 'Aunty Margo' in front of her colleagues, but make it clear that we were her *cousins*.

My sister Jennifer arrived two years after me. Close in age, we were, and remain, close in life. Our family, the four of us, lived in a small but comfortable bungalow in the Royal Burgh of Rutherglen, on the south side of the Clyde, a few miles from the centre of Glasgow.

My parents could hardly have been more different in character. Apart from the sizeable age gap, in personality they were polar opposites.

My father, who had a good job and a position of some responsibility in the vehicle trade, was gregarious and outgoing, the life and soul of the party. He had a large circle of acquaintances, some of them business contacts, others friends of long standing. He enjoyed socialising, and in such a setting he was usually to be seen with a cigarette in one hand and a glass in the other. A pose I myself would come to feature regularly in later years.

My mother, on the other hand, was self-contained, reticent and restrained, and at her happiest in a domestic setting. Possibly because she was aware that she had moved up a step socially in marrying my father, she was the *sine qua non* of middle class rectitude and propriety. She was considered attractive, even beautiful, and when she dressed up to attend some function or other with my father, perhaps a party or a business dinner-and-dance, she shone, however reluctantly.

Unlike my father, she was a non-smoker, and drank very rarely. And unlike him, with his easy-going and relaxed attitude, she had a fiery and easily-roused temper. We children, particularly myself, were never spared a whack if we misbehaved, to an extent that would probably be considered barbaric today. But this was at a time when physical chastisement was considered acceptable, even desirable, both within the family and in an educational environment. I can't see that it had any long-term ill effect on me and my generation. On the contrary, I feel that a little more of the same, judiciously applied, might considerably reduce the severity of some of the problems society struggles with today.

It was my mother who was the main presence in my childhood. My father's business commitments, meetings with clients, he claimed, kept him away from home regularly; and I came to understand that it didn't take much to persuade him to stay out just a little longer and have another drink or two. Another trait I seem to have inherited.

The irregularity of his hours and the unpredictability of his comings and goings became an increasing source of friction between my parents as I grew up. Their frequent noisy arguments when he arrived home several hours later than he had promised—and sometimes that was very late indeed—caused me considerable anguish from time to time. Maybe because I already felt insecure for other reasons.

As a child, I didn't really feel I knew my father well, and it was to my mother that I turned when things troubled me. But there were matters going on in my head that I could not share even with her.

I'm not sure if I wondered if I was really a girl because I was attracted to boys, or if I fancied boys because I had a suspicion that I might be a girl. Whichever it was, this odd delusion stayed with me for a long time.

I was sexually aware, and aware of my difference, from a very young age, indeed from as far back as I can remember. I can recall these feelings very clearly, and a psychiatrist I discussed the matter with in later life confirmed to me that a few children are indeed tuned in to sex and sexuality from a very young age, from three or four years old, or even younger.

As it no doubt continues to do, the cinema played a large part in forming my generation's personal image of Who One Was. But while my male peers were identifying with the square jawed heroes of the latest macho epic, Roy Rogers, John Wayne, Audie Murphy or Rory Calhoun, I was seeing myself as Linda Darnell or Veronica Lake.

I didn't mind, now and then, assuming the rôle of the Good Girl, the pure and virtuous heroine, Ivanhoe's Rowena or Robin Hood's Maid Marion. But I much preferred being the Bad Girl, Barbara Stanwick in *Double Indemnity* or Lana Turner in *The Postman Always Rings Twice*. The girl who dominated men and used them for her own advantage; who flaunted her sexuality to get what she wanted; who was 'in charge', and who was almost masculine in her proactive attitude; and who usually ended badly, but had a hell of a time on the way.

I didn't encounter the unique Mae West until later in life, but if I had, she would have been my ideal. She had all the qualities I have described, but added to those a seasoning of outrageous humour. And I have always had a taste for the light touch concealing the iron will.

But for the time being I was Bette Davis in *The Letter* or Marlene Dietrich in *Witness for the Prosecution*.

And it was a source of deep concern to me, and the cause of much interior anguish, that I knew that this was, in some hazy, undefined way, Wrong.

Initially, these feelings were emotional and vague, though uncomfortable and troubling. They weren't directly sexual. But all that changed one day.

I am playing 'doctors and nurses' with a few local children, two girls and a boy, innocent enough experimentation, inquisitiveness, nothing more. I am about seven or eight. An errand boy, fourteen perhaps, is passing on his bike, and stops, seeing what we are up to.

"What do you think of this?" he says, unbuttoning his trousers, and displaying his erection. I am simultaneously scared and enthralled.

I will dream and fantasise about this event for years to come, wishing it would happen again.

No doubt some people might consider it was that very incident that shaped my sexuality, that made me the way I am. But I don't believe this to be true. My gender uncertainty dated from much earlier in my life. What this event did, though, was in some manner to fix it, to focus it and clarify it, and to tie it up firmly and irrevocably with the body and with sex.

As a child, most of my time was spent in the small town where I grew up. It was there I went to school, socialised and played. But the city of Glasgow was only a short bus ride away. And later, as I grew into my teens, and began to question my own nature, it was in the city that I spent an increasing amount of my time.

1951–1955

I didn't really, all in all, have many problems at school. I was, I am sure, noticeably soft-natured and effeminate, and I have heard from people I came to know later, friends who share my tastes, that they suffered bullying, and that their childhoods were made miserable as a result.

There is no doubt in my mind that my schoolmates knew, without

9

understanding exactly how, that I was different, that I was a kind of alien. Children, unencumbered by preconceptions and received wisdom, sense these things. I was made aware, or became aware, without anything being said directly, that I didn't quite fit the mould.

And all through my childhood it remained with me, haunted me. That sexual curiosity, the need to know, the urges, the desires, unformulated but insistent.

Several times between the ages of eight and twelve I seized the chance to experiment with male playmates as curious as myself. Nothing that could be counted as true sexual activity took place between us. But I was fascinated by the differences in size and conformation, and by the phenomenon of erection.

I am eleven, and in the eleven-plus class, then called 'the qually', or Qualifying class. I have a huge crush on Alan Maitland, a classmate who is the son of a well-to-do local butcher. Alan is my best friend in school, a handsome boy who always has money and sweets which he shares with me. But I am far too shy where my feelings and emotions are involved to suggest or even encourage any physical intimacy.

However, at the same time, Gordon Andrews, who sits next to me in class, is forever nudging me and indicating the bulge inside his trousers, which he makes tense and twitch under my fascinated gaze.

Stuart Logan, no relation, and no more than twelve at the time, tells some of the other boys in our class about how often he masturbates, and about the quantity of spunk he is able to produce. When he gives a demonstration to two of us in the cloakroom, it is all I can do to keep my hands to myself.

I no longer recall exactly why I decided that I wanted to learn to play the piano. But I do remember that music entranced me from as far back as my memory goes. My father sang well, and had hoped in his younger years to follow in the family theatrical tradition. However an insuperable stage fright apparently prevented him from pursuing this ambition. But my sister and I were familiar with his choice of music from our earliest years.

He had spent some time in America, and, since he was so much older than my mother, his tastes were those of an earlier generation—we listened to Sophie Tucker, we enjoyed the music of Bing Crosby, Jimmy Durante, Sid Phillips and his band, and the like.

But somehow—and who knows where it came from?—I acquired a taste for what we at that time called 'classical' music. *Housewives'*

Choice, broadcast every morning, played the occasional sample, and I remember being particularly caught up by the music of Tchaikovsky— its open-hearted emotionalism resonated with me, and seemed to give expression to the well-hidden personal uncertainty I lived with. For my awareness of my own difference continued to trouble my thoughts constantly, despite the fact that I soon learned to mask my feelings under a calm and apparently placid exterior.

But it was another favourite that, I think, set me firmly on the road. This was a novelty record called *Sparky's Magic Piano*. It told the tale of a young boy who despaired of his piano lessons, until the day he discovered that his piano was a 'magic' one, one that could play anything. I remember the thrilling and turbulent racket of Chopin's 'Revolutionary' Etude, and Sparky's ecstatic reception as he played for an appreciative audience. I decided that that's what I would learn to do. They would be applauding me; I would be admired and validated.

How fortunate I was that my parents agreed. A baby grand piano was purchased (no simple domestic upright for the Logan family), and I was enrolled at the age of seven with a local piano teacher, Miss Burns.

I certainly seemed to have a natural talent. I don't mean to imply that a child prodigy was suddenly revealed to the world. But after a year or two it was obvious that I was going to make a competent musician.

I had a remarkably acute ear. I was able after a few years of lessons to reproduce just about anything I heard. Not perfectly, not note-for-note; but a convincing facsimile. This facility, the ability to fake, caused me to neglect my sight-reading, and to this day I don't sight-read fluently. Oh, I can read music perfectly well. But I am nowhere near those who can sit down and pump out the bare notes of anything put in front of them with ease.

After three or four years, I moved on to another local teacher, Mr Moyes, who was considered to be a step up from Miss Burns. Mr Moyes was blind, but a well-schooled, rounded, and knowledgeable musician. He had an enormous collection of gramophone records, which he would loan to me from time to time. Under him I progressed rapidly, passed all the standard piano examinations, and even won a couple of regional competitions. My proud parents decided it was time I moved onto higher things.

I was fifteen when I started taking lessons with Miss Kathleen Belford, who, apart from teaching, was a professional pianist of some distinction. Miss Belford taught at the Royal Scottish Academy of Music, in Glasgow city centre. So every Friday evening I would pack

11

my brief case and catch the bus into Glasgow for my lesson.

1955—1961

When I moved on to secondary schooling, my 'alien-ness' was as much a source of interest as of criticism; and for one or two, happily, a source of fascination. Though I was occasionally on the receiving end of the odd derogatory comment—'jessie' would have been the term, implying effeminacy and girlishness—there were usually as many ready to defend as to criticise. I quickly learned the benefits that accrue from cultivating the friendship of the rougher element in my classes. For the 'tough' boys I became a sort of weird *protégé*. And they were just the type that I admired most—they were masculine and everything that I was not. To them I was strange, odd. But witty and smart-mouthed, cheeky and defiant of authority.

I only got away with that because I always did well academically. I was, and remain, about the laziest person in the world. But I have wide interests and a retentive memory. I practically lived in the library, read constantly, anything and everything. I passed exams easily and without doing much studying. Though I was not the best student in my class, I was in the top two or three.

And not only was I an A-student—I was artistic. All the gifts, apparently, had been showered upon me.

I regularly played the piano for school events, for the shows we put on every year in the Rutherglen Repertory Theatre. I impressed my schoolmates on one occasion by following up a performance of some dazzling Chopin piece or other with my own version of *Roulette*, a 1959 hit record by pianist Russ Conway.

Shortly after that, myself and two friends who played the guitar formed what we called a 'pop group', which had some success locally. We played for school dances and at local parties; the hits of the day, pop tunes of the time—Bobby Rydell's *Wild One*, Cliff's *Living Doll*, Freddy Canon's *New Orleans*. I think we were regarded with slight suspicion by a few parents and other adults. Maybe we were a little on the wild side; maybe we were going to lead their kids astray; maybe we would encourage them into inappropriate behaviour with our espousal of this wicked pop music.

And I was only too happy to lead their offspring into inappropriate behaviour now and then, if not quite in the direction that concerned them.

I suppose I am twelve or thirteen when I first wank Darren Finlay off, in the cellar under our house. Darren is two years older than me, good-looking and something of a heart-throb among the girls in the school playground. And Darren loves displaying his considerable assets to anyone who is interested. I am definitely interested.

I am by now maturing physically myself, and my feelings start to harden along with everything else. Encounters are no longer motivated by an unfocused but sexual curiosity, but by an urgent lust. A couple of boys with whom I have experimented innocently enough in the past share stolen moments with me now and then. The object, hazy and ill-defined before, has now become clear. Orgasm is the goal.

Ian Moorhead and I are concealed in a secret spot together during a game of hide-and-seek. I am surprised (and delighted) when he takes my hand and pushes it firmly down on the erection in his trousers, then moves my hand back and forward on it, his intention unmistakable. I unbutton him and toss him off vigorously.

I am even more surprised when, a day or two later, his brother Andy, a year older, does the same thing.

Am I getting a reputation as a bit of a flirt?

There was never any hint of affection in these encounters. Kissing? No, certainly not that, much as I would have relished it. I instinctively understood that any move in that direction on my part would have been decidedly unwelcome. But it was what people did, wasn't it? If they were 'in love', or even just about to embark on a conjunction, sanctified or otherwise. You'd see it on screen, those lips pressed together, obviously it felt good and was a part of the whole experience. But I hadn't had the chance to try it.

He, whoever he might be, wanted me for mechanical manipulation, for my *otherness*, for the feel of a foreign hand on the part that up till then had only known the grip of his own.

Kissing? Ah well. maybe I have not been entirely accurate there. What about good old Ginger? How could I have forgotten…

May 1958

I am in second year, aged thirteen. Among the older pupils, those in fourth or fifth year, around fifteen or sixteen, there are a few boys who seem to have passed from boyhood to adulthood painlessly, who have become young men without ever having been adolescents. They are the boys the girls in my own year drool over. Darren Finlay, already mentioned, is one such, Ian Hetherington another. David Gourlay of the Brylcreemed hair is dark and impossibly handsome.

Yes, I drool over these young gents too. As I have mentioned, I have actually come to know Mr D. Finlay's physical charms quite well, but of course that is just a hand job, nothing personal at all in it, I might as well have been a cunningly designed and well-oiled machine.

'Ginger' Hastie is definitely not one of those gods of the fourth year. He wears glasses (as do I); he is thin and intellectual looking, with flaming red hair, a studious type; and I don't think I have even given him more than a passing glance; till the day I wake from a solitary sun-bathing doze in Stonelaw Woods to find him on top of me.

Kissing me.

Well, if this is kissing, I don't get it. He is pushing his mouth against my lips so hard he is in danger of loosening my front teeth, which have never been my best feature, and need to be maintained at the just-about-reasonable level of straightness they currently occupy.

He is grinding his pelvis against me, which, on the other hand, I find quite acceptable, indeed, agreeably stimulating. But this kissing thing; what is all the fuss about? It's just uncomfortable.

"Open your mouth," he grunts.

I don't really have a choice, it's that or suffocate.

So I do.

Ah, now I get it. They don't do it quite like that in the movies.

Just to clarify the picture, we are both completely dressed, the only skin-to-skin contact is in the facial region.

A few more pelvic thrusts, a groan or two, and it's over. The whole thing hasn't lasted more than thirty seconds. OK, maybe forty.

'Hastie' by name, hasty...

He gets off me and stands up. And undoes his belt and trousers.

Now? Was that just a warm-up, then? Is the real business just about to start? If so, I don't mind.

But no.

He pulls down his underpants, and removes what appears to be a sock from his subsiding manhood. He takes a handkerchief from somewhere, wraps the sock (a cock-sock?) in it, and puts the entire humid mess in his pocket. Then does up his clothes, leans towards me, muttering, 'You tell anybody about this, you're dead', *gets on his bike (which I hadn't even noticed), and is gone.*

I don't tell anyone.

I suppose I've been mildly ravished. I mean, I didn't actually give my consent.

Not that my consent was sought. And even if it had been, I doubt I would have withheld it.

No complaints, really.

A few weeks later, blazing hot June, it is our school sports day. Not an event at which I am likely to shine, I am definitely not the athletic type. I take part in a three-legged race and an egg-and-spoon race, failing miserably at both. Well, at least I have shown willing.

Later, queueing at the ice-cream van for a '99-er', I realise Mr Hastie is directly behind me.

"Hello, George," he says.

"Hello."

Apparently there's a bird's nest in a tree not far away, in a little wooded area, and he wonders if I am interested in having a look at it.

I must have seen several dozen birds' nests over the years, and found them less than fascinating; but I have a feeling that this particular one will be much more interesting than the others.

We head off together, unnoticed by the attendant throng, who are apparently fascinated by long- and high-jumps to the exclusion of all else.

This time it lasts considerably longer than at the première, though we both remain fully clad as before. He seems to like it that way. And certainly, it makes for an easier re-arrangement if we should hear anyone approaching.

It will be a few years before I learn that this friction-sex is actually a recognised thing, and become familiar with the term 'frottage'. Or as a friend of the future, Bongo Betty, will refer to it, 'a dry ride'.

During the course of our mutual frottage, I have a strange thought. I understand that, for this very brief period, I could probably make this boy do almost anything I wanted, as long as I am prepared to go along with his wishes. If I made him stop—and I could quite reasonably, this outdoor business is actually quite risky, especially for him, as he is considerably older than me—he would be frustrated and try to persuade me to continue. Then...

The problem there is that I actually don't want it to stop any more than he does.

Even so...

When he has finished, we go through the sock business again. And since he seems in a better humour today, I have to ask.

15

"Why the sock?"

He looks up.

"Makes things easier; no mess."

"You must get through a lot of socks."

He grins.

"Not really. Just rinse them out under the tap when I get home, and put them in the wash. My mother doesn't notice."

He smiles again.

"I suppose she thinks I must have smelly feet."

He hesitates. "Though I don't."

"Oh, right."

"Means I can have a pull inside my trousers any time I feel like it — had one earlier today."

I suppose that's why this encounter lasted rather longer than the previous one. He hadn't had time to completely restock.

I wrinkle my nose.

"That sock must be in a state."

He does up his trousers.

"No, that was a different one. I always have a pair on me."

"Matching?" I ask.

"Of course," he frowns/smiles.

The next time it happens, I feign a mild reluctance, and manage to persuade him to part with half a crown in consideration of my acquiescence. Out of his pocket money, I suppose. The pocket which usually accommodates a couple of soggy socks.

After the summer holidays are over, and we've both moved up a year at school, it never happens again.

I suppose I am by now a bit too old for him.

Or maybe just a bit too expensive.

I was around this time that I got to know Mary McKellar.

Mary was my first really close friend. Oh, I had palled about with other kids, we were 'a gang'. There was Johnny McKellar, Mary's cousin, our daring ringleader; the aforementioned Moorhead brothers, both of whose physical attributes I had gradually come to know almost as well as they did themselves. There was good-looking Ewan Harvey, one of my guitar-playing buddies, with whom I was passionately in love, and with whom, inevitably, I had no sexual contact whatsoever—it seemed to be the rule in my life that sex and love were destined to be forever separate. Not that I wouldn't have wanted to take things further with Ewan, but he showed no signs at all of even the slightest interest, try as I might to make my desires obvious.

There were one or two others who joined in our adventures from time to time, but we five were the hard core. Our gang activities were nothing remarkable. We enjoyed causing a minor nuisance around the neighbourhood in the winter evenings, robbing apples, knocking on doors and running away. In summer we would be up in the local park, playing games, larking around, and if I was lucky, I might get a little fun in the bushes with this one or that one now and then.

Mary McKellar was a year older than me, and in some quite inexplicable way, she seemed to understand me. We never discussed 'it'; that is, we never examined the facts, nor even the idea, of my peculiar sexuality. But she seemed to recognise it and accept it.

Mary was buxom; not unattractive, but definitely on the larger side. She was a virgin, I knew, we had discussed it, we discussed everything except for That Thing. One of the main reasons for my fascination with her, and the pleasure I took in her company, was her wicked, surprisingly adult, and slightly perverse sense of humour. She was fun to be with, and we laughed a lot together.

I remember bumping into her on the corner of Main Street and Mill Street one evening around five. She appeared to be a bit agitated.

"Oh, George, thank God—stay with me, there's a man following me."

As we hastened up Mill Street, I looked over my shoulder, and, sure enough, there was a guy of about twenty walking behind us. As I turned round, he winked.

"Don't look, don't look," she said, in a panic.

I was puzzled.

"But what's the matter? You're usually running after boys, not away from them."

"Yes, I know," she muttered, "But he's not a boy, he's a man!"

Eventually we had to tear off like mad to evade Mary's determined suitor.

Later, as we sat on a wall, panting, both of us knackered, I asked her, "So how did that happen? Why did he think—well, you know?"

Mary was still trying to catch her breath.

"I was in the library, looking for something to read, and he was in the reference room. Older, too old for me, but quite good-looking, I thought. So I was just messing about, you know, giving him glances, the come-hither, having a bit of fun."

That was the kind of thing I often longed to do. But I restrained myself, aware of how very deranged such behaviour might appear to your average gentleman.

"Then, just as I was leaving, he was standing at the desk, where you check out your books. So, as I passed him, I thought I'd try to appear a bit sophisticated, maybe say something in French.

"So I did. I meant to say *au revoir*, 'goodbye', but you know my French is not very good. What I actually said was *aujourd'hui*, 'today'. And he followed me all the way along Main Street, just couldn't shake him off."

Mary had somehow managed to gain the reputation—quite unjustified—that she was 'easy'. That is, that she had 'done it', and might do it again. In fact she hadn't, and wouldn't, but, maybe because she was not in the top five most desirable girls in school, she hadn't gone to any great lengths to dispel the myth. The result was that if we were out together, maybe in the park, or sitting together in Sam's Café over a sophisticated cup of Bovril, it was not long before we would be surrounded by two or three horny youths, usually boys a year or two older than we were. This was fine with me; particularly as they seemed to accept my presence as a necessary inconvenience, and indeed, tended to treat me as a kind of honorary young lady.

We didn't get up to anything seriously saucy. But if we were playing 'Truth or Dare', it was usually not long before one of the boys had his hand inside Mary's blouse (but outside her bra).

On one occasion, Mary dared John Byres, whose younger brother was in my class at school, to put his hand down my tee-shirt, which he did without turning a hair. He even tweaked my nipple gently. Maybe since he was unable to tweak Mary's through her sturdy underpinnings. Any port in a storm, I suppose.

It was all very strange; but it was a kind of acceptance.

But if, for myself, love and romance seemed but a very remote and unlikely future possibility, at least I would do my best to help out a friend.

Mary had a deep and abiding passion for Ian Hetherington, one of the deities of the fifth year. He was 'going steady' with a certain Jennifer Young, one of our local teenage lovelies, and sadly was not at all interested in Mary. However, I had an idea about that.

"She won't let him, Jennifer," I told Mary. "Do it, I mean. And it's driving him mad."

18

"How do you know?"

"Darren told me. They're big pals, him and Ian."

"Darren Finlay? I suppose you were lending him a hand at the time of this conversation?"

Yes, Mary knew all about my manual relationship with Darren.

"Yes, actually. And I was thinking... If Ian thought he might have more chance with you... If he thought hat you *might*... I bet he would be tempted."

Mary's negative was emphatic.

"Certainly not. I fancy him a lot, yes, but I'm not doing *that* with him."

"But no, you won't have to," I insisted. "That's part of my plan. You see... Here's how it will work..."

I had it all in my head already.

"I give him to understand that you *might*. Without promising anything for definite. I just say that you are keen on him, and want to get to know him better. I arrange for you to meet up with him somewhere quiet—the cemetery's a good place, don't you think? And then... Well after that it's up to you."

Mary frowned.

"But what if he gets—you know—insistent? He's a big guy."

"Well, if he does, I will be there, hiding behind a tombstone or some such. If it all gets too much for you to handle, you shout something like 'Oh dear, I think I dropped my bracelet in the grass' and I will pop out of hiding, as if I was just passing."

"Hmm," said Mary. "Just passing? In the cemetery?"

I reassured her.

"But I'm sure you will be able to control him. And that way, after a bit of chat, he will get to know you better, and find you interesting."

Mary was *much* more interesting than Jennifer, though, it must be admitted, not nearly as lovely.

It looked as if Mary was gradually coming round to the idea. But she had a further concern.

"All very well, George. But if he *does* become determined to have his way, and you appear—well, no offence but he's three times your size. I doubt we could control him between us."

I smiled

"True. But you haven't heard the rest of my plan."

Drew Miller was in my year, a nice enough lad, though not at all bright. But he was as strong as an ox. And he had a passion for Mary.

Mainly because, once again, I had given him the impression that she was one of those girls who *might*. So I told him that Mary fancied him (which she did, actually, to a small extent) and would be waiting for him in the cemetery at half past eight. I added that I would come with him to oil the wheels of conversation, then disappear when the time was right.

I also told Ian Hetherington that Mary was longing to meet up with him in private. 'At quarter past eight, in the cemetery'.

And that—'You never know—she *might*.'

My plan, of course, was that if Ian got too forceful, big lad Drew could jump out and defend Mary's honour. He could easily deal with Ian, and would thus appear in the agreeable rôle of protector of maidenly virtue.

Winners all round.

Unless of course Ian *didn't* become insistent; or Mary decided insistence was fine with her and consented to yield.

But these both seemed fairly remote possibilities.

Drew and I arrived at Rutherglen cemetery at the appointed hour. We concealed ourselves in some long grass on a little rise overlooking the cemetery Whence we could clearly distinguish Mary and Ian already comfortably ensconced in a hollow between two tombstones. Just chatting at this stage, but encouragingly close. . .

That's when it started to go wrong.

"Who's that with her?" whispered Drew.

"It looks like Ian Hetherington. You know, fifth year."

"But I thought she was meeting *me*?"

By this time Mary and Ian have progressed to a slightly tentative embrace.

I invented rapidly.

"Yes, so did she. I guess Ian must have just wandered past at the wrong moment. The right moment."

"Wandered past? In a cemetery?"

Drew was becoming incensed.

"So she just lies in wait here in the cemetery for the first guy to go past, and grabs him, eh?'

I had to restrain my laughter at this picture of Mary as the local lurking nymphomaniac cum succubus. But I had to quieten Drew down, in case the happy couple heard us.

"Ssh! Well, no, not at all. I guess maybe I got the day wrong or something. Sorry."

"You got the *day* wrong? You mean you have to book a *day*? What a fucking tart!"

"Who, me?"

"Not you, *her*!"

He got to his feet.

"I'm off."

I really didn't know what to say. And he was getting loud again. So loud that…

"Piss off, you two, pair of perverts."

Oh dear, Ian must have heard us. He was on his feet and he was angry. But fully dressed, I was relieved to note.

"Go on, fuck off, what's the matter with you, you little creeps?"

We had little choice, and fucked off as requested. There wasn't much else we could do.

A disconsolate Drew wandered off homewards, decidedly unhappy— and of course blaming me for the entire *débâcle*. Justifiably enough, under the circumstances.

I moved a little further off, but stayed hidden. I supposed I would just have to do my puny best if Mary dropped her bracelet. I settled down in a little corner behind some bushes, about twenty yards away.

And fell asleep.

Just what passed between the love birds, Mary always declined to describe. But she still had her bracelet the next time I saw her. Whether she had preserved that other less material thing, I have no idea.

I was sixteen when I started having regular encounters with a friend of my own age. Almost always outdoors in some quiet spot. We were both constantly on heat, and relieved each other relentlessly whenever we got the chance. It never went further than that, and it was not any kind of a relationship but it met an urgent need.

Then, one Saturday afternoon, I was in Glasgow, Buchanan Street.

I am looking in the window of Patterson's music shop, wondering how long it will be before I have saved up enough from my pocket money to buy a copy of Maria Callas: Mad Scenes, *when I notice that there is a man staring at me, both of us reflected in the glass. Much older than me, maybe thirty.*

I walk away, and am aware of him following behind. A little further on, I pause and look back. He has stopped too, at the corner of a narrow lane. He indicates with a twitch of his head that I should follow him, and turns into the long alley that runs between Buchanan Street and

21

Queen Street. My heart in my mouth, I head back, and turn off in the same direction. He seems to have disappeared. I continue down the passageway, curious.

And there he is. He is pushed back in the gap between two telephone boxes, leaning against a wall, masturbating.

Why do I run? Is it because he is so much older? It isn't because he's unattractive, some hideous old perv, he isn't, he's nice-looking, even handsome. Whatever the reason, I race off torn between overpowering terror and overwhelming lust.

I began to spend a lot of my spare time in Glasgow. After that last incident, I had come to be aware that there were at least some possibilities of adventure there; stranger encounters, maybe, adult encounters, perhaps. But how did that work? Where did you find them? Were there special places where these things happened? I had no idea. But there was a door somewhere, I sensed it. The door I thought of as the Green Door, behind which lay the answers to all my questions.

Just after leaving school, and before starting University, I applied for, and was offered, a Saturday job in Caldwell's, a large music shop in Glasgow. So between my piano lessons on a Friday evening, and my Saturdays spent working in the city, by dint of perseverance, I began to uncover the very edge, the merest hint, of the secret world I was sure existed; and one or two of the places where, if one were lucky, one might learn more.

That's how I met 'The Man with The Van'.

I was in the waiting area of Waterloo Street bus station; Friday night, on my way home from my music lesson. I didn't know it, of course, but these identical circumstances would soon lead to perhaps the most significant encounter of my life to date. But that was still some months in the future.

I knew that the toilet here was one of those places I have mentioned. Thus I was not surprised when a young man standing near me at the stalls began staring at me fixedly. Not surprised, but excited. But how did this work? I had no idea.

Unsure how to progress this, eventually I left the toilet, and plonked myself back down on my bench.

He followed me out, and sat down next to me.

He was maybe nineteen or twenty, and not at all unattractive.

We had some utterly meaningless conversation—the subject of sex was not approached—before he offered to give me a lift back to Rutherglen. In his works van.

How foolish it was of me to accept, I now realise. But there were no untoward consequences. Indeed, no consequences of any kind. Though I suppose there might easily have been. Like most kids, I had been severely warned about accepting lifts from strangers. But he hadn't offered me sweets, which, I had been told, was the usual warning sign, so on balance, I thought it was probably OK to say 'Yes'.

He dropped me off in Rutherglen Main Street. Throughout the journey, about half an hour, inconsequential conversation had continued. He might just as well have been a friend giving me a lift.

I cannot express how deeply disappointed I was.

Until, just as I was thanking him for the ride, he asked if I was interested in meeting up again.

Of course I was,

I waited for half an hour in St Enoch's Square for him.

He didn't show up. I was not only disappointed. I was angry.

Unluckily for him, I was a bright child, and had made a mental note of the name of the company that employed him—it was written on the side of his van. A couple of minutes scrutinising the Glasgow telephone directory and I had the address.

The next day I made my way to his place of employment, near the St Andrew's Halls, and hung around for an hour or so, across the road, inconspicuous. Eventually his van rolled up, and I saw him park it, get out and go into the main entrance to the works yard

Now exactly what was my plan? Confront him and loudly accuse him of toying with my affections? Hardly. In fact I had not made any plan at all.

So I just crossed the road and parked myself right outside the entrance to the yard. After about twenty minutes he came out again and headed for his van.

"Hello," I said. "Did I tell you I'm only fourteen?"

I was sixteen, in fact.

I was satisfied to see his jaw drop and his face turn white.

I turned around and went home.

*

I am in Central Station, Glasgow. A place that will feature regularly in

23

this narrative, and one meriting a detailed description.

Central Station is bounded by four major thoroughfares. To the south is Argyle Street, and it is in the southern part of the station that the departure platforms lie and the 'throat' of the station is located. Trains head out from there over the Central Bridge, 'The Hielan'man's Umbrella', which crosses Argyle Street, and on to destinations local and distant.

The flanking streets are Hope Street to the west and Union Street to the east. To the north lies Gordon Street. It is within the 'U' formed by these three that the concourse of the station lies.

Imagine you are standing just in front of the magazine and cigarette stall in the centre of the station, your back to the counter. You are facing north. From here you will be able to see the various portals of this, Glasgow's largest and busiest railway terminus, and are about equidistant from all of them. They are important, these entrances and exits. For as well as being a transport hub, Central Station is a stage; those who wish to perform thereon have to know which portal will lead them into the glare of the spotlight, and which will conduct them safely back into the wings.

Over to your left, west, is the narrow passage leading in from Hope Street, designed primarily for the use of taxis arriving to deposit passengers, but also utilised occasionally by those on foot. Immediately adjacent are the offices of the Railway Police.

Some little way clockwise, north-west, is the porticoed entrance that leads via a revolving door directly from the Central Hotel into the station, provided for the use of those travellers solvent enough to afford the dubious pleasure of the hotel's faded splendours. These old British Rail hotels are not what they were, but still manage to exude a degree of cumbersome and antiquated Victorian charm.

Continue to turn in the same direction. North, directly in front of you, is the entrance from Gordon Street, wide and imposing. This is the major access to the station, and outside is the departure taxi rank, arcaded for the convenience of passengers awaiting transport. Later, in the small hours, it will provide a degree of shelter for the few homeless who congregate there near the hot air vents. On your right, north-east, as you look down towards this entry, you will see the left luggage office.

Continue to turn clockwise. You are looking eastward now, to the exit that leads via a set of stairs into Union Street. On its left, the Travel Information and Ticket Sales Office with its floor-to-ceiling windows. On its right a further set of stairs leads down to the Gents' toilets. Beyond that a weighing machine. Adjacent, the station buffet, and further along, the Ladies' facilities.

No point in turning any further, southward there is only the real business of the station, dull as can be, the gates to platforms one and two. But we are interested in the station—and particularly, this eastern part of it—as a social structure, a gathering place, not as a point of departure or arrival.

Look around. Take it in. Travellers arriving, leaving; meeting by The Shell, a metal relic of the Second World War; parting at the gates to the platforms, one to thirteen, unlucky for some.

A gang of lads, average age about eighteen, noisy, boisterous and just a bit threatening, although apparently in the best of humours, have just got off a train and head for the exit on your right, leading out to Union Street.

Just next to the stairs which go down to the public toilets, between the station buffet and the weighing machine, stands a conspicuous figure; lantern-jawed, with a Brylcreemed teddy-boy quiff, drainpipe trousers, suede shoes, and a suspiciously matt complexion. In a brilliantly white rain coat, tightly belted.

As the group of lads passes, one blows him a kiss. The target turns away slightly, without reacting.

A great place for hanging around, Central Station. People come and go at all hours, you can loiter with or without intent undisturbed, unless you make your intent that wee bit too obvious.

This person is definitely loitering. Now and then—not too often, he doesn't want to draw attention—he descends the stairs to the toilets, and then returns to his post by the buffet.

I watch intently. I know nothing about him at all. But I do know what his game is, and what he is looking for. I am looking for the same thing myself.

2. The Great Pretender

Oh-oh-oh, yes I'm the great pretender,
Pretending that I'm doing well.
My need is such I pretend too much;
I'm lonely but no-one can tell.
The Platters, 1955.

December 1961

I huddle under the overhanging arch of the doorway in a vain attempt to shelter myself from the freezing rain. Gathering my determination, I take a deep breath, press the doorbell, and listen for the sound of approaching footsteps.

I am only slightly nervous. After all, what is the worst that can happen? I have thought myself into the character I mean to assume. I am respectably dressed, and carry an official-looking attaché case. I *am* official, I convince myself. I am legitimate, I am here to disinfect the pay telephone, nothing more.

I am seventeen. And I am on a mission.

My co-conspirator and best friend, Ian Hall, is waiting round the corner, inside a telephone box, anticipating my call. At least there he is out of the rain, which is more than I am.

The two of us have attended performances of *West Side Story* religiously at least once a week since the national tour reached Glasgow. The show is scheduled to play at the King's Theatre for ten weeks in total, and the run is about half-way through.

We have become obsessed—there is no other way to describe it. By the magic of the show itself, the music, the dancing, the cast. Not particularly by the principals, although David Holliday is handsome, Jill Martin pretty, and both sing well and are moving and convincing as the star-crossed lovers. But it is the dozen young and attractive men who take the minor rôles of the gang members who are our particular fascination.

We have, individually and jointly, done all we can to engage their interest and attention. We have waited for autographs at the stage door, whence the persons of interest tend to issue in groups of two or three after a performance; we have followed them in the street (discretely, distantly, but determinedly) to ascertain where they are lodging; we have arranged to pop up unexpectedly in a restaurant or café where one or other of them happens to be eating. But so far our efforts seem to have had no impact. As a final throw of the dice, I persuaded my friend and fellow addict to stage a faint directly in the path of a group of them. But they simply stepped carefully over and round him. In their world, it appears, we don't exist at all.

Our researches have revealed that at least three or four of these gods have accommodation at this address. So, after pressing the doorbell once more, I look up at the imposing façade of this large mansion to look for any sign of life at the windows.

I see nothing.

I, the elder, and ringleader of our duo of determined stalkers, have racked my brains to come up with some method of inserting ourselves more effectively into the consciousness of our idols. It is only a few days since inspiration finally struck—and from an unlikely source. I hazily remembered the plot of a book I had read in years gone by, *The Bridesmaids*, by Pamela Brown. A 'girls' book, but no matter—I have a catholic taste in literature. I recalled how the plucky and daring heroine had managed to obtain access to a suite of offices (where vital information apparently lurked among the filing cabinets) by disguising herself as a telephone cleaner. That is, as a representative of a company whose business it was to pay scheduled visits to office premises in order to disinfect the telephone equipment installed there. In the book, our enterprising protagonist had been able to come and go unremarked, and investigate whatever-it-was to her heart's content.

Why, I wondered, should this ruse not be equally successful in a domestic setting? I couldn't remember the name of the company in question, and the book itself has long since disappeared from the library shelves. But these operatives are ubiquitous—indeed, I have seen them at work, and have watched them, intrigued.

Despite my ingenuity, I have not been able to obtain anything resembling an official uniform, and I hope that the conservative pale grey coat I wear will serve. It is unlikely, I think, that these theatricals will have any clear idea of how an employee of *Phonocleanse Limited* (the name I have invented) ought to be attired, but just in case they do, I have rehearsed the line, '*Oh, they've done away with our uniforms recently—it's a new policy.*' An artistic friend at school has prepared a lapel badge, reading *Your Phonocleanse Representative—Your Health Is Our Business*, in gold letters on a black background, which will, I think, survive casual scrutiny.

I have carefully packed a small attaché case, purchased at a local jumble sale, with what I hope will pass as suitable equipment—some soft cloths, tissues, a plastic squeezy bottle of Jeye's fluid, and a large rubber bone of the type designed to engage the attention of a dog—this last an eleventh hour inspiration. When an expert in this field is engaged in his work, I have noticed, it is naturally necessary he take the telephone handset off the base unit; and, unless some compensating weight is placed on the receiver rest, the hideous howling noise that indicates to a subscriber that his telephone is off the hook will go into action. I have seen too that those officially qualified in this arcane art of telephone sterilisation arrive equipped with a rubber-coated metal weight designed for this precise purpose.

The dog bone is about the right size and shape. I have scraped the white colouring off it and it is now a greyish-black. It isn't as heavy as the genuine article, but it works reasonably well on our phone at home, and I think it adds a convincing touch of professionalism, provided one doesn't examine it too closely.

You might ask yourself just what we hoped to gain from this insane plot; but at the time I don't think it occurred to me to wonder. Access was the goal—what might happen after that was an unknown quantity. Perhaps I would be able to skulk through the house and investigate the domestic habits and lifestyles of our heroes, and report back to my fellow fan. That would depend on whether or not there were many people at home and on how closely my activities were monitored. Perhaps I would be able simply to observe the comings and goings of the household. Maybe (the mere thought is enough to make my heart race) one of the objects of my desire might even speak to me:

'Hello—who are you? Fancy meeting up for a coffee after the show?'

At any rate, I would have proximity, and—well, who knew what might follow?

There seems to be no-one at home.

'God, they can't all be out.'

It's 6 pm, Friday. They have a performance at 7.30.

'Surely they must be readying themselves for the evening, making sure they look their best, limbering up, doing vocal exercises?'

Such was my fantasy of the lifestyle of a touring actor in those days. How far from the reality I now appreciate.

'Maybe they've already left for the theatre.'

But that's unlikely. I and my co-conspirator have been watching the place for hours, and in that time no-one has entered or left. We know that at least three, maybe four, male members of the cast lodge in *The Palace*, this large and well-maintained double-fronted property in smart Hill Street. What's going on?

I lean on the bell push once more, and examine the fancy framed card next to it. It reads *Lyon* above, and *Hart* beneath.

'*Lyon-Hart,*' I think to myself, distractedly. '*It's a sign! Lionheart! Yes, that's me.*'

I ring again.

And, finally, yes! I hear a footfall from inside, and a peevish and distinctly Scottish voice intones, "Coming, coming… Huv ye forgot yer key again, Kevin?"

1961 has been a year full of incident. I finished my schooling in June, and turned seventeen in July. I flew in a plane for the first time. I spent a few weeks in Brittany, on a school exchange visit, (where I actually contrived to have a brief connection with one of the cousins of my host) then a few more in conventional employment, helping out in the offices of a company where the boss is a friend of the family.

I passed all my examinations successfully—the *Highers* which were then the equivalent of what are today *A-levels*—and was accepted to start my further education at highly-regarded Glasgow University in September, my course an Arts degree in the rather unusual combination of Music and English. Music, my choice, English, that of my parents; the compromise between what I wanted to do, and what they (or more specifically, my mother) thought I should do, 'just in case'. Like most compromises, satisfying no-one, and potentially a problem.

And there remained the bigger problem. My secret. My difference. The difference that seemed to me so glaring, but that most other people appeared to be unaware of.

As far as indulgence was concerned, I continued to contrive the occasional rushed liaison with some fellow-adolescent whose testosterone overload helped to overcome his reluctance and render him temporarily gender-blind.

"God, if only you were a girl," groaned Danny Rice, eyes closed, as I squeezed and pumped his erection firmly.

Eddie Leigh, more adventurous, was keen to attempt The Deed, but I certainly wasn't ready for that, and he had to be satisfied with more primitive forms of stimulation.

More recently, I had begun to discover there were other avenues open to me. On my sojourns to the city, I came to be aware that certain hidden corners sheltered others, strangers, who were eager to share an anonymous ten minute conjunction.

But it was this very anonymity, the air of rushed shame and a shared guilt that surrounded them, that made these mutual fumblings as unsatisfying as my earlier exploits.

Sex was all very well. Sometimes it was very well indeed. But without any personal dimension it remained shallow and ultimately empty.

I constantly pondered this facet of my character. I was certain there existed somewhere and somehow a solution. I was convinced that there was a door somewhere, behind which waited enlightenment, and a world where my desires—for affection, friendship, maybe even love— were accepted and understood.

The Green Door—thus I pictured it in my imagination. Like most people of my age, many things in my life were permeated by the music and the lyrics of the popular songs of the day, or of the day before:

> *'There's an old piano and they play it hot*
> *Behind the green door.*
> *Don't know what they're doin' but they laugh a lot*
> *Behind the green door.*
> *Wish they'd let me in so I can find out what's*
> *Behind the green door.'*

Yes, along with Mr Frankie Vaughan I wanted to laugh a lot and find out what. I already had the piano, and played it as hot as I could.

This image of the Green Door haunted my imagination, the Green Door for which I would need to find the key.

But first I needed to find the door.

But *this* door, which is not green, but a smart and glossy brown, is finally opened, and I find myself face to face with a plump and pleasant-looking gentleman of about sixty.

Damn! I have been expecting one of the tenants to answer. Foolishly, I haven't anticipated the presence of a landlord. At least, I assume that is what this person is.

He looks at me in some confusion (as well he may) and after a moment, eyebrows raised, he says, "Oh—sorry dear, Ah thought ye were Kevin— one of our lodgers, you know—well, ye *widnae* know…"

Oh, but I *do* know. Kevin's the reason I'm here. One of the reasons. My stomach does a little jig.

The gentleman continues, "... well, never mind that, anyway... it's usually Liz that answers the door, Mr Lyon, that is, but she's oot at the moment."

He seems to become aware that his genders are not perfectly in sync, takes a deep breath, and continues in a rather more composed manner.

"Fred didn't mention we were expecting onybody the day, and he usually does if we are—he knows Ah forget. Mr Lyon, that is..."

I decide to let this rather confusing speech ramble to its natural conclusion. Then I realise it already has, and that it is my turn to contribute.

"I'm sorry to disturb you, sir," I start, all professional politeness, "but I'm from the agency."

Understanding appears to dawn. "Oh—from the agency."

I am relieved at his lack of surprise. But then a frown passes over the pleasant, slightly vacant face.

"Dear me, really, they ought tae phone first, they're supposed tae phone, they ken that very well."

I hadn't actually considered this, but realise that, yes, it's natural that an appointment would be arranged in advance. I improvise unblushingly.

"Oh, I believe they tried to phone you, sir, but there was no reply."

The eyebrows rise again.

"Really? But Ah've been in aw day, and the phone's no' rung once."

The brows crease in thought, and he leans against the door jamb.

"Well, hang on, it *did* ring this morning, but that was just the butcher aboot the liver, nae lamb's, only pig's, and Liz disnae like pig's, too strong-tasting. And then big Olivia phoned for a wee chat aboot two o' clock, but apart fae that..."

"Perhaps the agency rang while you were on the phone, sir?"

This is considered. The head nods.

"Aye, you're right, that could be it."

The face assumes an expression of sympathetic commiseration, and he continues.

"Anyway, dear, Ah'm sorry you've had a wasted journey, but we've nothing available, nothing at all—we've got half the cast of *West Side Story* in at the moment, the show at the King's, and we're full till the end of January. Such a pity yiv had a journey for nothing. Ah'll get Mr Lyon tae speak tae the agency in the morning and make sure they know not to send anyone round until they've spoken to one of us."

I grasp the misunderstanding, and interrupt again, after a quick glance at the names on the door. "No, no, Mr—er—Mr Hart, is it?"

It has to be—he has already mentioned Mr Lyon.

"Aye."

I realise that the agreeable Mr Hart is luckily not the sharpest knife in the box, and thank my guardian angel that Mr Lyon, obviously the brains of the outfit, is absent. All may not yet be lost.

"I'm not from the accommodation agency, sir. I'm from the telephone agency."

Confusion once more descends.

"Telephone agency? But we've already got a telephone."

"No, sorry, sir."

If this all goes wrong, at least I can run quite fast.

I take a deep breath and lie my head off.

"The telephone *cleaning* agency—*Phonocleanse*—you have an arrangement with us. To disinfect your telephones. Once a month, sir. It's a recent contract, I believe."

"Really? Do we?"

Mr Hart looks even more bewildered. I feel slightly guilty at deceiving this pleasant elderly gentleman, but reassure myself with the thought that I don't actually mean him any harm, I just want to get into his house.

"Oh dear. It must be something Liz has arranged. Funny he never mentioned it. And what is it you say you do?"

I am back on my script by now.

"We come round once a month, sir, to your home or your place of business, and we disinfect your telephones—you know, for health reasons. A lot of people, all using the same telephone, it can cause— well, you understand…"

The truth is I have no idea at all what it can cause, or what the health implications of sharing a telephone may be. But I struggle on.

"I believe you have a public telephone in the house, sir? That is, a shared telephone?"

This is a complete shot in the dark, but seems likely.

"Oh aye, we have two, one on the first floor and the other upstairs on the second. Coin phones, ye know, for the paying guests. And ye disinfect them, ye say? Ah see. Well—yid better come in."

He opens the door wide and stands to one side to allow me to enter.

"Straight up the stairs and turn left. The other phone's up another flight, same place. Ah'll leave ye to it, dear, Ah'm sure you know whit yer doing."

'*You couldn't be more wrong,*' I think to myself.

But I give Mr Hart a reassuring smile. He turns and heads towards a door at the end of the passage that runs down one side of the imposing flight of stairs that rises up into the unknown.

"Pop in and have a cup of tea when yiv finished," he calls over his shoulder. "Just come down here to the hall and give us a shout."

Then he turns back, grins, and winks at me in an unexpectedly conspiratorial manner.

"Oh—and the boys'll be getting ready tae go tae work, washing, shaving and the like. I hope yil not be too shocked—if a naked man passes you in the hall, just pay no attention."

I gulp and my stomach loops the loop once more.

And this slightly strange gentleman who addresses me unconcernedly as 'dear', turns back and disappears down the hallway.

Most of my family can at least sing or perform in one fashion or another. I have a vague notion that I will eventually carve out a career in music, precise details unclear, but since my parents are not enthralled by that prospect, despite our family traditions, this ambition has caused quite a few domestic tremors; harbingers of the far more violent upheavals which will follow in the next few years.

Despite my misgivings about the direction my personal life is likely to take in the future, and my confusion and concern about my sexuality in general, I have been lucky enough to find a kindred spirit of a sort. Ian attends my school, and, like myself, is 'artistic'—he also plays the piano. Adequately. Apart from any other shared traits, we both have a mutual interest in assiduously avoiding anything associated with sport, or physical exertion in general—we are wimps, and happy to be so. Both of us acknowledge our unusual personal tastes between ourselves without ever discussing the larger implications. We simply accept that we are different, but different in the same way. We have never contemplated, and never would consider, sharing a physical intimacy. Even within our secret world we understand that there is a divide, and we sense that we are both on the same side of it.

From time to time one or the other of us develops a fascination with some classmate or acquaintance, as adolescents do. But we have come to realise vaguely that the world of the stage is something of a haven for people of our inclinations, and tend to spend a lot of our free time attending performances in one or another of Glasgow's several theatres. And we are usually to be found after the show, lurking at the stage door, clamouring to add to our autograph collections.

Or so we claim. The truth is that we are desperate to be approached, befriended, maybe even (God save us!) chatted up, by one of the denizens of this fascinating world.

And best of all, if a member of my family happens to be appearing in the show, as is sometimes the case, we have Access All Areas, which ought to increase the possibility of An Adventure.

But up till now it hasn't arrived.

I remember an aunt, an inveterate devourer of the *News of the World*, warning my mother that she should be wary of allowing me to hang around backstage.

"Be careful," she hissed, "The theatre's full of men of *that* sort. You know—men who might take advantage of a young boy."

If that's true, how is it that I seem to be unable to find any of them?

As Mr Hart disappears into the depths of the house, I turn and start to mount the wide staircase that runs upwards from the centre of the hallway. Now that the moment of truth is approaching, I am beginning to feel just a little nervous. But all is quiet for the moment.

As I reach the top of the stairs, I register that there are two doors on my left and two on my right. Two further flights of stairs continue upwards, one on either side of where I stand. It is clear that this large and beautiful house has been lovingly maintained, and that the elaborate staircases are an original feature. The paintwork throughout is immaculate, modern wallpapers imitating Victorian patterns clad the walls, and the black and white tiled floor gleams in the glow from a lamp set on a table in the centre of the hallway.

My goal, the public payphone, a jarring contemporary note, is on my left, on the wall between the two doors, one of which is closed and the other ajar. As I head towards it, I can see that the door which is half open leads to a large bathroom. From behind the other I can hear faint music.

First things first. My friend is expecting a call from me—I have jotted down the number of the telephone box where he waits, and we have arranged that I will contact him, report my progress, and pass on the number of the pay telephone here, in *The Palace*. Essential, as we see it, to give us contact with the present occupants. But also useful as a long-term investment—we know that this house is popular with theatricals on tour, and who knows who may end up staying here in the future?

I take the necessary change from my pocket, insert the coins into the box, and dial. After barely one ring, my friend Ian picks up.

"You're in, I take it—good, it took you long enough," I hear. *"Anyway, what's happening?"*

Rather offended by this lack of recognition for my daring—after all, this was all *my* idea, and I feel I deserve a little more credit for my enterprise—I press Button A, and the call is connected in both directions.

"OK, Ian—have you got the pencil and paper? Here's the number…"

My eyesight has always been bad. I wear glasses as a rule, but am inclined to remove them from time to time, if I feel I need to startle the world with my desirability. This is one of those occasions.

I clutch the phone to my ear and squint at the centre of the dial where the number is printed. And just at that moment, the closed door on my left opens, the volume of the music from within rises—I recognise immediately the voice of Edith Piaf—and a young man who is unfamiliar to me appears in the doorway. Despite being taken aback by this apparition, I somehow contrive to switch into 'professional' mode. I speak into the phone.

"Head office? It's Andrew here, operative 42."

I pause to allow time for an imaginary response.

What I actually hear is, *"What are you talking about? What's going on?"*

God, I think, why could I not find a lieutenant with a little more flair?

"Yes, that's right," I carry on, regardless. "I'm at the premises now, and just about to start inspection. I'll give you the number—make a note on my time-sheet, will you—er—Ruby?"

"Afternoon," says the attractive, dark-haired young man, as he passes me and heads towards the bathroom.

"Hello there," I reply, as I tuck the phone between my shoulder and my ear, and busy myself with the catch on my attaché case, wondering who the hell he can be.

"What do you mean, Ruby? Who are you talking to? Who was that?"

"Oh, shut *up*," I whisper into the phone through gritted teeth as the bathroom door closes and is locked. "Just write this down."

I shut my attaché case, take the phone once again in my hand and proceed to quietly repeat the telephone number, which I can make out only with some difficulty. I heave a sigh of relief when Ian reads it back to me correctly. At the same time I am attempting to peer through the door of the room recently vacated to see if I can glean anything; any little snippet of information to pass on; any personal detail; anything at all, in fact. I can just make out the corner of a bed and some clothes— jeans and a sweater—hanging over the back of a chair. I edge my left foot forward, thinking that if I can ease the door open just a fraction more… It creaks as it swings inwards.

"That you, Sarah?" comes a voice, accent definitely English, from inside the room, causing my heart to leap into my mouth in shock. "Come in, have a gin, it's the cocktail hour."

I call out, "Er—no, sorry, just caught the door with my foot."

I can feel myself going red.

"*What's happening now?*"

"Nothing," I hiss.

At the same time, from the bedroom, I hear, "Oh, OK, no problem. Who's that, anyway? Liz?"

"*Who's that talking? Who is it?*"

"Never mind," I whisper, and then raise my voice to normal level. "No, it's just…"

The bathroom door opens and the first, the unknown man, comes out. At the same moment, the bedroom door is thrown wide and… It's *him*. The muscular, fair-haired one, Ian's particular favourite. Funny, he's not as tall as I thought he would be. Nevertheless…

"Oh, sorry—I'm just here to…" I stutter.

"*Oh come on, who's there?*"

I hastily bang down the receiver on the rest—I just can't cope with the overload.

"…to disinfect the telephone."

The phrase sounds utterly stupid, like a bad joke. I am sure to be caught out, I feel.

"Good thing too, it probably needs it." The unknown man smiles at the other. "Larry was on the phone to his friend last night, and, my dear, the *filth*…"

"Oh—you must be with the phone people," interrupts the blonde one.

He looks at me, a question in his devastatingly blue eyes. I nod dumbly.

He examines my badge. "Oh yes, *Phonocleanse*. I see."

He smiles and leans against the door jamb. "Yes, I remember I did some work for one of these companies the last time I was between jobs—a year or two ago now, it must be."

He straightens up, loose-limbed and relaxed.

"Anyway—time we were on our way. Dance class in ten minutes, vocal warm-up at six-thirty."

He smiles and turns to his friend. (His lover?)

"Give Larry and Kevin a knock, Paul, and we can all walk down together. Maybe get some chips on the way if we hurry?"

"OK," the one called Paul replies, and crosses the hall towards one of the doors on the right. I am left face to face with whatshisname.

Ah! *This* is what I came for.

And the phone rings.

We both reach out to grab it, but he gets there first.

"Four two five nine." He listens for a moment. "Yes, he's just here—I'll pass him the phone."

He turns to me. "It's your office for you, someone called Ruby."

He hands me the receiver, smiles, says, "See you later", and re-enters his room.

"Hello?" I say. "Ruby?"

Paul knocks on the door opposite. "Larry? Kev?"

It's Ian. He seems to have calmed down.

"I'm just about to start," I say. "I'll report back when I've finished, OK?"

"Yes, fine, good luck—I'm going for some chocolate—there's a queue outside and they're looking nasty—tell me all about it when you get back. I'll be outside the phone box."

'*Oh God,*' I think, '*Chocolate? At a moment like this? As if you're not fat enough already.*'

"Fine," I say. "See you later."

I replace the receiver on its rest. And suddenly everything seems to be happening at once.

The door on the other side of the hall opens, and Paul is joined by Larry and Kevin, both faces I know very well. Another young man I recognise—Eric is his name—comes down from upstairs, along with one of the girls from the show, who is carrying a tiny fluffy white poodle in her arms. From the door by which he left comes the blond one, closing and locking it behind him. I think he's called Gerry. He smiles and winks at me. My own favourite, Kevin, is only a few yards from me, chatting to the girl who carries the little dog. It's enough to make my head spin.

In the face of this sensory deluge, I decide that now would be a good time to busy myself with my alleged duties, while continuing to observe. No-one is paying me particular attention, it appears. I place my attaché case on the table next to the telephone, open it, and take out the gadget I have prepared. I pick up the receiver and place my contrivance on its rest. I take the heavy Bakelite handset firmly in my left hand, while my right deals with the spray bottle, and then with the polishing cloth. Spray—cloth—spray—cloth… I get a nice rhythm going eventually.

Unfortunately, the payphone at *The Palace* has a much heavier action than does our phone at home, and the rubber bone is not heavy enough to keep the receiver rest in the depressed position. I don't notice this at first, and am still in the throes of spraying and rubbing at the handset in what I imagine to be an appropriately professional manner, when I become aware of the sound of the 'your telephone is off the hook' howler, with its steadily increasing volume and surprisingly piercing siren sound.

I notice one or two heads turn in my direction in reaction to the noise, so I casually rest my right elbow on the receiver rest in order to silence the damned thing. In so doing, I dislodge the weight, which falls to the floor. With a joyous bark, Fluffy leaps from the arms of his mistress, seizes the rubber bone expertly in his jaws, and heads off with it down the stairs. It then becomes the goal of everyone in the hallway to help me to retrieve it.

A mild chaos ensues.

Eventually, order is restored, my equipment ("*Well, it does look like a dog's bone*," says someone) is returned to me with profound apologies (it has rather suffered from the thorough chewing it has received) and gradually people begin to drift downstairs towards the front door in ones and twos. Everyone says goodbye to me on their way out. The girl shakes my hand, smiles, and once again apologises for the naughtiness of unpredictable Fluffy. For a moment, I almost feel I belong.

Above the laughter, I hear the front door downstairs bang. All the residents have left, and I am alone.

I consider it is only fair that, before beating a strategic retreat, the least I can do is to fulfil the duties I have laid claim to. So, after I have done a reasonable job on the first floor payphone, I mount the next flight of stairs and attend to the one on the second floor. I try a couple of the doors, just in case someone has been unwise enough not to lock up behind them, but with no success.

As I make my way downstairs afterwards, I hug to myself the joyous delight in a job well-done, a mission accomplished. Not only have I seen the animals in their native surroundings (hence enjoyed a kind of safari), but have actually spoken to some of them. Wait till I tell Ian.

"Ready for that cup of tea now, dear?" Mr Hart is lurking at the bottom of the stairs and intercepts my exit, making me jump.

I turn towards him.

"Oh—I should be getting back to the office—I have another call-out to attend to. It's very kind, but…"

"Och, c'mon, dear, what's five minutes? The kettle's on."

I consider my options. While I am anxious to re-join my friend and give him the full story of my adventures, I realise that the chatty Mr Hart might be a source of all sorts of tasty titbits. After all, he has been living cheek-by-jowl with these deities for weeks, and will no doubt have had the chance to observe them closely.

"OK, thank you, Mr Hart, I will."

"Good, dear, good, come through."

He indicates a door to the left of the bottom of the stairs. He leads the way.

"And it's *Donald*, please," he says, over his shoulder. "*Mr Hart* makes me feel like a pensioner."

I follow him into an elegantly furnished sitting-room, thinking, with the hard arrogance of the young, '*Well—if you're not a pensioner yet, Mr Hart, you soon will be.*'

"I'm Andrew," I say. I'm not, of course.

"Well, here you are, Andrew."

He pulls out a chair for me, and we sit down.

As we do, I think, '*Oh dear, this was a mistake. Nice old guy, but what on earth are we going to talk about?*'

But my fears prove unfounded. I soon discover that Donald can talk quite unassisted for what threatens to be an indefinite period. After the tea is poured, and delicious scones proffered, Mr Hart launches into his monologue.

I learn that he and his friend Mr Lyon have run *The Palace* for the unbelievable period of forty years; that prior to that he was in the army ('*Would have been the First World War,*' I think, astonished); that they have always catered exclusively to a theatrical clientele ('*Although with all the theatres closing down, business is not what it was. Luckily, Liz and I…*'); that the theatre itself has sadly declined and is no longer the theatre as it was ('*I mean, it's before your time dear, but I remember…*')

Watching Donald relax and continue to expand on his memoirs, I am confirmed in my earlier suspicion. Yes, I may be very inexperienced, but I am pretty sure Mr Hart is One Of Them. Or One Of Us, I suppose I should say. I wonder if I can profit from this, and if so, how? He's much too old for me to be interested in him in *that* way; and anyway, his manner is distinctly reminiscent of a kindly old aunty. My goal, in the unlikely event of me making a foray into gerontophilia, would be something more in the naughty old uncle line.

I have just managed to steer his soliloquy round to the present day, and his current clutch of lodgers, when I hear the sound of the front street door shutting, and footsteps crossing the hall.

"I'm back, Sarah. God, what a day, and it's just starting to rain again," a voice calls out.

"In here, Fred," responds Mr Hart. "Just made a fresh pot of tea. Come in, ye must be perished."

The *Fred* receives an unusual emphasis.

The door opens, and another gentleman of about Donald's age appears. Tall and slim, this one, elegant in a tailored overcoat, cavalry twill trousers, leather gloves and highly polished boots, he is in complete contrast to Mr Hart, whose style of dress, at least around the domestic hearth, could charitably be described as 'pipe and slippers'. The newcomer's face is aquiline, the features sharp, the greying hair swept back from the temples in a pompadour, held in place, I would guess, with more than a hint of lacquer. But it is the eyes that make the biggest impression. Bright sapphire chips, shrewd and penetrating.

'*Oh dear,*' I think. '*Not much chance of fooling this one.*'

Mr Hart bustles, and helps the newcomer out of his coat.

"Come in, come in and get warm, Fred. Cup of tea? As ye can see, Ah'm entertaining."

The newcomer puts his coat over a chair.

"Really, Donald? Personally, I have never found you to be so. But yes, I will have a cup of tea, thank you. And who is your young friend, may I ask?"

I stand up and offer my hand, but it is not taken straight away. Instead he looks down at it, and up again, enquiringly.

Donald busies himself with the pouring of the tea.

"This is young Andrew, Fred, from the phone company."

"The phone company? Oh? Which phone company is that?"

Mr Lyon removes his gloves and places them next to his coat. I let my hand drop to my side, move back to the table, and sit down again.

"The company you forgot tae tell me about—the phone *cleaning* company. The one you've taken out a contract with. *Phony* something."

Mr Lyon in his turn approaches the table, and looks at me hard.

I just *know* I have been caught out. Making a dash for it might be a possibility—they are old, and I am fleet. The one thing I can't do is to confront that steady gaze.

"Oh, I see," he says, never taking his eyes off me. "*Phony* something. Well, there's certainly something phoney going on here, if I'm any judge."

Mr Hart is oblivious to any tensions. "Aye, Phony something. Here, come on, sit down and enjoy yer tea."

Mr Lyon joins us at the table. He sips his tea, then leans over, and examines the badge pinned to my lapel.

"Oh—Phono*cleanse*," he reads.

His glance rises and our eyes finally meet. His mouth puckers in a tight little smile. He reaches for my hand at last, and shakes it.

"Nice to meet you, Andrew."

He turns to Mr Hart.

"Sorry, Donald, I forgot to mention it. The contract, I mean. Silly of me. Yes, I've arranged a visit from them every—how often is it, Andrew?"

Once again the blue gaze meets mine. He *knows* I am completely bogus, but for some reason has decided to play up to my story. I am utterly embarrassed and confused. All I want to do is to get out of there.

"Er—every month, I think it is," I mumble.

Once again the thin lips contract into that secret, intimidating little smile.

"Oh? So Donald and I are going to have to wait a month before we have the pleasure of your company again? Shame, that."

I mumble something incomprehensible.

He picks up the plate of cakes.

"Have a scone. Sarah was up all night making these. Weren't you, Sarah?"

This last is addressed directly to Mr Hart.

I realise that Mr Lyon has somehow seen right through me. Right through to my secret core. He is passing me a coded message. I glimpse the Green Door. If we had met under other circumstances, not in the midst of this foolish charade, I might have learnt...

But I am scared to death. I am too young. It is too soon.

I summon all my courage. He is playing a game with me. There is only one thing I can do.

I remember my rôle and return to it. I will be impenetrable.

I smile and hold up a hand.

"No, I won't, thank you, Mr Lyon. It's high time I got back to work—I have an appointment in about ten minutes. Please excuse me, both of you."

I place my teacup on the table and stand up.

"Well, if you really must go, Andrew, we won't detain you, will we, Sarah?"

Somehow, suddenly, Donald is playing too, though I would wager that, although he knows the rules, he is not sure of the name of the game.

"No, of course not, Elizabeth," he says to Mr Lyon.

41

And turning to me, "Lovely to meet you, dear, see you next month. Let me show you to the door," he says, as he rises to his feet.

I know now who and what they are. I long to stay. But it is time to leave.

"No, really there's no need," I protest, "I can find my own way out."

I turn to go.

With my hand on the doorknob, I turn back. "Thank you again, both of you, for your kindness."

As I walk down the hall towards the street door I am grateful that neither of them can see me. My knees are shaking.

When Ian and I next visit the theatre, he suggests that as usual we head for the stage door after the curtain falls on *West Side Story*. I make an excuse, saying that after my recent escapade I think it might be unwise.

"One of them could recognise me," I say. "It would be hard to explain. Let's leave it this time, OK?"

He is not too happy about that. He realises that my excuse is just that, but doesn't understand the reason for it. I'm not sure I do myself.

But I feel, in a confused way, that I have somehow moved beyond these childish games. I have finally glimpsed the outlines of the Green Door. Indeed, I have stood with one foot on its threshold.

But how to find it again? And if I do, if I am that lucky, will I dare to reach out, grasp the handle, turn it, and push the door wide?

3. Saturday Night at the Movies

Saturday night at the movies
Who cares what picture you see?
When you're huggin' with your baby
In the last row in the balcony.
The Drifters, 1964.

January 1962

One evening a few weeks later, after a late class at University, I have decided to pay a visit to the cinema before heading for home. I join the line at the confectionery counter.

I don't know what film is showing, indeed I don't care. It's raining, and in this particular cinema I know that there may be the chance of an adventure. There are half a dozen people in front of me. Idly, I tune into the conversation going on at the head of the queue.

"Poppets or pastilles, Sarah?"

"Oh, both, Ah think, Elizabeth, don't you?"

Suddenly I am on full alert—I look towards the counter ahead.

My God, it's them again! Mr Lyon and Mr Hart. Fred and Donald, Laurel and Hardy, Elsie and Doris. No—they are 'Elizabeth' and 'Sarah', I remember.

I turn up my collar and allow my shoulders to drop. I am wearing my glasses. I do not want to be recognised. It would be too embarrassing after our recent encounter.

Mr Lyon, once again elegantly attired, remonstrates.

"Sarah, my dear, you're never going to regain that figure of yours stuffing yourself with sweets. Aren't you supposed to be on a diet?"

"Well, Ah am, Liz, sort of. But this is a special occasion—it's no' often we get a chance for a night oot at the pictures these days. So, Ah've decided Ah'm going to spoil masel', so Ah am."

If anything slightly stouter than he was when we last met, he gazes in admiration at the gaudy poster advertising *The Tattered Dress*.

"Jeff Chandler! That man holds a special place in my heart."

The other sighs theatrically.

"Ah yes, Sarah—your heart; that fallible organ. No doubt by now sheathed in a layer of fat an inch thick."

With a shake of his head, he continues in a resigned tone, "Oh, very well, Madam Bernhardt, just this once."

Ah—Sarah *Bernhardt*.

But how can they address each other in this way, in front of a horde of the most ordinary Glaswegians imaginable? And with such *sangfroid*?

Turning to the girl behind the confectionery counter, Mr Lyon adds, with a conspiratorial smile, "I suppose we'll have to humour her, won't we, dear? Right—I'll take a box of your Payne's Poppets, if you please. The sixpenny one."

The taciturn young lady serving reaches for the requested item.

"Aw, make that a big box," Mr Hart wheedles. "Go on, Liz."

"Very well. A large box, hen, if you don't mind. And a tube of your best Rowntree's Fruit Pastilles, please."

"Make that a box, too. Ah cannae manage they tubes wi' ma rheumatics."

'Liz' has had enough. 'She' faces 'her' companion.

(Messy-looking, that. So in the interests of readability, let's lose the quote marks.)

"Good heavens, Sarah, is there no end to your gluttony? *No!* This is for your own good, I'm being cruel to be kind. A *tube* of pastilles. I'll help you unwrap them."

She continues in a conversational tone, now addressing the disinterested assistant, who is placing the sweets in a paper bag.

"You'd never believe it, hen, but The Divine Sarah here had a *lovely* figure when she was a young girl. Men went mad for her curves. And look at her now."

"That'll be one and six," says the uncommunicative salesgirl.

"Thank you *so* much."

Elizabeth takes the sweets, counts out the exact money and places it in the outstretched hand. She and Sarah turn and head for the box office.

"Pair a' queers," mutters the girl to herself as her customers leave.

"And fuck you too, ya fat slag," calls fat Sarah in a polite tone over her shoulder.

"Sarah, really! Such intemperate language! Have forty years at *The Palace* taught you nothing?"

"Sorry, Liz, it just slipped out. And speaking of which…"

"Oh, please, enough, Sarah, if you don't mind! Now—seats. What do you fancy—stalls or circle?"

"Oh, circle, Liz, I think," says Sarah. "After all—we're on a night out, aren't we? Let's go mad."

After paying, they head for the stairs.

Helpless, unable to resist, I follow them.

This particular cinema, the Green's Playhouse, in Glasgow's Renfield Street, first opened its doors to the public in 1927. At that time, it was the ultimate in entertainment luxury—as well as the beautifully appointed cinema auditorium, it boasted both a ballroom and a tea-room. But thirty-five years later, it has lost ground to more up-to-date venues, and is indeed considered something of a flea-pit.

It has a loyal following, however, among a certain element of Glasgow society, and frequently the activity in the stalls and the gentlemen's facilities far outstrips in energy and inventiveness anything to be seen on the screen. Indeed, *The Green's Playhouse* is habitually referred to by *aficionados* as *The Players' Greenhouse*.

Due to its diminished reputation, the *Playhouse* is never host to a first run of a major movie, and on this particular evening, *The Tattered Dress*, a late experiment in *film noir*, is receiving its second or third showing in Glasgow. It is, frankly, a pretty minor example of the genre, but its star, Jeff Chandler, is a popular favourite, and the fact that it also features the glamorous Elaine Stewart (who set male pulses racing in a small rôle in *The Bad and the Beautiful* a few years earlier) is enough to ensure that, on this occasion, the screening is well-attended.

Elizabeth and Sarah settle into their seats in the front row of the circle, immediately on the left of the centre aisle, and, while waiting for the programme to commence, take a look around the crowded house.

"Now," says Elizabeth, donning her glasses—plain black frames with a discreet touch of *diamanté*—"what stars have we with us this evening?"

"You have a look round and tell me, Liz, Ah'm a bit busy here," replies Sarah, frowning intently, as she wrestles with the tricky cellophane wrapper on her box of chocolates.

Captive, I manage to find a seat in the row behind them, slightly off to one side. Why shouldn't I? After all, this is a place of public entertainment. And frequently, of pubic entertainment.

The large auditorium, once a symphony of gilded plaster mouldings, delicately executed *putti*, and sumptuously upholstered red and yellow plush *fauteuils*—the Scarlet Divans and the Golden Divans— is undeniably looking its age. The peeling walls show here and there traces of intruding damp, the seats are worn and patched, the curtains which mask the screen during the intermissions in the programme are noticeably darned and shabby, and the enormous chandelier which depends from the roof is missing a good third of its bulbs. Nevertheless, a spectator can obtain a fleeting impression of the unimaginable luxury that awaited working-class Glasgow in the nineteen-thirties, if he half-closes his eyes.

But Elizabeth's eyes are wide open as she scans intently the acres of stalls beneath. Leaning carefully over the low railing in front of her, she peers downwards.

"I think that's Ava Gardner in the scarlet divans, with someone I don't recognise. But I can't be sure—it's high time I got new glasses."

She turns round and cranes her neck in order to better take in the tiered seats of the Grand Circle. I sink further down in my place.

"Ah—there's Olivia de Havilland two rows back, with Susan Hayward."

She waves. "Good evening, Olivia, Miss Hayward."

"Hello girls, ur yiz aw right?" calls back a raddled young man with a ruddy, pitted complexion and bloodshot eyes. Around twenty, he is seated in the row behind mine, next to a plump, sleek, older gentleman, round-faced, with hair of an unlikely ash blond, arranged in an improbably youthful style.

"Hang oan, Olivia and me'll come doon and sit next tae ye."

"Oh *must* you," groans Elizabeth, *sotto voce*, as she and Sarah stand up and shift along two places to leave room. "Olivia's a dear friend, and a person of some class, but that Susan Hayward is such a *common* girl. Well at least I'll have *you* between me and them, Sarah."

The two newcomers leave their own crowded row with many apologies, and join Elizabeth and Sarah in the two seats adjoining the central aisle.

It strikes me as at least slightly odd that none of the other patrons in the vicinity seem to be aware of anything unusual in this group's behaviour. And *they* are just the usual heterogeneous cinema crowd. Maybe it's only me who can hear them. Maybe they are talking to me.

But they are not. It is simply that the rest of the audience is not paying particular attention, and for most of them, these interactions blend into the background babble.

The one they called 'Susan Hayward' is bubbling over with enthusiasm as he seats himself next to Sarah.

"Ah'm really lookin' forward tae the film—gie us a Poppet, Sarah, there's a guid lassie—oh aye, Ah just *love* thon Jeff Chandelier."

"It's *Chandler*," corrects Sarah, passing over a single sweet. "Jeff *Chandler.*"

Susan glances down resentfully at the meagre offering. "Aye, that's what Ah said."

"No Alec with you the night, Olivia?" Elizabeth asks, leaning forward to speak across the two others.

Olivia, settling herself at the end of the front row, gives her carefully teased hair a quick pat. "Naw, Liz, he's no' a big movie fan, my Alec. He's went out for a few drinks wi' yon Connie Stevens."

The plump cheeks crease into a little smile. "Just a drink, ye understand—I ken well she's got a fancy for him. Always running after him. I've told him not to encourage her, though I know for a fact there's nothing—well, personal—going on there."

The little smile broadens. "Believe me, by the time I've drained my Alec, he hasn't the strength for a wank, never mind anything more energetic."

Elizabeth shudders delicately at this *franc-parler*.

Olivia goes on, shaking her head from side to side. "Aye, she lives in a world of fantasy, poor Connie, daft bitch. But I've given Alec strict instructions, just to be on the safe side."

"Oh, ye dae right, Olivia," says Sarah, managing to cram two chocolates into her mouth at the same time, and placing the box on the floor well out of Susan's reach. "That Connie Stevens bears watching. Nice enough lassie in her way, but Ah wouldnae trust her wi' ma man, if Ah wis you."

Olivia appears unperturbed, and laughs girlishly. "Och well—you know what I always say, Sarah—if yiv got a licence for a dog, ye can let it run wild."

This sally is greeted with an appreciative laugh from Elizabeth and Sarah, but Susan raises an eyebrow.

"Ah hope you're no' referrin' tae ma brother as a *dog*, Miss de Havilland?" she says. "He'd no' be too pleased tae hear that."

Olivia sighs.

"Just a figure of speech, Susan dear. Not that you would know what one of those is, of course."

Her little smile is sour. "I keep forgetting my Alec's your brother. There's not much of a family resemblance, after all, thank God."

Susan appears mollified. Stretching out a hopeful hand in Sarah's direction, she continues, "Anyone else in, Liz?"

Sarah is blind to the invitation to contribute, while Elizabeth turns her head and scans the auditorium.

"Well, Susan, I *did* see Judy Garland and Bridie Gallacher in the queue. Maybe they're down in the stalls." Once again her eyes weigh up the occupants of the circle. "Oh—and there's Kay Starr and Vivien

Leigh over on the other side."

She points across the centre aisle.

"Oh aye, Ah see them."

Susan stands up and waves. "Good evening, Miss Starr, Miss Leigh. Awright, Miss Newton?" she bawls.

Olivia winces, and, while Susan's attention is otherwise engaged, Sarah struggles to retrieve a chocolate which has fallen near her feet.

Elizabeth looks up. "Oh? Miss *Newton*?"

Susan turns back. "Oh aye, Liz—that's Zoë Newton ower there, sittin' wi' Kay and Vivien."

"Really, Susan? Zoë Newton? And who's she, when she's at home?"

"She's a New Face," says Susan, sitting down. "Well, *fairly* new. I've only met her the once, masel'."

"I see. But who is she *named* for?" Elizabeth asks. "I don't know of any star called Zoë Newton."

Susan laughs. "Ye need tae get yersel' a telly, Liz. She's oan the adverts. Zoë Newton, the Milk Girl."

Elizabeth raises her eyebrows. "I already *have* a television, thank you, Miss Hayward. I just don't watch all the rubbish on STV like you do. BBC only for me and Sarah. Adverts indeed! What kind of actress names herself after somebody in an *advertisement*?"

There seems to be no answer to this.

Comes a pause in the conversation, during which Elizabeth continues to survey the audience.

"Nae sign of Miss Stewart, then, Liz?" asks Olivia, in her turn scanning the stalls. "Ah thought for sure she'd have been here tonight. After all, she's the star of the film."

"No, not at all, Olivia," corrects Sarah, round a mouthful of chocolate. With some difficulty, she swallows. "She's *featured*. The *star* is Jeanne Crain. Elaine Stewart only plays a cameo rôle. She's the slut at the start that gets her dress ripped aff."

"Aye, an' slut's about right," sniffs Susan, still eyeing Sarah's chocolates. "Ah saw Elaine Stewart oan ma way here, no' half an hour ago, in the Central Station. She wis bevied tae the gills, makin' a right exhibition of herself. Ah don't know why, but she always picks on *me* when she's pissed. Screamed me up an' everything—I was that embarrassed—everybody wis staring at me. Aye, slut's the word, right enough."

Elizabeth, turning round, fixes the speaker with an intimidating glare.

"Now, now, Susan, that's ungenerous. I'll not hear a word said against

Elaine, if you don't mind. She has problems, certainly, with the drink and that, but a nicer person you couldn't meet. A good heart, too, and nobody's fool. She's had a difficult life, that's all. If she's been drinking, it's best to avoid her altogether."

"Ah wis jist saying…"

"Yes, Liz is right," says Olivia, ganging up against the unfortunate Susan, "so you can shut yer trap, you."

She raises herself up in a fine taking and turns to her companion. "Anyway, *you've* a nerve to criticise Elaine—you've more than a taste for the drink yourself. What about that time you fell off the Suspension Bridge? Sober then, I suppose?"

Susan bridles. "Ah didnae fall—Ah wis *pushed.*"

"Pushed? Really? Well somebody had the right idea. Elizabeth is right. Miss Stewart's a decent soul. At least, she is when she's off the booze."

Olivia nudges a straying wave back into place.

"Onyway, we'll no' see Elaine the night. No, no. It's Thursday, her buroo day. She'll have got her dole money, and when she's got a pound in her pocket, that's it. All she thinks about is getting hold of a couple of bottles, and drinking herself senseless."

Just at that moment, the lights are lowered and the program commences.

I am all ears. I haven't missed a word of my neighbours' conversation. I don't understand all of it, by any means. But I know that the Green Door is near.

The first feature, a dim western starring war hero Audie Murphy, appears to be of little interest to anyone, judging by the subdued murmur of conversation which accompanies most of it.

The Fox Movietone News which follows arouses a little more enthusiasm.

"Lovely lassie, the Queen," whispers Sarah. "And disnae her mother look well? That's *you*, ye ken, Liz. You're not the Queen any longer, no, you're the Queen Mother now."

Elizabeth shudders delicately. "Sarah, my dear, you know perfectly well that I *never* described myself as the Queen. I have always remained Elizabeth, Duchess of York, which she was many years ago. Furthermore, I wouldn't want to be confused with that dreadful creature, the *real* Queen Mother."

"The real Queen Mother?" asks Olivia. "Auld Queen Mary? Don't tell me that one's still alive! She must be a hundred!"

"Very much so, Olivia. She's eighty-something. She doesn't go out much these days, she spends a lot of time in bed with her leg. But she shows her face now and then outside the pubs at closing time, hoping to pick up a bit of rough."

Olivia purses her lips.

"Really? Imagine that... Ah've no' seen her in years, myself. Ah wis sure she must be dead."

She takes out a cigarette and lights it before continuing.

"Is she still in yon big house in Renfrew Street, just up the road from you two?"

"Yes, Olivia. Mind you, she's not able to look after the place properly herself, now she's a bit incapacitated. She has that Maggie Wilde character living with her, lets her have a room there. Supposed to help her with the cleaning an' that."

Olivia nods. "Oh aye, Maggie Wilde, Ah know her, Ah think. Hangs around the Central Station. Always in a white trench coat, belted tight enough tae stop your circulation—is that the one?"

"Yes, that's Maggie, by the sound of it."

After a moment, Olivia returns to an earlier topic.

"But yer quite right tae keep your original name, Liz. That's the tradition. Once you're named, that's the name you stick with."

She smiles rather maliciously across Susan. "Not that it would be a problem for The Divine Sarah there, since she's been dead for forty years."

Sarah, unheeding, engulfs another Poppet.

"Ssh, girls, Ah'm trying tae *watch* this," protests Susan.

Next on the bill are the Pearl and Dean commercials. Everyone wonders which twin has the Toni, and thrills to the novelty of Bachelor's Soups, Chicken Noodle Flavour. They learn they are never alone with a Strand, and that Persil washes whiter.

And that a pretty blond recommends that they 'drink more milk'.

"That's *her*, Elizabeth," whispers Susan, trying to regain some points. "The one Ah wis talking aboot. Zoë Newton, the Milk Girl. Over there. The one sittin' wi' Kay and Vivien."

Elizabeth and Sarah simultaneously turn in the direction Susan is indicating, and inspect the claimant to the title.

"Well," says Elizabeth, looking back at the screen after a short pause. "I can see a resemblance, a certain similarity. Blond. Short hair, gamine style."

"Yes," agrees Sarah. "And about the right age. Should we recognise her claim, this Zoë Whatsit?"

"Oh, I think we can go that far, Sarah. We will acknowledge her for now and see how things develop. But I would say she has possibilities, myself. Of course we've yet to meet her. But, all things considered…"

"Aye. And she'll have to be formally presented."

Sarah pauses and looks round, feigning inattention, rather in the manner of someone waiting patiently to swat a crafty fly.

Then…

"And why don't ye buy yer *own* chocolates, Miss Hayward, instead of scoffing mine?" she exclaims triumphantly, bringing down her foot sharply on Susan's sneaky hand as it attempts a surreptitious flanking movement.

"Aargh!" yelps Susan. "Yiv near smashed ma wrist, ya fat cow!"

"Sorry, dear, Ah'm breaking in thae high heels for a friend." Sarah smiles smugly.

The commercial presentation draws to a close and the cinema lights go up to signal the intermission. The curtains draw together, and the auditorium is filled with the syrupy sounds of the Mantovani Orchestra playing that perennial favourite, *Charmaine*. A young lady with a glued-on smile and a slightly grubby white uniform tittups down the central stairway, a tray slung from her shoulders. As a spotlight hits her, she turns and takes up her station at the foot of the stairs, back to the railing, the rictus on her features revealing a major dental nightmare.

"Oh aye, a choc ice, that's for me," says Sarah, struggling to her feet and pushing past Susan in the direction of the salesgirl, before whom a queue is already forming. "Oh, sorry, Olivia, wis that yer foot?"

"Ice cream, now," shudders Elizabeth, turning to the others. "What am I to do with her? She's like the side of a house already."

"Maybe she's eating for two," smirks Olivia. "There's certainly room."

"Get us an ice cream, Sarah," calls Susan after the retreating figure, at the same time sneaking a chocolate from the box lying on the floor.

"Get yer own, ya tight bun. Whit am Ah, the Royal Bank a' Scotland?"

Conversation continues in a desultory manner until Sarah returns to her seat with two chocolate ice creams, and breath-taking news.

She passes one of her ices to Elizabeth, and sits down.

"She *is* here!—Elaine Stewart. Right at the back o' the circle. Oh, pissed, well pissed, by the look of her. Ah jist saw her—Ah don't think she clocked me. Have a look, Liz—back row, on the left, two in from the aisle. Ye cannae miss her, there's naebody else in the row bar her."

As one the four heads turn. And so does mine, carefully.

"Watch out," hisses Sarah. "Discretion! If she sees ye looking, she'll cause a scene. Ye ken whit Elaine's like when she's had a few."

There appears to be little likelihood of that, as the person in question, a short insignificant-looking man, seems to be entirely engrossed in the contents of a brown paper bag which sits in his lap. Occasionally it is raised in the direction of his mouth, then replaced.

He appears to be initially unaware of the interest he is arousing. No more than five foot six or seven, mid to late twenties, shabbily dressed and solidly built, and with a head of thick, dusty-looking brown hair, he continues to swig contentedly from the concealed bottle. Pencilled eyebrows of an improbably rich chestnut brown and lashes with a coating of mascara, along with ticks of eye-liner at the corners of the eyes, are complimented by a beige complexion of an unnatural uniformity.

But suddenly, and for no obvious reason, the benign appearance changes. The chin goes up and the head is thrown dramatically across the right shoulder, itself thrust forward. The eyes glare, the eyebrows rise. The teeth are bared, the lips drawn back in a smile that resembles a snarl.

"It's a *lie*! No photographs, *please*!"

This, delivered at top volume, appears to be addressed to no-one in particular.

"Oh aye, here we go," murmurs Olivia, turning back. "For God's sake, Susan, stop staring, don't catch her eye."

But it is too late. Whatever the level of inebriation of the newcomer, there is obviously no problem with the eyesight.

"*I* see you, Miss Hayward, you *slut*. Don't you *dare* touch Fury!"

"Oh—she's featuring Bette Davis tonight," says Elizabeth, turning away. "That's from *Another Man's Poison*. Olivia's right, best not to look, it only encourages her."

"Oh, Jerry, don't let's ask for the *moon*—we have the *stars*…"

"Aw, fer fuck's sake, shut up, ya bam pot."

Surprisingly, this, contributed by a gentleman sitting with his lady friend in the row in front of the newcomer, appears to have some effect.

And at this point the cinema lights are lowered, and everyone settles down to enjoy the main feature.

A United Artists production, in Cinemascope, the titles proclaim. The stars next appear individually in vignette and voice-over—handsome Jeff Chandler, appealing Jeanne Crain, soulful Gail Russell. Suddenly, the driving, rumbustious title music changes to a siren-like and seductive strain, strings swoon, muted trumpets croon orgasmically, and a well-upholstered blond, back to the camera, turns her head and looks invitingly over her shoulder.

"*...and Elaine Stewart, in...*"

A hand reaches out from the surrounding darkness, seizes the back of the low-cut gown and rips it.

"*...The Tattered Dress.*"

And all hell breaks loose.

A clattering of feet is heard as the little person from the back row suddenly gallops down the steep central staircase towards the front of the circle. Arrived there, he turns his back to the low railing and faces his audience.

"It's a *lie*! I am the *real* Elaine Stewart."

"Oh no..." groans Elizabeth.

"Whit the fuck?" mutters a gentleman further along the front row.

"You tell them, hen!" guffaws Susan.

"What a *dump*!" exclaims the newcomer, eyes popping.

"*Beyond the Forest*. Oh dear," says sympathetic Sarah.

The eyes flash again, and Elaine continues her rant.

"Fasten your *seat* belts—it's going to be a *bumpy* night."

Obviously 'the *real* Elaine Stewart' has an ample supply of quotes from Bette Davis's most admired films.

"Fer God's sake, somebody get the manager," shouts a lady from downstairs in the stalls.

Susan by this time is convulsed with laughter.

"Gawn, Miss Stewart," she yells. "Gie's a show. Naebody really wants tae watch this load of old shite."

Unfortunately this remark is not appreciated by the star of the film.

The head turns, the eyebrows rise.

"How *dare* you criticise my latest vehicle, Miss Hayward!"

Eyes glittering, Elaine approaches the end of the row and leans past Olivia.

"Excuse me, Miss de Havilland, always admired your work," she says politely. "But let me get at that skinny hoor, if you don't mind."

And stretching across Olivia, she slaps Susan smartly across the face.

"Kssh! Take that, you bitch."

"Ow—ya pure cunt!" shrieks Susan, clutching her face, and rising from her seat. "Yiv burst one of ma boils wi' yer fuckin' nails!"

"Such *language*, really!" protests Elizabeth, covering her ears.

"And were you saving that particular one for a special occasion, dear?" Olivia asks Susan nastily.

"Oh, for Christ's *sake*!" shouts someone.

In the background, *The Tattered Dress* continues to unreel before a suddenly disinterested audience.

Elaine returns to her position against the circle rail as Susan attempts to push past Olivia in pursuit, screeching, "Jist you wait till Ah get ma hauns on *you*, Miss Stewart."

Olivia sticks out a foot, and unlucky Susan trips over it.

"Sit down, Susan, *please*, you'll only make things worse."

Sarah saves Susan from a nasty fall by grabbing the back of her *faux* leather jacket, which gives way with a loud ripping sound.

"Och, fer fuck's sake, this jacket's *new*!"

Susan, almost in tears, and still clutching her oozing face, turns back and resumes her seat.

She pulls her hand away and examines its contents.

"Huv ye goat a hanky, Sarah?"

Sarah shudders delicately. "No, sorry dear. But have a Poppet, Susan, yil feel better."

"This is a disgrace! Will somebody please inform the management?" demands a rather posh lady on the other side of the aisle.

Intrepid and triumphant, Elaine, once more in charge, confronts her audience.

"Yes, the *real* Elaine Stewart is *back*. In those days, we had *faces*."

"She's Gloria Swanson now—*Sunset Boulevard*…" murmurs Sarah.

The hands reach out. "And I love you all, you little people out there in the dark."

A sentimental tear or two spills from the painted eyes, and tracks mascara down the cheeks. Some wag in the audience starts to applaud. Very quickly more join in, and soon the circle echoes to the roar of clapping hands and stamping feet. Elaine tucks her paper bag under one arm, leans back and hoists herself up onto the narrow circle rail, where she balances precariously.

She retrieves the bag, raises it, takes a quick swig, and, stretching out her arms in a gesture of gratitude, beams love at her fans.

"Oh no, I can't look, she'll go over that rail in a minute," whispers Elizabeth.

Susan's eyes gleam.

"Oh, Ah hope so—and maybe if Ah wis tae…?"

"Don't you move, Susan, I'm warning you, or it'll be *you* that goes over," threatens Olivia.

"Ah don't know why yiz are aw picking oan me, it's *her* that's makin' a show of herself," whines Susan.

"A pastille, Susan?" says kindly Sarah.

Elaine's embrace becomes wider as the applause continues to grow in volume. Still clutching the paper bag firmly in one hand, visibly moved, apparently unconscious of the ironic nature of the accolade, she first draws her hands together to her chest, and then, still seated, inclines her head graciously.

Tears trickle down the cheeks, taking much of the make-up with them. *Oh, the glamour, the acclaim!* As she raises her head again, balancing carefully, the paper bag is once more raised to the lips, and then waved in a general benediction.

"Thank you, thank you. I love you all."

And just at that moment, two burly commissionaires thunder down the stairs, and flank Elaine, one on each side.

"Come oan, son, quietly now, time tae go," says the first.

As Elaine confronts the newcomers, the eyes glare and open even wider, and the lips are once again drawn back from the teeth in a snarl.

"Unhand me, you traitorous dogs—my people, arise, defend your sovereign! It is I, your mother, the Tsarina!"

The second official says, not unkindly, "Ah don't care if ye *are* Mother Teresa, pal—it's time tae leave."

"What? Mother Teresa? The ignorance of some people!" tuts Sarah, incensed. "Really! '*Your mother, the Tsarina.*' That's *The Scarlet Empress*—Marlene Dietrich."

The first gentleman, obviously unaware or careless of his colleague's inexcusable gaffe, takes a firm hold of an arm.

"Let's go, pal."

On the other side, the second commissionaire grabs the other.

But Catherine the Great is not to be taken so easily.

"Release me, you ruffians! Summon Potemkin and the Imperial Guard!"

Shaking off the clutches of officialdom, she raises her arms beseechingly to the crowd.

"Sons of Holy Russia! Rescue your empress!"

Arms still outstretched, imploring succour, she leans backwards.

And vanishes.

The applause dies away as quickly as it had begun, and every breath is bated, every eye riveted on the unfolding scene. What a night for one and six! Not only two films and an exhibition of total lunacy from a deeply disturbed person, but a suicide!

However, obviously accustomed to dealing with such situations, the two officials manage to neatly grab a leg each at the last moment, and

Elaine hangs briefly suspended upside down in mid-air over the stalls beneath. Arcing into the void, the contents of her pockets are followed by the contents of the brown paper bag. There comes a resounding *clunk* as the bottle that was inside finds a target.

"Right, young man, time tae go, it's back tae Paramount for you."

"Warner Brothers, if you don't mind!"

Elaine is dragged forward, dusted down, and set upright. Each of the uniformed gentlemen takes a firm grip under an armpit, and the reluctant star, paddling air, is hoisted upward towards the exit.

As the unlikely cortège moves off, Elaine has a final word to say.

"Lord Cecil, Lord Burghley—conduct me to my chamber!"

"*The Virgin Queen*," says Liz, relaxing back into her seat. "Nice exit line."

As I leave the cinema later, I ponder the scenes I have witnessed. Who *are* these extraordinary creatures, these men who call each other by feminine names, apparently unselfconscious and comfortable with their assumed identities? Why are they 'named' after notable female figures, the majority of whom, it appears, belong to the Hollywood pantheon?

I put on my gloves, wrap my university scarf firmly round my neck and tuck the ends into my coat. It is getting late. Ten-thirty, early January, Christmas just past, and it is *cold*, Glasgow-cold. A few constipated snow-flakes are attempting to fall, and glitter fitfully under the twinkling Christmas lights.

I head towards the bus station, and continue to reflect on the nature of these unusual characters. Seated directly behind them in the cinema, I had relished every word of their occasionally surreal interaction. I want to know more. In some undefined way, I want to know *them*, perhaps even to belong to their company.

The Green Door looms before me, just out of reach. I sense the proximity of excitement and danger at the same time, perhaps in equal measure. It appears that, just as I have suspected, there is a whole side of life of which I have been completely unaware.

How does one *join*? There seems to be no obvious answer.

But my reverie is interrupted brusquely. Just on the corner of Waterloo Street and Hope Street I see a by now familiar figure. Obviously the bottle of whatever it was has been replaced, but this time without the benefit of a concealing paper bag. Elaine Stewart is once again laying off to anyone interested enough to listen. By and large, the late night crowd pays little attention—just another mad drunk cluttering up Glasgow's streets, harmless enough in all conscience, nothing more than a minor oddity.

The litany is much as before—quotes from famous films, lines expressing womanly chagrin, heroism, despair and resignation. I begin to appreciate that it is more of an internal monologue than a speech. The flashing Christmas lights paint the made-up face now red, now yellow, now a ghastly blue like the bloom on week-old beef. There appears to be no reason why the performance should ever end.

But end it does. While I watch, once again the guardians of moral authority—this time two uniformed police constables—have decided it is time to step in and restore order. The little figure is trundled off, this time in the direction of the police box at the end of the street.

On my way home, I continue to turn over in my mind the events of the evening. This is a mystery I need to investigate further. I have become aware recently of the hurried intimacies that may occur in some of the many public conveniences that dot the cityscape of Glasgow's central area. And of the furtive goings-on in darkened places like the cinema I have recently left. But that there may be a social side to this hidden world is news to me.

'He danced under the lights', reads the headline in the Daily Record a day or two later. I learn that Michael Feeley, of no fixed abode, was arrested in Waterloo Street for the offence known as 'breach of the peace'. Fined one pound, he claimed that he had been out celebrating the birth of a child to his brother, and had perhaps consumed more drink than was wise; that he was very sorry; and that he could promise the court it would never happen again.

The unlikely nature of this assurance becomes clear when it is revealed that this is the defendant's nineteenth conviction.

4. *What's Your Name?*

What's your name? Is it Mary or Sue?
What's your name?
Do I stand a chance with you?
Don and Juan, 1962.

February 1962.

Upstairs in Glasgow's Waterloo Street bus station is the waiting area, a harshly lit cavern that runs the entire width of the terminus beneath. Four hard wooden benches form a line across the middle of the floor for the convenience of those awaiting their homeward transport. Seated thereon, you will see facing you the mouths of five or six staircases which lead down to the departure platforms. Behind you, windows look out onto Waterloo Street. To your right, the conveniences, ladies and gents.

A Friday evening, eight thirty. I have just left the Royal Scottish Academy of Music after my piano lesson. I am currently tussling with Schumann's G minor sonata, which is giving me considerable problems. Why does the damned thing have to go so *fast*?

Only a few people are about, sitting carefully apart on separate benches. The one nearest to the toilets is unoccupied. My bench is next. A young mother with a child of perhaps two is seated on the adjacent one. And an older man, half-reading his *Glasgow Herald,* half-asleep, is at the far end.

I am here to catch my bus home. I will have about half an hour to wait, and am reading a book to pass the time. Though it's a quiet evening so far, it pays to keep your wits about you in rowdy Glasgow, particularly on a weekend night. But the pubs won't close for another hour and a half, and at the moment all is peaceful.

I am aware that the gentlemen's toilet here is regularly used as a pickup point, and is even the scene, now and then, of a rushed intimate encounter when urgency overcomes caution. I have struck lucky there once or twice. The experience was exciting, but oddly shameful, and far from comfortable. Needs must, from time to time, naturally. But tonight, it appears to be completely neglected.

I turn a page of my book.

After some time, the sound of voices floats up from downstairs:

"…so she says tae me, *'Oh aye, we all know whit you are. Don't think ye fool me, or anyone else in this close. My man says it's a disgrace.'* So Ah says, *'Well he should know—Ah've had him'.*"

"You never! And have ye?"

"Och no, he's an ugly bastard."

The volume of the conversation rises as the speakers mount the stairs to the waiting area.

"Miss Eaton! Mind yer big feet—ye nearly had ma sling backs aff!"

"Well, if you will wear they peerie heels at your age, Connie."

As the group of young men reaches the top of the stairs, I see there are four of them. Vivacious, extravagant of gesture, self-confident, loud, nonchalant, apparently careless of the impression they create. Yet this is also a performance; they move as though on a stage, larger than life, consciously playing to an audience.

As I catch sight of them, I immediately feel uncomfortable. I am riven, simultaneously spellbound and scared. I don't dare look directly at them, but am half-aware that it is as if someone has switched on a rose-coloured spotlight, illuminating this drab corner of Glasgow. Around the edges dark shadows lie, where nameless menace may lurk. But the centre of the light is hypnotic, bright and inviting. And it is theirs, they carry it with them. I understand that they know secrets. And half afraid, half attracted, I sense our kinship. These are not elderly dowagers, like Sarah and Elizabeth. These are people of my own age.

Two of them approach my bench. The taller, indeed, very tall, broad-shouldered, with a long pale face, a large nose and a head of tightly-curled coppery hair, sits down at the far end and lights up a cigarette. The other, slighter, with short, crisp brown hair and a cratered complexion stands behind.

"Gie's a light, Wilma," says the latter.

Wilma obliges and passes a lighter back. Their two friends are still lingering by the top of the stairs, deep in some private conversation.

"So, Connie—whit's the score wi' you and Alec McGowan?" Wilma asks without turning round. "Is it oan or aff or whit? Is it real or is it aw in yer heid? Ah cannae keep track, masel'."

The other takes a deep draw on his cigarette and leans forward confidingly.

"Aw—you know the way Alec is, Wilma—here wan minute, gone the next. But he's ma husband, when all's said and done. Ah've warned him, mind, Ah'll be suing for divorce if he's no' careful. Then Ah can retire tae Florida on ma Alamo money."

This last with a girlish giggle, a shrug of the shoulders and a toss of

59

the head.

I am guessing that *Alamo money* may be *alimony*.

Wilma looks dubious.

"Nae offense, Connie, but yer wasting your time chasin' after Alec. He's jist using you tae buy him a drink or a meal now and then. Big Olivia's got him under her thumb. She's a crafty auld bitch, her. OK, ye may say that she's auld enough tae be his mother, but she's no' short of a bob or two. And Alec'll always be where the cash is."

Connie dismisses this.

"Och, there's nothin' like *that* goin' on, Wilma, him an' Olivia. If she wants tae take Alec oot and spend a few bob on him that's fine wi' me— she jist likes tae be seen around wi' a nice-lookin' fella, it's good fer her image, as she sees it. It's no' as if Alec has tae actually *dae* anything for it. Nothin', well, ye know…"

"Oh? Is that whit he tells ye?" Wilma sniffs.

The arrival of the group has not gone unremarked. Indeed, the atmosphere has altered perceptibly from weary to wary. Young Mum has gathered her child up on the bench beside her, and Glasgow Herald, fully awake now, has put down his newspaper and sits there looking disapproving and uncomfortable.

Meanwhile, the other two newcomers have joined their friends. One short, handsome, dark-haired and smartly-dressed, the other taller, with a pale, freckled complexion and red hair. They cluster round the seated Wilma. Connie disagrees with some remark the redhead has just made.

"Naw, Shirley, Ah'm telling you, I saw them last night, in the *Strand*, holding hands. 'S that no' right, Nicky?"

"Aye, that's right," says good-looking Nicky, "love's young dream. All over each other, they were."

Shirley seems unconvinced.

"Well, Miss Strasberg told me Patrick smashed her over the head wi' a bottle for nae reason at all. Jist the other day, it wis. Ah'll tell you this, if any man of mine treated me like that, ye'd no see me for dust."

"No' that you've ever hud a man longer than five minutes," Connie snips, "as far as Ah can remember, anyway."

Shirley doesn't rise to this. She shakes her head in a motion of exaggerated despair.

"Ah'm tellin' ye, it'll end up in murder wi' they two."

"Naw, it's just the way they are. They're mad about each other really," says Nicky.

"Aye, an' mad's the word."

The one called Wilma hasn't taken any part in this exchange, but has stood up and is looking round, taking in the other passengers. I try to appear as inconspicuous as possible. Difficult, since they are gathered around the far end of my bench.

However, attention is directed elsewhere for the moment.

"Aw, look at the wee lassie." Wilma strolls past me towards the mother and child seated on the neighbouring seat. "Ah love weans, so Ah do."

She bends down to examine the child more closely. The latter looks up at her, eyes bright with curiosity.

"Aye, jist a shame ye cannae bear them," responds Shirley, with a laugh, following her. "And it's a wee boy, anyway, no' a wee lassie."

Young Mum can hardly be unaware that she and her offspring are the object of scrutiny. But she carefully avoids reacting either by word or by look. Like me, she senses that this exchange is in some manner a prelude to confrontation and challenge.

Wilma is not convinced. Straightening up and turning to her friend, she continues, "Don't be daft, Shirley, you can see it's a wee lassie. Ask Connie, see what she thinks."

Shirley sneers. "How would Connie know? Her mammy had her in pigtails till she was forty-two."

Connie, hearing this, moves to join the other two. "Miss Eaton, dae Ah hear you scandalisin' me? Ah'm twenty-one, fer yer information."

The one they called Nicky sits down on the other end of my bench, takes out a pen knife, opens it, and starts cleaning his nails.

Shirley continues. "Naw, Connie, nae offense, we just wanted your opinion. Now—would you say that wean was a wee boy or a wee lassie?"

The child's mother, although obviously uncomfortable at being the subject of this discussion, and at the proximity of the group, continues to ignore them.

However, support is about to arrive from an unexpected quarter.

"Why dae yiz no' just leave the lady alone, you lot?"

It is the man who has up till now been sitting further along with his newspaper.

"She's no' bothering you, is she?"

And turning to the lady, "Just ignore them, hen. You can see whit they are, can't ye?"

Whether she can or cannot we will never know, as she is clearly not prepared to discuss the subject. Starting to button up the child's coat, ('*Come on, pet, our bus'll be here by now,*' her accent marking her as a denizen of Newton Mearns, or of some equally affluent suburb), she prepares to leave.

"Aye, best ye get off, hen," continues her defender, folding his newspaper. "Ye don't want to be sitting around here wi' thae lowlifes."

Still unresponsive, the mother carries her child towards the exit stairs, which lead to one of the departure platforms.

But she is not permitted to leave entirely unscathed.

"Aye, gawn, hen, yer man'll be wanting his tea." This from Wilma.

"Ah hope yiv something hot in the oven," laughs Shirley.

"If yiv no', send him roon tae me," Connie concludes, as mother and child disappear from view.

Satisfied with their victory, the three sit down on the vacated bench.

Mr Glasgow Herald, however, decides it is time to continue his contribution.

"Here, now, enough of that kind of talk. That lady wis no' botherin' anybody. You lot should learn some manners."

"An' what's it got to dae wi' you?" asks Wilma, looking over. "Ah wis just showing a friendly interest, that's all."

"Aye—an' if Ah wis you, Ah'd mind ma ane business," Connie adds.

The gentleman rises to his feet and continues, "Ah'll tell ye this—it's your sort that gets this toon a bad name."

He wags his folded newspaper in the general direction of the group. "Nae wonder decent people are feart tae walk round on their own."

He focuses on Wilma.

"An' if Ah wis your faither, ma lad, Ah'd gie you a good skelp roon the ear, so Ah wid, big an all as ye are."

He takes a step towards Wilma, who, in mock panic, leaps to her feet, claps hands to face and runs behind the bench, screeching, "Help, Nicky, help, Ah'm being molested."

Nicky has taken no part in the preceding encounter, but now stands up and saunters over. His entire demeanour has shifted in an instant from good-natured and likeable to aggressive and threatening. This change is not lost on Mr Glasgow Herald.

"You lay a hand on any of them and you're in trouble, pal. You'd better go and get your bus while your legs are still workin'."

No more than that. Still holding his pen knife, he moves protectively in front of Connie and Shirley. And the air is suddenly charged with menace. This is serious. Or may become so at any minute.

"Imagine—threatening a woman in ma condition," sobs Wilma in the background. "Yer no gentleman, sir."

"Did ye no' hear me?" says Nicky, his knife hand raised, advancing a step.

"Aye, go on, beat it." Shirley and Connie stand up and join him, confident now the cavalry has arrived.

Wisely, Glasgow Herald decides discretion is the better part, and limps away, shaking his head and muttering to himself, "It was a sad day when they stopped the National Service."

He turns again, raising his voice. "A couple of years in the army…"

"Aw, bugger off, Hopalong," Connie interrupts before he can finish.

"Ah'm pregnant," Wilma wails.

But the wee man's not leaving without firing a final volley.

"Bunch o' fuckin' jessies!" he shouts as he disappears down the stairs.

"How did he know?" wonders Shirley with unsubtle irony.

Connie heads off towards the toilet. And amid gales of laughter the other three make themselves comfortable on the neighbouring bench.

Now we are alone.

I should probably leave, I think. They have managed to intimidate everyone else, now they will start on me.

But somehow I can't. I am fascinated and petrified.

Sure enough, it is only a moment or two until the one called Nicky approaches me. He folds his pen-knife and puts it back in his pocket.

"Have ye got a light, dear?"

I look up from my book, as if I had just this moment become aware of the group's presence.

"Sorry, I don't smoke."

He raises his eyebrows and smiles. "Really? You should give it a go, it would suit your look. Sophisticated."

I have already registered him as attractive. But face to face, he is more than that.

"Here," he says, "Try one of mine."

Almost visibly shaking, in an odd mixture of delight and terror, I take the proffered cigarette. Not quite my first.

He turns towards the others. "Hey, Wilma—len' us yer lighter."

Focusing again on me, he goes on, "And just who are *you*, dear?"

Wilma throws her lighter to Nicky. He catches it neatly.

"My name's George," I mutter, as he leans towards me to light my cigarette. As he gets closer, I see that his eyes are dark brown, and that his thick black hair is obviously dyed. He smells pleasantly of after-shave. Not the ubiquitous *Old Spice* but something subtler, warmer. He sits down on my right.

"George? Och, yer no way a George."

'No? What am I then?' I wonder.

"Wilma, Shirley, get ower here a minute."

The two others approach and Shirley sits down on my left, while Wilma settles herself next to Nicky. I am flanked, trapped.

'Shit,' I think, *'I'm in trouble. I should have left when they arrived. Too late now.'*

Nicky leans across me. "You're good at this, Shirley. We need tae find a name for this lassie."

He turns towards me again. "This yer first time on the scene, dear?"

I am not really sure what that means, but guess that *'Yes'* would be the right answer.

"Yes," I say.

Nicky smiles, while the other two inspect me. "Aye, Ah thought so. Now, we need tae find ye a name."

He wrinkles his brow in thought.

"How about Rita Hayworth?" suggests Shirley? "That red hair…"

"No," says Wilma, "her hair's no' red, Shirley. *Yours* is red. Hers is auburn. Lovely colour."

My hair is indeed the shade known as auburn.

"That's it!" says Nicky, looking delighted. "Auburn. Audrey Auburn. Audrey Hepburn. That's the name for you, hen."

He examines me intently. "Yer tall, yer slim—it's perfect. You're Audrey Hepburn now. Unless you object…?"

Why would I? He could have picked someone I detested. But I have always admired the delightful Miss Hepburn.

"No, it's fine, I like it," I say.

Amazingly, slowly, the icy lump in my throat begins to dissolve. These people appear to accept me as one of them. Without a question, they know who and what I am.

I am Audrey Hepburn.

The hinges of the Green Door creak alluringly.

"Jist right, Nicky," says Shirley, clapping her hands. "Audrey Hepburn. Aye, ye're her tae the life, hen. As Nicky says, tall an' slim—and nae tits!"

This provokes an outburst of laughter in which I join slightly nervously. But I am beginning to get the smallest inkling of how these interactions work.

Just then, Connie returns from the toilet.

"Over here, Connie," Nicky calls. "There's a new star in heaven tonight. Connie Stevens—meet Audrey Hepburn. Audrey—Connie."

Connie sits down on the other side of Shirley.

"Awright, Audrey?" she smiles in a friendly way. "Got a light, Nicky?"

Nicky still has Wilma's lighter, and stretches across me and Shirley and lights Connie's cigarette.

"Hello, Connie," I say.

As we sit and chat, I examine my new friends more closely. Nicky wants to know more about me and my background, but I keep my answers vague and general. My local newspaper, *The Rutherglen Reformer*, would have a banner headline were it ever to come to its notice that Audrey Hepburn lived locally. I am relieved to learn that none of the present company knows Rutherglen at all well, or, as far as I can tell, knows anyone else who lives there. Even so, I will play my cards close to my chest until I become more familiar with this new world.

'Connie Stevens', otherwise Jim, apparently, is twenty-one. Tall and slim, he would be good-looking were it not for the remains of adolescent acne which mar his face. He comes from Shawlands, an area of southern Glasgow with which I am unfamiliar. I will learn later that his earlier reference to *Alamo money* was no deliberate shaft of wit, and that his occasional malapropisms are inadvertent. He seems to suffer from a kind of verbal dyslexia, and words, often short and simple words, tend to come out wrong. I note for now that, though he is pleasant enough, his attempts at humour are distinctly second-hand.

'Shirley Eaton', or Archie, of medium height, tending to plumpness, with a pale complexion, freckles and red hair, is older, perhaps twenty-five. He works, in his own words, *'in the brothel above Lyons' Book Shop'*. I know the Sauchiehall Street shop well, but had no idea that its upper floors housed a *maison de joie*.

"Oh yes," says Shirley, "I'm the madam. You know, take the money, buy the johnnies, make sure the girls are safe, that sort of thing. You'll have to come round for a cup of tea one afternoon, Audrey, meet the girls."

Me, in a house of prostitution?

"Oh, yes, I'd like that," I say.

Shirley strikes me on the surface as being light-hearted, agreeable and obliging, but I sense a certain hard core and a self-serving quality beneath the amiable exterior. It's well concealed, but it's there.

'Wilma Flintstone' is an oddity, even in this company. Perhaps twenty-two, he is about six foot two, and built in proportion. Deep chest, broad shoulders, a long pallid face, large hands and feet, hair of an unlikely

65

bronze shade, tightly crinkled. More than a hint of make-up, foundation and powder. The dainty gestures and fey remarks seem more than usually unlikely, issuing from this robust frame. Yet under the improbable exterior, I recognise a warm and engaging personality, and his talk brims with self-deprecating wit and humour. William hails, I learn, from Blackhill, a notorious outer Glasgow satellite estate known colloquially as *The Ponderosa* for the level of crime and violence it houses.

I have never been there, but know its reputation.

I am interested too, to discover that this name game has a wider remit than I had at first imagined. Not only is 'Wilma Flintstone' a fictional personage, but, bizarrely, a cartoon character.

Nicky is a complete contrast to the others. He is just *Nicky*, it seems. I will find out when I come to know him better that that is not his real name, that the 'Nicky' is as assumed as the 'Connie' and the 'Wilma'. Smartly dressed and notably attractive, he differs sharply in his style and deportment from the others. Whereas they cheerfully and unselfconsciously flaunt feminine mannerisms, speech patterns and names, he is distinctly masculine both in appearance and behaviour. He certainly seems at home in this company, and I get the idea that he looks on the others as 'his girls'. His earlier defence of them when it appeared as if violence was about to erupt reinforces this impression. He comes from Bridgeton, I learn, an inner city area of Glasgow with a rowdy reputation. The *Saracen's Head*, or 'Sarry Heid', at Bridgeton Cross, is one of the most notorious of Glasgow's watering holes. Unlike the other three, he has a regular job. He is a bus driver, it appears, working for Glasgow Corporation, the orange and green city buses, not the red SMT buses which run from this garage out to the suburbs.

I am already half-smitten. He is not tall, maybe five foot eight. Solidly built and broad shouldered, he has a round, handsome, and oddly innocent face; a mobile mouth above a dimpled chin; and dark, liquid eyes. But it is more than his looks that turn my knees to jelly. He exudes a warmth and sympathetic quality that I find irresistible. He is one of those people who, once they turn their attention to you, give you the impression that you are the most interesting and fascinating person in the world. And that is something that is hard to fight against.

Although all four intrigue me, he does so in a very different way from the others. He seems to be taken with me, too, although I understand that this is partly because of my novelty value, and the fact that I am the newest addition to his stable of 'stars', his latest creation.

Of the fact that, this evening, Frankenstein-like, he has unchained a monster that will take to the perfumed swamp of gay Glasgow like a duck to its home pond, he is for the moment unaware. As is the monster itself.

"C'mon, let's head over tae Central Station," says Connie, standing up. "There's eff-all daein' here."

Shirley also rises to her feet. "Aye, OK, Connie—this place is dead."

Just dug up, it looks as though I am about to be reinterred.

"Right," says Nicky, getting up in his turn. "You coming, Audrey?"

"Yes, alright."

Why would I refuse? Buses run up to eleven or later, I'm in no rush.

"Wilma?"

"No' me, Ah'm off tae Clyde Street tae meet Lena fae work. Ah'll catch up with yiz after, you lot, OK?" says Wilma, yawning.

"Awright, Wilma, see ye later, keep yer hand on yer halfpenny," says Connie as Wilma traipses off. "C'mon, Audrey, Shirley."

Inside my head I hear a *snick*. Somehow or other, the Green Door is unlocked. It opens just enough for me to peep through. Soon, I know, it will swing wide.

What, I wonder, lies on the other side?

The four of us troop down the stairs towards the exit, turn left, and cross Hope Street. A few yards further on, we arrive at Central Station. Next to the Central Hotel, we enter through a narrow passage, which debouches into the main concourse.

It is always busy here. Too early yet for the drunks who will swarm in after the pubs close, hoping they have retained enough of their faculties to locate their homebound trains. But a sizable crowd of commuters of all ages already throngs the main part of the station. I follow my new friends through the press, and we head for the far side, where a further exit leads down a flight of stairs into busy Union Street. To the right of the top of these stairs is the opening to another flight, which leads to the gentlemen's toilets. A weighing machine is on the far side of this entrance, and next to that the station's licensed buffet.

We arrive outside the bar, where we stop. Nicky explains to me that this is the position of choice, and that any regular denizen of 'our' world will usually stop by here if in town, to see who is around, to share gossip, and to generally catch up. And possibly to try their luck in the public toilet, which has, as I am already aware, a reputation as a pickup point.

"Mind you," says Connie, "If bucking the cottages is your thing, Audrey, the best one is the bust deposit. It aw goes on there."

I already know that 'cottages' is gay slang for public toilets. But— 'bucking'? And 'the bust deposit'? Somewhere you leave your bosom to be looked after?

But no, of course… As I have said, I am not entirely unfamiliar with the activities which can go on in the bus depot we have just left.

"St Vincent de Paul for late at night. Or The Black Hole, if yer feeling daring and yiv had a few," laughs Nicky. "Or so these two tell me. Ah'm not one for the cottages, masel'. Ah've nae trouble finding a bit of fun without hangin' round places like thon."

I would, I think, be only too happy to provide as much fun as required. But—how does that work? What is the acceptable way to express my interest?

What a lot I have to learn. I keep quiet.

Nothing happens for a moment or two.

Then, "Oh, fer fuck's sake, will ye look at that!" exclaims Shirley.

That is a young man in a tightly belted white raincoat—collar turned up, hands thrust deep into pockets, shoulders and hips competing for maximum sway—who is swivelling his way towards us from the direction of the magazine and book stall in the centre of the station.

I recognise this one. I have seen him round here before.

"Maggie Wilde," murmurs Connie. "How aboot that walk? If ye could bottle that ye'd make a fortune."

Her expression sours. "Gets oan ma nerves, she does."

'*I sold my heart to the junkman…*' I hear the newcomer singing to himself, as he heads our way.

"Aye. Maggie Wilde." mutters Shirley, drawing on her cigarette, as he approaches. "Always on the scrounge, that one."

'*…and I'll never fall in love again.*'

He reaches us, and looks round the group.

"Awright lassies, Nicky?"

"Aye, OK Maggie, yersel'?" says Nicky.

"No' bad, no' bad. Huv any of yiz saw Big Dora Doll? We wis supposed tae be gawn tae the pictures, but Ah waited half an hour for her an' she never turned up. Bloody freezing ma arse off outside the La Scala. Probably picked up a bit of trade, the slut, she's man-mad, that one."

If she is expecting a response, there is none forthcoming.

"Onyway, Ah'm off doon the *El Guero* fer a coffee. Onybody fancy it?"

There is a further pause.

"Onybody goat a fag?"

Total silence.

Maggie waits, looking from one to the other of the group.

"Aw, c'moan, wan of yiz must have a spare fag!"

Shirley sighs heavily.

"How is it yiv never goat ony fags, Miss Wilde? If ye want tae smoke, buy yer ain."

Maggie shrugs. "Ah've jist run oot."

"They sell them ower there," says Connie pointedly, indicating the bookstall a few yards away.

"Oh, by the way," Nicky suddenly says, filling the ensuing silence, "you'll not know Audrey, she's new. Audrey, meet Maggie Wilde. Maggie—Audrey."

The newcomer registers my presence, and turns to me with an ingratiating smile.

"Hello, Audrey, nice tae meet ye. Goat a fag, hen?"

"Audrey disnae smoke, Maggie." This is Connie.

Maggie looks me up and down, puzzled.

"Ye don't smoke? Why? Huv ye stoaped?"

I'm not sure how to respond. "Er—no. I haven't started yet."

This provokes an outburst of merriment. Shirley, particularly amused, throws a friendly arm round my shoulder.

She turns to Maggie, resigned, shaking her head. "See *you*, Miss Wilde…"

She takes her own cigarette from her mouth. "Here, fer Christ's sake, ya tight bun, huv a draw oan this. Just the one, mind."

She passes her half-smoked cigarette to the newcomer.

"And dinnae make a cow's arse of it wi' they slobbery lips of yours."

Maggie takes the proffered cigarette, greedily sucks in a lungful of smoke, and passes it reluctantly back.

Shirley examines it critically, then puts it back in her mouth.

"An' now ye can fuck off," says Connie. "Wheel yer arse doon tae Clyde Street, flog yer fud fer five bob and buy yersel' a packet of fags."

Maggie sniffs disdainfully.

"Very well, Miss Stevens. I know when I'm no' wanted."

"Really? Did ye huv a revelation?" wonders Shirley.

Maggie chooses to ignore this. She turns to me.

"Lovely tae meet ye, Audrey. If yer new in the toon, maybe you should be a wee bit careful about the company you keep, dear? Not Nicky, he's lovely…"

Oh yes, I know.

69

"…but this pair of sluts."

Connie sighs and turns away. Shirley, after grinding out her cigarette with her shoe, immediately takes another from her packet and lights it spitefully.

"Gawn, piss off, Maggie. If Ah see Dora, Ah'll pass oan the message, OK? The *El Guero* ye said?"

"Aye. Thanks, Shirley, see yiz around, girls."

And, turning, Maggie gives an unnecessary tug to the already tourniquet-tight belt of her raincoat and heads off in the direction of the stairs leading out of the station, the exaggerated hip swing drawing more than one bemused look from members of the public.

Connie's tone is acid. "Pain in the arse, that one."

Shirley draws on her cigarette. "Och she's harmless enough, Maggie. Just a bit of a pest, wi' her scroungin' aw the time."

I begin to appreciate that the catty remarks and put-downs which have characterised this recent exchange are a convention of sorts in the company I am now in, and are not intended to be taken over-seriously.

'*How,*' I wonder, '*do you express yourself if you genuinely want to be offensive?*'

"Anybody fancy a drink?" says Nicky. "Still an hour till the pubs close. Audrey?"

I don't want to explain that I have up till now never set foot inside a pub. In fact, I am still under the legal age for drinking. Not that I would have any difficulty, I imagine—I have been talking my way into X-certificate films since I was thirteen. But I am reluctant to say anything about that. I'm already branded naïve as a non-smoker, and am desperate to appear at least a little worldly.

"Yes, good idea, Nicky. Connie? Shirley?"

"Sure, why not," responds Shirley.

"Ah'm skint," says Connie.

"Nae problem, Ah've a couple of bob, Ah'll treat yiz all," Nicky offers.

"In here, then?" I turn towards the door of the station bar.

As one, my three new friends stare at me in amazement.

Oh dear; a *faux pas*, apparently.

Shirley guffaws. "Why wid we want to drink in there?"

"Well—why not? Is it a dump or something?" I say, not sure why my suggestion has provoked such a strong reaction, but agonisingly aware that I seem to have perpetrated a major social gaffe.

I see the already narrow opening of the Green Door shrink to a fine line of light.

"Audrey, dear," smirks Connie, "Yon's a *straight* bar."

What, I wonder, is a *straight* bar?

"Aw come oan, Jim, gie the boy a chance," Nicky says, springing to my defence. "He's new tae all this."

He turns to me, and puts a protective arm round my shoulder. "If we're going to have a wee drink, George, we'll go tae a gay bar."

A *gay* bar? There *are* such places?

"Much more fun, and time for you tae see the way the other half lives. *Your* half now. OK?"

"Yes."

OK, indeed. And the warmth of his encircling arm is OK, too, even if he has to stretch to reach my shoulder.

"Awright," he goes on, "Where's it tae be, ladies? *The Strand* or *Guy's*?"

"Ah'm barred fae *The Strand*," says Shirley. "That bastard, Robert…"

Connie interrupts. "And Ah'm no' welcome in *Guy's* for a week or two at least. Since Ah had that wee disagreement wi' Olivia de Havilland."

"Jesus, whit a pair. Right—it's the *Royal* then, is it?"

"Och, Ah *hate* the *Royal*," whines Connie. "Full of snobs and posies."

"Posers," corrects Shirley. "Aye, Jim's right, thon's the debutantes' bar." Her tone turns querulous. "Not really *us*, is it?"

Nicky is exasperated. "Look, you two—between the pair of ye wi' yer shenanigans, we cannae go anywhere else. And Ah want George here tae see a gay bar, it's his first time."

He drops his cigarette and steps on it. "Och, c'moan, it's a drink, isn't it?"

The other two's initial resistance is overcome when Nicky suggests that, if they prefer not to join us, he and I will go on our own—'*And youse two can please yerselves*'.

I would be very happy with that arrangement—'*He wants to get me on my own,*' I think.

But gradually the grumbles subside, and we set off together to walk the one hundred yards or so to West Nile Street and the *Royal*.

As we turn into the doorway of the pub, I am unsurprised to see that it is painted a bright emerald green. Nicky pushes it, and the door swings wide.

5. Don't Play That Song for Me

I remember on our first date
You kissed me and you walked away
I was only seventeen
I never dreamed you'd be so mean.
Aretha Franklin, 1970.

The events of that night in 1962, now more than fifty years in the past, had consequences for me and for my future life that would be difficult to overestimate.

My tentative investigations of literature treating the subject (such as it existed at that time) had led me to form a pessimistic view of my personal prospects. Ploughing through *The Trials of Oscar Wilde*, or Peter Wildeblood's *Against the Law* was a depressing experience. The few works of fiction that dared to handle the matter were no more encouraging—though generally sympathetic, the picture they painted was not an encouraging one. In Paul Buckland's *Chorus of Witches*, Rodney Garland's *The Heart in Exile* and Stuart Langer's *Winger's Landfall*, nearly everyone ended badly; unhappy, unfulfilled, suicidal, blackmailed, murdered, or at the very least on heavy medication. Or worse, undergoing some nameless 'cure' designed to adjust them, in spite of their innate orientation, to function according to the accepted mores of society.

So my view of what I might have to look forward to in my private life was not a cheering one, and this, in my adolescent years, and notwithstanding the occasional hidden adventure and the similarly inclined friend I had found, caused me terrifying feelings of alienation.

I felt on the outside of everything. As my peers groped forward into the world of dating, relationships, and the things the majority take for granted, contemplating my own future was a depressing exercise. And the concern that somehow or other my natural desires and inclinations might become common knowledge in the small town where I grew up, and the anticipation of the problems that might bring to my family, was an additional burden and a source of equal concern.

It is certain that eventually, sooner or later, bit by bit, step by step, I would have discovered that in any city of reasonable size there existed a thriving gay community. Not, as I had imagined, just a few isolated, unfortunate, despised outcasts, criminals according to the law of the day. And I would have eased my way into this foreign territory carefully, gradually, tentatively, until I became familiar and comfortable with it, and learned its geography, its history and its culture.

But it didn't happen that way. Instead, my life was changed in an instant, and changed forever. I was thrown in at the deep end without a life jacket.

Rather, I closed my eyes, pinched my nose, and jumped. And I didn't sink. I swam.

That night, it was revealed to me that there were not just a few odd people like me, people who could, at best, hope for some tolerance from the broad-minded, and who might, if they were very discreet and careful, avoid ending up in prison. No, there were hundreds, maybe thousands, in Glasgow alone, and this revelation had an effect on me that is, to this day, hard to convey. This was the Great Answer. Overnight, it seemed, my burdens dropped from me; in a very real sense I felt reborn. Among my new friends I acquired a confidence I had never known before. And I knew that, whatever the cost, I would not give up this precious gift for anything. That here, finally, was where I belonged. This was owed to me. The Green Door had opened wide to welcome me, and I knew that it would never be closed for me again. I felt as if I had suddenly been released from prison. Though it would be a couple of years before I would actually know what *that* feels like.

If I had been a little older, or even a little more experienced, perhaps I would have been more cautious; if I had been more cautious, I might have avoided some of the pitfalls that were to follow; if I had avoided those pitfalls, my passage through life might have been considerably easier in some respects.

I went too far too fast. But I was seventeen, and starved of the simple joy of belonging.

'Oh brave new world that has such people in't.'

The *Royal* is a small, brightly-lit lounge, crammed, it seems, with gentlemen, most of them standing by the bar or sitting at tables in small groups. Smartly dressed, for the most part (no belted white trench coats here), hair painstakingly coiffed, occasionally sporting a *very* discreet touch of make-up, their conversation is loud and vivid—

'My dear, when he told me he lost it in the war, I thought he meant his ration book.'

'Her? She spends so much time at the clap clinic they should give her a room.'

'Who, the big one? Oh, that's the Countess of Cardonald, dear, don't

let the butch appearance fool you, sucks up a bit of cock like a sweetie.'

—and their gestures animated and flamboyant. Their accents in general mark them as denizens of the middle class, or at least aspirants to that rank. The class to which I belong.

I notice the two ladies serving behind the bar. One of them, the manageress—Madge, apparently—is holding court surrounded by a little group of obsequious queens. Outwardly affable, she is a type I will come to know well. This is her little kingdom, which she rules with a rod of iron. The sycophantic, toadying group that surrounds her flatter and fawn, desperate for an approving word. They know only too well that she holds their fate in her hands. One word out of place, one compliment missed—*'Oh Madge, love the dress, is it new?'*—and they will be consigned to limbo, banished to the outer darkness. In other words, they will be barred. And what will they do then, the poor little orphans of the storm? There's a big bad world out there that hates and despises poofs, and this is the only place they can let their hair down and be themselves.

So it's *'Madge, dear'* this, and *'Madge, darling'* that. And the hard-faced old harridan sucks it up like a drug. In fact, she despises her customers utterly, as they do her. *And they all know that.* But, terrified of exclusion, they treat her like royalty; while, in truth, outside these walls, she is a total nonentity. But in here she has a power and knows exactly how to use it.

She is a horror, and an ugly cow into the bargain.

Nicky pushes his way to the bar and buys a round of drinks—pints of beer for Connie and Shirley, a 'wee whisky' for himself, and a lager and lime for me. The latter is Nicky's suggestion, as I have no idea what to order, or what I might enjoy.

"Lager and lime? That's a virgin's drink," sniggers Connie.

"And why not?" says Nicky as he passes it to me. "I bet George is still a virgin, aren't you, dear?"

Yes, I am, technically.

'But thank you for the interest, maybe that's an issue we can tackle together?' I think, glancing in his direction.

Immediately I can't control my blushes, brought on both by my awareness of my virginal state, and the thoughts that are running through my head. Luckily no-one seems to notice.

"Oh aye, Ah remember when *I* was a virgin," sighs Shirley.

"What a memory," laughs Nicky.

"Aye, when Eden was in bloom," says a passing stranger who has

74

overheard.

"Cunt," says Shirley, entirely without malice.

She buys the next round of drinks, and I feel bound to apologise to the company for my lack of funds. I have just enough, I explain to Nicky, for my bus fare home, but hope to be able to make up for that on a future occasion.

"Nae problem, George, yer oot wi' friends. This is yer debut, it's only right that we treat you."

I want to hug him. I am out with friends.

I am aware that neither Jim nor Archie appears entirely comfortable in this, the debutantes' bar. And I can imagine why. The bulk of the people around us affect a rather grand and 'ladylike' attitude that these two obviously find grating.

But why should it also irritate me? After all, many of the regulars here appear to come from a background similar to my own.

Is it because I sense in Shirley and Connie (and particularly in the absent Wilma) an alluring aura of life lived on the edge? Of disapproval confronted and vanquished? Of risks taken whatever the consequences? Of a reckless and admirable disregard for any price that may be exacted? Perhaps.

All I can be sure of is that something is stirring in me, something new, a kind of revolt, a desire to finally be able to say '*Fuck you!*' to the rest of the world, instead of contorting myself to fit its patterns. Just as Shirley and Connie undoubtedly would; and as the others, the regular patrons of this bar, would not. *They* are, I sense, undercover. How I know instinctively that the majority of them probably lead a kind of double life, I cannot say. But it is a great revelation. I understand that I have a choice. And unhesitatingly I am anxious, indeed determined, to join the dark side.

I notice that, of the other three, Nicky is the only one who appears to feel entirely at ease here. He seems to pass freely and comfortably from one side to the other. He is obviously well-known and well-liked everywhere. Even the gargoyle Madge treats him differently from the others.

I wonder why?

"Right at home, here, isn't he?" I say quietly to Shirley, watching him.

"Oh aye, welcome everywhere, Nicky. He's a man, isn't he? No problem for *him*."

And that is absolutely correct. On reflection, it is obvious. Technically we are all men. But Nicky's masculinity, and, in a way, his ordinariness, his *realness*, are in such sharp contrast to the sea of pretentious, artificial behaviour which surrounds him that he is a sought-after figure.

"Aye," says Connie, "they'd aw like tae get Nicky interbred, every one o' they queens."

It is a few seconds before I realise that no-one actually wants to get Nicky interbred, but rather, 'into bed'. It will take me a little while to adapt to Connie's quirky speech patterns.

"Nae chance of that, though, eh, Shirley?" She winks.

Shirley laughs. "Naw, nae chance, Connie. He likes his ane kind, Nicky does."

'*Good,*' I think, and smile in secret satisfaction. '*Then that is the kind I shall be.*'

But had I thought to pursue the subject further, I might have saved myself some difficulties later on.

We leave the bar at closing time, ten o'clock.

"Well, what did ye think, Audrey? Enjoy yersel'?" Nicky asks me, as we stroll down West Nile street.

"Yes, it was great, thanks, Nicky. A wee bit pretentious for me, maybe."

I am already assuming the rôle I think is made for me.

"Aye, it is, yer right," he goes on. "Next time Ah'll take ye tae the *Strand* or *Guy's*. A bit rowdy and noisy, but mair fun. Much more your style, I think, and much more mine."

Next time? This sounds almost like a date.

Nicky suggests we all head for the *El Guero* for a bite to eat. Once again I mention my lack of means, but my protests are brushed aside once more.

"Ah've a couple o' quid left, Audrey, enough for a snack for all of us. Spend it while yiv got it, that's what I say."

As the other two seem quite happy to allow Nicky to treat them, I say no more.

The *El Guero* is a cavernous self-service restaurant in the basement of the Cad'oro building in Union Street, offering a range of uninspiring sandwiches, hot meals, and teas or coffees. No alcohol. Only specially licensed night-clubs are permitted to pass the ten PM alcohol curfew in puritanical Presbyterian Scotland.

The *El Guero* offers little in the way of *haute cuisine* or arresting décor. The food is ordinary minus. The seats are either red rexine covered booths seating four or six, or hard plastic chairs surrounding melamine topped tables. The lighting is so bright as to present a hazard to the eyesight of anyone coming inside from the dark. But the place is obviously popular. Almost every table is occupied, the majority of the customers being weekend revellers anxious to enjoy some social intercourse to fill the gap which yawns between leaving the pub and their last transport homeward.

A good percentage of the clients, too, I am guessing, are refugees from the gay bars in the city centre. A few faces from the *Royal*, I note, along with others I am coming to recognise by type, if nothing else. We find a booth against one wall, and the social acknowledgements commence. Indeed, the sheer number of names bandied about by my friends makes my head spin.

Connie points. "There's Hayley Mills ower there—awright Hayley, Susan?—she's sittin' wi' Pat Calhoun and Susan Strasberg. Oh, and there's Judy Garland, too."

Shirley says, "Brenda Lee (she's wan tae avoid, Audrey). Liz Taylor fae Greenock and Princess Margaret Rose. Polly Fulton..."

Nicky takes up the refrain. "Terry Moore, wi' Kay Kendal and Johnny Mason."

Of course, the people indicated are all unequivocally male.

"Oh, and we *are* honoured," Nicky goes on. "Look—the Duchess of York and The Divine Sarah."

My ears prick up, and I follow his pointing finger. Sure enough, the two mature gentlemen I remember are ensconced directly in front of us about two tables away in the company of someone else I recognise, their friend from the cinema, the one they had called 'Olivia de Havilland', plump, jolly and blond. Olivia has her back to me, but the flaxen hair and the buxom figure are unmistakable. A young man I don't know sits opposite her.

I am tickled to see that someone of the party has actually brought along a table-cloth.

Wanting to appear just a little worldly and in-the-know, I say, "Isn't that the one they call 'Olivia de Havilland' sitting with them, the one with her back to us? Opposite the scruffy-looking guy with the Elvis quiff?"

Shirley just manages, "Yes, that's Olivia..." when Connie springs to her feet.

"What?" After looking over to the table in question, she turns and glares at me. "Scruffy? How *dare* you, Miss Hepburn. That's mah *husband* you're talking about!"

And she turns and sweeps off in the direction of the toilets.

"Good God—did I say the wrong thing?" I ask, baffled, turning to the others.

But both Nicky and Shirley are laughing.

"No, no, not at all," replies Shirley, calming down. "In fact, *scruffy* is a bit kind, if anything."

"Don't worry about it, Audrey," says Nicky. "That's Alec, Alec McGowan. Connie's crazy about him. God knows why, he's a right waste of space."

I look over again. I can see that the rough-looking young man in question is in fact not unattractive, in a blowsy, overfed kind of way. In his twenties, he has a plump face, rosy cheeks, greasy Brylcreemed hair tumbling onto his forehead, a leather jacket. He has pouting, spoilt lips, but nice teeth and attractive twinkling eyes. Since he is sitting down, that is all I can see at the moment. He has an amiable, foolish grin on his face, apparently he is amused by some remark Olivia has just made. My first impression is that, like Nicky, he is essentially a masculine character, not a queen, as I have only this evening learned to call my sisters in Sodom.

Nicky enlightens me.

"Let me gie ye the story, Audrey. Alec McGowan's been aroon the toon a good few years now. Harmless, bit of an idiot. The old queens like him, he's a big, butch-looking guy, and he makes a few bob goin' off wi' one or the other of them from time tae time. Particularly Big Olivia, there, who's nobody's fool, but who seems tae have taken a fancy tae him."

His voice drops. "But Alec's real taste is fer the young, pretty things, Hayley Mills or the like."

He indicates a fair-haired, willowy young person seated at a nearby table. Very young, possibly even younger than me.

"Our Connie has fallen for Alec hook, line and sinker. But she disnae qualify under either category—nice lassie, but permanently skint, and nae beauty, as yil have noticed—so he just uses her when it suits him. Ah'm pretty sure nothing ever happens between them, not in the bedroom department. But according to Connie, Alec's her husband, she's got that fixed in her heid."

Shirley interrupts. "Oh quiet, Nicky, here she comes."

Connie emerges from the toilets with a determined expression on her face. But instead of heading back to re-join us, she makes for the nearby table where Olivia and company are seated.

"Oh dear," says Nicky, "I feel one of ma heads coming on."

Shirley's attention is on the unfolding scene.

"Oh no, Connie, whit are ye up tae?" she mutters, and looks away.

Connie has by this time attained the enemy camp. Olivia looks up enquiringly, but Alec has not yet registered the arrival of his 'legal' spouse, who is standing behind his chair.

"Why, good evening, Miss Stevens," says Olivia politely. Alec raises his head from his lasagne and glances over his shoulder. His mouth drops open and a piece of something unidentifiable falls from it onto his lap.

He puts down his knife and fork, and, still seated, turns round, one hand raised, palm outwards. "Now Jim, hang on a minute, don't start..."

He half rises to his feet.

Connie, or Jim, puts a large hand on his shoulder and effortlessly pushes him back down into his chair.

"Start? Me? Not at all, Alec. Just popped over tae say *hello* tae you and yer mother there, and tae remind ye that yer a married man."

Olivia smiles pleasantly.

"Aw, as if he could forget, Connie dear. Considering that you're forever hanging around him, panting after his cock."

She in turn puts down her cutlery, and adds in a tone of mock despair. "Aye, as persistent as a dose of the clap, and about as welcome."

The one I remember as Elizabeth shudders. "Olivia, *please*. There are ladies present."

The other, Sarah, is far too engrossed in her cottage pie to contribute.

Sensing the imminence of drama, diners at adjoining tables allow their conversations to dwindle away.

Connie's scowl darkens. "Is that right, Olivia? Is that how ye see it?"

She assumes a casual tone, leaning on the back of Alec's chair, head on one side.

"Well, think on this. Whit's he daein' wi' *you*? He's only here for what he can get out of you. A few bob here, a pair o' jeans there, a pint or two now an' then. If it's no' for that, Ah repeat, whit's he daein' wi' *you*?"

Olivia takes up her knife and fork once more.

"Oh, Ah know just what he's doing wi' me, hen."

"Oh aye? And whit's that?"

Olivia leans forward towards her rival. "Everything you dream about. Twice a night."

Connie, straightening up, has had enough.

"Right, that's it, ya fuckin' auld bitch!"

Leaning forward again, she draws back her right fist. As it pistons forward, Alec again half rises from his seat and turns to face her. Raising his hands in a placatory gesture, he says, "Now Connie, hen, hang on a minit. Let's no'…"

Too late. The meaty punch meant for Olivia catches Alec a glancing blow on the side of the jaw. He falls back into his seat with a slightly dazed expression on his chubby features.

He immediately gets to his feet again a little unsteadily. He moves away from his chair, gives himself a rapid shake and faces Connie squarely.

"OK, Jim." His head goes back and he raises a finger. "Ah understand. Ye're angry. But—Ah'm warning you—that's enough. Yil no' dae that again…"

Oh dear. This time Connie catches him solidly on the point of the chin, and I think I actually see his feet leave the ground, his head rocking back. As it rolls forward again, he staggers sideways and, turning to face the table, clutches the edge of it for support.

There is a second or two suspended in time. And then, taking the table-cloth and everything on it with him, he falls backwards and clatters apparently unconscious to the hard tiled floor.

The entire place erupts into a storm of spontaneous applause. Connie, although cheated of her prime objective, the facial reconstruction of Olivia, wisely realises that she has somehow scored an even more telling victory.

Nursing her bruised hand, she returns to her seat at our table.

I make a mental note never to get on the wrong side of that fist.

"Oh, well done, actress, well done! That'll teach him, the rotten bastard," enthuses Shirley, greeting the returning heroine.

"Aye, nice job, Connie," says Nicky, getting up. "Now, let's get oot o' here afore the polis arrives."

We leave our table and head towards the exit. In the distance I can hear Olivia's soothing tones.

"Aw, come on now, pet, get up from there. Come on, Alec, you know you can if you try. You'll be fine—Mummy's here, she'll look after you."

Elizabeth is looking the other way, as if to dissociate herself from the current goings-on. Sarah is busy scooping the remains of her supper from the floor back onto her plate.

Midnight. Nicky and I are alone, walking down Ropehouse Lane, a narrow alley that leads from St Enoch Square down to the River Clyde. I have missed my last bus home, but I don't care. The Green Door is gaping wide, and I'm in love. I have had the foresight to telephone home and explain that I am invited to a party and will be staying over with a friend from University. I am anticipating an interesting night.

Connie and Shirley have left us, the former to catch a bus home, and the latter for the late shift at the brothel.

"Oh aye, Ah'll be on the go till three, Audrey. Friday night? Business will be non-stop, and Ah'm on commission."

She scribbles a telephone number on a scrap of paper.

"Give us a ring when ye want tae come round, just ask for Shirley. If a man answers, hang up. Unless it's me, of course!"

And in a gale of laughter, she is gone.

My new friends have spent the last hour or so showing me the attractions of late-night Glasgow. A selection of public toilets, mainly, all of which, according to them, are likely pickup points for those interested in such things. As my attention is, for the moment, entirely focused on Nicky, I keep my observations non-committal. But the information is being filed away for future reference. One never knows, after all.

I am particularly intrigued by the fact that one of these monuments is referred to in conversation as *Saint Vincent de Paul.*

What is the connection with the revered saint?

The reason becomes clear when I look up. This large public convenience is located in Saint Vincent Place.

Or, as the street sign has it, *St Vincent Pl.*

Ropehouse Lane is an ill-lit tunnel linking two major thoroughfares.

"So how long have you been a bus-driver, Nicky?" I ask.

"Och, not long—maybe six months or so."

"Like it? As a job, I mean?"

"Aye, it's OK—gets a wee bit lonely stuck up the front in that cab aw day. An' it's shifts, so cuts intae ma social life a bit. But it's no' a bad job on the whole."

Conversation falters. I rack my brains for something to say. Because I fancy him a lot, I am feeling tongue-tied and a bit shy.

"Dark, isn't it?" I say eventually.

Nicky takes my arm and links it through his.

"Don't be scared, George, yer safe wi' me," he chuckles.

Yes, that's more like it. But not *too* safe, I hope.

Suddenly a figure detaches itself from the gloom of a doorway on one side of the street, and I yelp in alarm. Nicky too gives a start.

"Awright, Nicky—huv ye seen Wilma? Ah must've missed her."

"Aw, it's you, Lena—nearly scared the wits out of us, so ye did. Naw, no' seen Wilma since earlier. She said she wis off tae meet *you*."

"Aye, but Ah had tae work late, missed ma usual bus from work, so Ah did. Any idea where she might be?"

Nicky ponders. "Ye could try the Broomielaw, Ah suppose. The docks, doon near *Betty's Bar*. She's there a lot these days, wi' yon Bridget character. She wisnae hangin' aboot in Clyde Street?"

"Naw, Ah've no' seen her at all. And Ah'm no' gawn doon the docks—too dangerous roon there. Ah'll get the late bus home from The Square, Ah've goat work the morra."

"Aye, OK, Lena. By the way, excuse my manners. This is George—Audrey Hepburn, that is. He's new. Audrey, meet Lena Martell."

The newcomer is revealed in the light to be a small, round-shouldered young man, perhaps nineteen or thereabouts. Sallow complexion, vaguely Italian-looking, with pleasant features and a warm smile.

"Hi Audrey, nice tae meet ye. See ye around, Ah'm sure. You an' all, Nicky. Take care, you two."

"Good-night, Lena," we both say in unison, as she totters off. Nicky once more links my arm through his and we continue on our way.

"She works all hours, Lena," says my swain. "She's a mental nurse."

It takes me a moment or two to realise that this is not an insult but a job description.

Eventually we arrive at Clydeside, the long and well lit road that runs parallel to the river from the High Court at the eastern end to the Broomielaw, Anderston Quay and the docks at the other. Nicky is anxious to show me the crowning glories of Glasgow-by-night, the twin public toilets he refers to as Clyde Street and The Black Hole; the former between the Albert and Victoria Bridges, near Glasgow Green, and the latter tucked in off the beaten track between Victoria Bridge and the Suspension Bridge.

Truth to tell, I am not really interested in seeing yet another example of the architectural glories of the Glasgow Corporation Public Works Department, but I stay with the programme, certain that sooner or later Nicky will run out of interesting local curiosities and turn his mind to more personal matters.

We first investigate the Clyde Street toilet—dimly lit, and still playing host to a couple of late-night enthusiasts, who spring apart and quickly re-arrange their clothing when we enter.

When Nicky says, "Sorry boys, just showing ma friend around, we'll leave you to it," I choke back a nervous laugh.

We then cover the couple of hundred yards to *The Black Hole*, which turns out to be something else entirely.

Tiny and completely unlit, you would not know it was there unless you knew it was there. We enter together, and it's impossible to tell if we are alone or not.

But by this time, I am ready to seize any opportunity. I put my hand on Nicky's solid shoulder, and lower my head. And suddenly it is happening. We kiss. And it is no timid peck. He seems as enthusiastic as I, tongues come into play; as he presses into me I am aware of his arousal.

My head spins. This is the very first time I have ever been kissed, properly kissed. I hope it won't stop.

But it does. He pushes me away.

"Sorry Audrey, sorry. Ah got a bit carried away there. Sorry."

He's *sorry*?

He turns to leave and I follow him.

"But why, Nicky? I was enjoying that as much as you."

He looks away.

"I know, I know. But it's wrong, it's not fair on you. This is all new to you, I can't take advantage, it wouldn't be right."

Gentlemanly scruples? All very admirable in their place, I agree, but there are limits, surely?

"But I want you to take advantage…"

"No, sorry, I would feel really bad if I did."

I am devastated and wounded. Worse, embarrassed.

After this awkward moment, we continue our stroll down Clyde Street, back in the direction of Glasgow Green.

After a moment, slightly sheepishly, he looks at me again.

"I'm really sorry, George. Hope ye didn't think Ah was leading you on?"

That is exactly what I think. But I try to sound dismissive.

"No, of course not. My mistake, don't worry about it."

This is too difficult. What a dispiriting end to a wonderful evening.

"I'd better be getting off," I say.

"Yes, me too. How will you get home?"

It's at this point that I realise that I have about sixpence to my name. My last bus has long gone, and Rutherglen is several miles away. There is a late-night bus service from George Square every hour or so, but that costs a shilling or one and six; at any rate, more than I have. A taxi at four or five shillings is completely beyond my means. I could walk, but it's February, it's cold, and I'm tired. Besides, my parents think I am out for the evening staying with friends.

'*Shit,*' I think to myself. '*What a mess! What can I do?*'

"I don't know, Nicky. I've no money. What will *you* do?"

"Och, I can walk, Bridgeton's no' far. But Ru'glen's miles away. And Ah've nae money left either—spent the last of it on that meal at the *El Guero*."

I look down.

He sighs heavily. "You'd better come hame wi' me. My maw'll find a corner for ye."

His *mother*? No, I don't think so. After recent events, and registering his reluctant tone, spending the night *chez* Nicky, I decide, is about the last thing I want to do.

"No, it's OK, Nicky. I'll walk. You get off."

"Walk? Ye can't. Don't be daft—yil freeze tae death. Let me think."

I let him think. Is he considering mugging someone? Begging a loan? Robbing a bank?

He seems to be struggling with something. I wait.

Eventually he comes to a decision.

"OK. Hang on here a minute. Got a wee idea. Ah'll be right back. Leave it tae me."

He turns away and walks back in the direction of *The Black Hole*, where he disappears.

'*Great,*' I think. '*Thanks a lot! Abandoning me here in the middle of Glasgow, in the middle of the night, in the middle of winter!*'

But I am doing him an injustice. Two minutes later he is back. And he is not alone.

"Audrey, this is Sammy, a wee friend of mine."

Sammy is old, maybe forty, short and fat.

"Hello Audrey," he burbles. "You're lookin' nice, so ye are."

I raise my eyebrows and look at the pair of them. Is this Sammy going to lend us some money, then?

Nicky seems a little uncomfortable. "Sammy, let me have a wee word wi' Audrey here, will ye?"

"Aye, sure Nicky, nae problem."

He looks over at me. "Awright, Audrey? Cauld night, isn't it?"

I still say nothing. Sammy turns away, and Nicky comes towards me.

"Audrey, Ah don't know just how tae put this. Ah swear tae ye, Ah wid dae it masel', but it's you he wants."

I suddenly know exactly where this is going.

OK, it's a solution.

'*But*,' I think, '*why make it easy for him?*'

On the surface, I am all innocence.

"Sorry, Nicky, I don't quite follow. It's me he wants for what?"

He squirms, and I relish his unease.

"Och, ye know whit Ah mean. For—well—for a bit of fun. For sex." His voice drops. "He'll pay."

Although I understand the situation, I'm still a little shocked at his bluntness. Couldn't he have skirted round the subject a bit longer?

"What? You want me to have sex for *money*? With that old guy?"

Sammy has overheard me.

"Aye, that's right. Five bob. Just a wee wank, that'll do it. Pull it off nice, and it's five bob in yer haun', nae questions asked."

He pauses, and then adds, a little indignantly, "And Ah'm no' *that* auld."

So—Nicky doesn't want me for himself, it seems, although he has spent the last few hours giving me the impression that he does. But he is quite happy to pass me on to this strange little man just to get out of being responsible for me.

OK. I see it's high time I took this situation in hand, he's messed me around enough.

I decide to play up my reluctance a little. From somewhere I conjure a sob or two.

"Nicky! How could you ask me to do that? I thought you *liked* me!"

He squirms some more. How delightful!

"Ssh, ssh, Audrey, Ah do, of course Ah do."

He pauses. "It's just—well when all's said and done, the money's no' for me, it's for *you*, for yer taxi home."

I have to concede that point.

"But I swear to you, if he'd wear it, Ah'd dae it instead. But he wants you."

He beseeches with one of his winning and irresistible looks, puppy-dog eyes well to the fore. "Just this once, eh? Shut yer eyes and it'll be over in no time."

I give in. "I don't seem to have a choice, Nicky, do I?"

I leave him and head towards Sammy. He isn't hideous or anything. Just old, fat and sad-looking.

"OK Sammy. Just a wank, mind, nothing else."

From my very limited past experience, I know that this is one particular manipulation in which I am expert.

"But that's all. A wank. I don't want you touching me."

"Oh aye, that'll be fine. A wank. Five bob."

"No, no. Ten bob." I hesitate. "I'm a virgin."

Nicky, who has joined us, is quick on the uptake.

"Aye, that's right, Sammy, a virgin. Ah guarantee it."

Sammy turns to him. "Ye *guarantee* it? It's a wank Ah'm efter, no' a fuckin' reference!"

Nicky warms to his theme. "Aye, Sammy, but look—brand new in the toon, too, first night. Young and fresh. Untouched."

Is this Clyde Street in Glasgow, or the auction block in old Algiers?

Sammy appears to consider, looking me up and down.

Eventually, "Aye, OK. Seven and six," he says.

I am adamant. "No. Ten bob. Final offer."

He shakes his head, and turns as if to leave.

Desperate, Nicky suddenly hits the jackpot. "Only fifteen, Sammy," he whispers urgently.

Sammy stops and turns back. "Fifteen, ye say? Is that right?"

He wets his lips.

"Yes, that's right," I say, picking up the cue. "Fifteen. Still at school."

He moistens his lips again, and stares at me. "Whit school wid that be then?"

Without breaking stride I say, "Laurel Bank."

"Laurel Bank, eh? Very nice."

Sammy doesn't appear to be aware that Laurel Bank is Glasgow's most prestigious all girls' school, a kilted Roedean. Possibly because he is too busy fiddling around inside his trousers to take it in.

After a pause, he says, "OK, ten bob. But Ah want *baith* hauns mind."

Despite my distaste, I am intrigued by the unexpected request for the use of *both hands*. Does Sammy's diminutive size conceal a remarkable anomaly?

No. He clarifies the situation.

"Aye, baith hauns. Ah want ye tae squeeze ma balls while yer pullin' it, OK?"

I don't hesitate.

"Deal. Both hands. Ball-squeezing included. Ten bob. In advance, please."

After some humming and hawing, and protestations of poverty, a crumpled ten-shilling note is produced and handed over, and the three of us make our way back towards *The Black Hole.*

The act is concluded in less than three minutes. Both hands are applied vigorously, alternately, simultaneously. Balls are squeezed till he yelps, "Ow! No' sae *hard*, Audrey, please."

Maliciously, I give them an extra tug, which causes him to spurt copiously and noisily.

Luckily I have a handkerchief, and *The Black Hole* a working sink. How did Lady Macbeth put it? '*A little water clears us of this deed.*'

I leave a presumably satisfied Sammy dabbing ineffectually at his groin.

'*He's going to have to have these trousers cleaned*', I think to myself.

Nicky manages to hail a taxi without any difficulty, and I climb in, having instructed the driver as to my destination. I relish the delicious warmth of the heater.

Nicky leans in the window to say farewell. He takes my hand.

"Great night, Audrey. I hope you enjoyed your debut?"

I certainly have. Some parts more than others. But on the whole, what progress! In a few short hours I have become Audrey Hepburn. I have also become an occasional smoker, a bona fide Glasgow queen, a connoisseur of the public toilets of Glasgow, a spurned lover, and a kind of prostitute.

Not bad for one night's work, all in all.

"Well, it has been an experience, Nicky. But yes, I've had fun."

He smiles, looking relieved. "Great. Hope we can do it again some time?"

"Oh, don't you worry, Nicky, you've not seen the last of me."

"Good. And sorry about the wee misunderstanding."

He looks down, then up again. Though I am still smarting from his rejection, I am reminded of how attractive I find him. That hurts a bit.

He clears his throat.

"Ah wis just wondering—since you got ten bob, ye could drop me off in Bridgeton on your road home—it's not far out of your way."

I simulate a regretful smile.

"Aw, I'd love to, Nicky, but I'm afraid I can't afford it. I need to keep the other five shillings for tomorrow, to get some cigarettes. For my sophisticated look, remember, your idea? Anyway, as you said yourself, Bridgeton's not that far."

Before he can respond, I lean over and kiss him quickly on the lips. Then I wind up the window.

"OK, driver, hit the road please."

6. *I Sold My Heart to the Junkman*

I gave my heart to you, the one that I trusted.
You gave it back to me all battered and busted.
I sold my heart to the junkman,
And I'll never fall in love again.
Patti LaBelle and the BlueBelles, 1962.

How quickly I fall into the routine. Since I am in Glasgow most days to attend lectures, it is easy to pass through Central Station on my way to and from University, and spend half an hour gossiping with whoever is around. I see Connie and Shirley regularly, and Wilma and Nicky from time to time. But in a few short weeks, my circle of acquaintances has widened enormously. In our little secret world, everybody knows everybody. Audrey has become a familiar face, if not at this stage quite as ubiquitous as she will be later on. Occasionally in the evening I stop off at one or other of the gay bars in the city centre, *Guy's,* or the *Strand*, for a drink or two before making my way home. As Nicky had predicted, I find the atmosphere of these two far preferable to that of the *Royal*. More edgy, more exciting, more fun.

But at University my attendance at classes remains as regular as ever. I will be playing a small rôle in a French language production of Molière's *Le Malade Imaginaire* in a few weeks, and have been invited to perform in a Music Department concert, playing a Mozart piano concerto with the University Orchestra. This will not take place until December, so I have months to practice.

In my first year there, I have made a considerable impact. The social side of University life, too, takes up some of my time. And living at home with my family as I do, I have commitments there. So, for the moment, I am keeping both feet firmly planted in the real world, and my visits to the wild side of life are restricted to my spare moments.

But the addiction is insidious. I imagine that most of my family and friends would class me as a quiet, studious person in normal life, unadventurous and conventional. Indeed, that is what I am, or have been, or have been compelled to be. But when I move into the company of my new friends, a side of myself of which I have always been aware, but have never dared to let out, appears. In imitation of my circle I begin to affect a hint of make-up. My hair is lightly back-combed and lacquered, my conversation becomes louder, and begins to take on a hint of the raw Glasgow edge that characterises the speech of those of my peers I am anxious to emulate. And I am now a smoker, although at this stage only a light one.

I consider my curtailed moment of intimacy with Nicky, and wonder why it didn't lead anywhere.

'*Perhaps*,' I console myself, '*it was just the wrong moment, the wrong place.*'

I see him from time to time, here and there, and he is as charming, flattering and affectionate as ever. He laughs in what appears to be genuine amusement about me leaving him stranded on Clydeside on that memorable evening when we first met. He doesn't seem to bear any resentment, or to have spread the word concerning my willingness to sell my personal services for a taxi fare. At least, I never hear mention of it. Perhaps he really is that rare thing, a gentleman.

I wish there were someone I could confide in, someone who knows Nicky better than I do. There is no question—I am head over heels. Perhaps someone else can explain to me where I went wrong, and how to go about the process of winning him. Despite my enthusiastic plunge into this new world, I am as yet very naïve and inexperienced.

I already know that it is not difficult to find casual sexual adventure, especially if one is young and not too fussy. But, breath-taking and exciting as they can be, these encounters leave a bitter after-taste, conducted, as they tend to be, in ill-lit, malodorous surroundings, hurried and anonymous. My nature is fastidious enough to appreciate that, however momentarily gratifying they may be, and however strong the imperative that prompts them, in the end these experiences are empty and unsatisfying. There must be, I think, something better than this.

And there is—what is known as *an affair*. In my new world that expression refers both to the relationship itself and the partner. Your boyfriend is your *affair*. And that's what I really want. A permanent, or at least a regular, lover, not a one-night stand.

I have already cast Nicky in that rôle. And in spite of the free and easy, anything-goes atmosphere of most of my new friends, with their lurid tales of sexual adventure and conquest, I come to appreciate that for most of them, too, that is the goal. It seems that, gay or straight, we all want to be one of two.

Among my new social circle, there are a few couples of an apparently permanent nature. But this is exceptional. The rest of us, huddling in our little groups in Central Station, in the *Strand* or in *Guy's*, gossiping and laughing, are all single girls.

And 'girls' we are. Our world is divided into two camps, the 'ladies' and the 'gentlemen'. The unwritten rule is that a *queen* and a *man* go together. That is, that one half of the partnership should be a lady—a Connie, a Wilma, a me. The other, a gentleman—a Nicky, an Alec McGowan. I am thoroughly indoctrinated with the belief that this law is immutable, and since my own objects of desire tend to conform to the stereotype, it never occurs to me to question it.

It isn't obvious to me at this stage that my particular circle is in a certain sense on the edge of gay 'society'. Among my close friends, the female names and mannerisms are the rule. This is not the general case.

Oh, in all such groups now and then feminine terms are used, but usually as a joke, or possibly as a put-down.

"Get *her*!" someone may say about a person who has offended or irritated them.

"Love the hair, Marilyn," if your best friend has had a bleach job.

"Don't be a bitch, Mary," and such like.

But in my own little world it is different. I am nearly always Audrey or 'Miss Hepburn', only occasionally George. Forever Audrey, in fact. Only on rare occasions is Connie 'Jim', or Wilma 'William'; perhaps when an outsider is in the company, and it is considered advisable to keep things discreet; again, when someone wants to address a serious topic, as opposed to making light-hearted conversation; and sometimes for no very obvious reason at all.

This can lead to odd effects—it's not that unusual to hear someone addressed by two different names in the same sentence.

Another situation where 'real' names tend to be used is between two who are together, who are an 'affair'. Pat Calhoun and Susan Strasberg are such a couple. But Pat, the 'male' half of the duo, always calls his partner 'Peter', never 'Susan'. To Johnny Mason, his other half, whom I know as 'Kay Kendall', is always 'Tommy'.

But even that rule is not always strictly observed. I will in the future have one or two more or less regular boyfriends who will happily call me 'Audrey'. As a group, we are infinitely flexible.

But we outrageous queens are a minority within a minority. Mainstream gay society, if there can be said to be such a thing, often affects to despise us, just as they may have been despised by the world at large. We all need someone to look down on, after all.

The truth is, I come to realise, that they find us rather frightening; our refusal to be inconspicuous and to blend into the background threatens them. Many, I think, long to be as bold and as upfront as we are, but either lack the courage or are in a job or a social situation where this is impossible. They claim to find us ridiculous. Just as we find those who affect an ultra-straight exterior ridiculous. They call us 'screamers.' We refer to them as 'male impersonators.'

So though we cling to the pseudo-male, pseudo-female conjoining, it is a fact that that the majority of gay men do not make these distinctions. Or if they do, the rules and rôles are considerably more flexible. But so imprinted am I by my early experiences that I continue for a long time to believe that this dichotomy exists and is immutable.

The term used in gay society at large for sexual congress is 'trade'. You 'have trade' with someone, or you simply 'trade' them. Based, I imagine, on a notional exchange of goods of equal value, a *quid pro quo*. If a person is sexually available, then he is trade. Or he is TBH, 'To Be Had'. There are no rigid rules as to who may have whom.

But in my own group it is different. Any couple breaking the law of one masculine male, one feminine male, is guilty of the heinous crime of 'tootsie trade'. Considered an unnatural and rare occurrence, as reprehensible in its way as incest, it is, I will learn, not really all that uncommon. But those indulging are likely to keep the matter to themselves, fearful of the social opprobrium they might incur. Although on the surface we claim to be liberal and liberated from convention, this is simply not so. Indeed, our social rules and stratifications are if anything even more rigid than those of the world we have abandoned. We have given up a tailored suit for a straitjacket. No, it is often reiterated, one 'lady', one 'gentleman', as nature apparently intended.

The problem is that there are far more ladies around than gentlemen.

As if my social calendar were not already full enough, I still have my part-time job. On Saturdays I am employed in the record department of Caldwell's, Glasgow's premier music emporium, located on the corner of Sauchiehall Street and Maitland Street. I have worked there for close to a year, and love it. Music has ever been my escape, my solace and my fascination. Classical music, that is.

Oh, I am not indifferent to the charms of the pop culture—like most people my age, certain of the anthems of the day come to have a special significance for me, and to reflect the teenage *angst* I am currently suffering. At the moment I am hooked on an oldie but goody, '*To know, know, know him is to love, love, love him*', dating from 1958, and sung by *The Teddy Bears*. No prizes for guessing the identity of the him in my mind.

Mawkish, in retrospect, but tear-stained truth at the time.

But in Caldwell's I am the acknowledged expert in the classical department. On Saturdays, that is. I'm not sure how the regular staff cope with a Beethoven or Schubert enquiry during the week. Maybe they ask the customer to come back on Saturday.

It is an oddity that while the full-time staff are exclusively female and of varying age, we Saturday part-timers are all male and in our teens. Two of us are students, and the other is a young man who is otherwise employed during the week, and makes a little extra money on a Saturday. Not that the wages here are exciting—one pound ten shillings for the day's work, although this goes up to two pounds after I have been there for a while. But the conditions are good, the surroundings pleasant and the company agreeable.

Popular record sales are at an all-time high, and on Saturday it takes all seven of us to cope with the demand for service. The occasional classical query is passed to me, but for most of the day I am weaving in and out in the cramped space behind the counter along with my colleagues, dispensing a copy of Acker Bilk's *Stranger on the shore* here, or the latest offering from Connie Francis or Bobby Vee there. Since I started at the shop, the former might have been heard *Breaking in a brand new broken heart*, or wondering why she and her man are not *Together*; while the latter was asking someone to *Take good care of my baby*, or suggesting that you *Run to him*. The Beatles are as yet unknown—they will make their first top twenty appearance late this same year with *Love me do*, and will sweep to number one in 1963 with a raft of hits including *From me to you* and *She loves you*.

Manageress Miss McClellan is a plump redhead, hair tightly permed, freckled pudding face powdered and lipsticked extravagantly. I wish that she were *Ellen* McClellan. I am fascinated by unlikely names. I have a fellow student at University who was unbelievably christened Daphne Gaffney, while at school there was a Roland Butter in my sister Jennifer's class. In primary school I sat next to a Gladys Smellie. Pronounced 'Smyllie', she insisted, though Gladys was neither especially smelly nor particularly smiley.

But Miss McClellan, forty-ish, is not an Ellen or even a Helen, she is an Iris. She favours tight-fitting black velvet two-piece outfits teamed with frothy blouses in white lace. Iris is something of a live wire, and we get on well. She is the first person I have ever known who actually goes abroad on holiday, to somewhere apparently called Torremolinos. Her claim to personal celebrity is that she once had a 'thing' with

John Leyton, pop star (*'Johnny, remember me'*) and later an actor of some note. I suspect it was probably a one-night stand, but she implies otherwise, and I haven't the heart to attempt to pin her down too closely.

Rosemary, early twenties, is extremely pretty, dark-haired and tall. Her appearance is marred by her unattractively thick legs and ankles. But, lower half concealed behind the counter, she is a popular favourite with male customers, and I quietly envy the attention she receives. She is a sweet-natured and kind girl. We are friends, and by the time I leave Caldwell's, she will be the only member of staff who was already there when I arrived. In fact, she will help to save my life, or at least my liberty.

Rita is something of the 'black sheep'. An attractive girl, despite her oily complexion and constellation of spots, she is a year or two older than Rosemary. She has a fine figure, of which she takes full advantage, in her low-cut, tight-bodiced, full skirted floral summer dresses. I like Rita, she is gallus and a bit wild. But she is a terrible time-keeper, and is almost always in trouble for being late. Miss McClellan has it in for her, there is no question of that, and I gather from overheard conversations that Rita is considered a bit of a free spirit. It is 1962, and a horde of horny American sailors are stationed at Dunoon and the Holy Loch. At the weekend they descend on Glasgow *en masse*. Their drinking place of choice is the Beresford Hotel, further along Sauchiehall Street, and I gather that Rita is a regular patron, and an enthusiastic follower of the fleet, both during licensing hours and later.

Marlyse, late teens, has not been there very long when I join the staff. She is hardly a natural beauty—she has the face of a Pekinese—but is full of personality and sparkle, and makes the most of what she does have. Petite and slim, Marlyse features heavily back-combed jet-black hair, stiletto heels, and lots of eye make-up. I am particularly entranced by her perfume, which she tells me is something called *Intimate*, by Revlon. I manage to save up enough to buy myself a small bottle of the stuff—the packaging claims that, apparently, it is renowned as one of the world's seven great fragrances. I wonder if I can somehow get my hands on the other six? I realise it would be a little tactless to feature *Intimate* when at work, but a liberal dose is applied when I am out on the town, as I tend to be increasingly as summer 1962 approaches.

Matters in general are very relaxed in Caldwell's. We staff are, unbelievably, allowed to borrow records from the shop, take them home and return them. There is a book in which these movements of stock are supposed to be recorded, but as often as not no-one bothers about it. All staff are allowed full access to the tills, and this at a time when virtually all purchases are paid in cash. There are no transactions which require authorisation from a higher level, and each member of staff—including we part-time Saturday employees—functions pretty much autonomously. It is in general a more trusting era.

April 1962.

It is about ten o' clock on a Saturday morning. The shop is still relatively quiet—our busy time is lunchtime and afternoons, and I am looking forward to my tea break, due in half an hour or thereabouts.

I am rack stacking. A boring job—when new stock arrives, the LPs are removed from their colourful sleeves and put on the shelves encased in plain cardboard, while the decorative covers are on display where customers can browse through them. Every rotating unit has a number of sections, each with a helpful sign attached. I am just in the process of tucking Petula Clark in between Shirley Bassey and Brenda Lee in the bay marked *Female Pop—Latest*, when a quiet but familiar voice is at my shoulder.

"Good morning, Miss Hepburn. Ah'd nae idea *you* worked here. Yiv never said."

It is Shirley. Horrified, I look round, and am relieved to see than there are no other members of staff within earshot.

"Um—oh—Shirley…" I mutter, panicking a little.

She smiles. "Relax, George, there's nae problem—Ah'm no' daft. We all have tae be a wee bit canny from time to time, don't we?"

The practice of 'screaming up' is something I have heard about. You scream someone up if you deliberately make their secret clear in situations where this is undesirable. Perhaps in front of a member of their family, a work colleague, or a straight friend—someone, at any rate, who is unaware of the victim's true inclinations.

Often it is achieved simply by addressing the victim openly using his 'camp' name, or by the perpetrator deliberately exaggerating his own effeminate behaviour. Sometimes by even more blatant means. However it is done, it is generally frowned upon, and considered unworthy and a low blow to subject someone to this sort of ordeal. You are expected to have subtler methods at your command if you want to get back at a person who has annoyed you.

So I am relieved by Shirley's understanding and discretion. But I have a slight difficulty.

"And," says Shirley with a little smile, "the name's *Archie*, by the way, remember?"

Shirley, in the persona of Archie, practically charms the pants off my colleagues, and in no time at all has them eating out of his hand. Iris suggests he join us in the staff room for a coffee and an Empire biscuit. I am still slightly concerned that unwelcome repercussions may result from this collision of two worlds. But Shirley/Archie never misses a beat. It's an impressive performance.

Later we chat briefly, and arrange to meet up for lunch. The shop has filled up, and Shirley buys Elvis's latest, *Can't help falling in love*. I slip a copy of Helen Shapiro's *Tell me what he said* into the bag as a thank you.

I have never done such a thing before. If I were to be caught, I would say the second disc must have already been in the bag. It happens sometimes when things are busy that you inadvertently pick up a bag that someone else is in the process of filling for another customer.

But I am not spotted.

'Hm. That was easy', I think.

"Six and six, please, Archie." A 45 rpm single costs six shillings and sixpence. About 33 new pence.

Archie hands me seven shillings. I ring the amount up on the till and give him the sixpence change.

"Thanks, George. See you outside about one, OK?"

"Lovely fella, that Archie, really polite, funny too. How do you two know each other, then?" Iris comments after Shirley has left.

"Oh, we're in a drama group together," I reply, fairly certain that this will account for any lingering odour of theatricality.

"Nice," says Iris, moving off.

No-one has noticed anything untoward at all.

"Nicky? Yer in love wi' Nicky?"

Open-mouthed, Shirley puts down her knife and fork with a clatter and stares at me. She starts to grin, and then, seeing I am deadly serious, puts her hand on mine.

"Oh, hen, ye're barking up the wrong tree there, Ah'm afraid."

We are lunching in *The Renfrew*, a fish and chip bar located opposite the Glasgow Art School in Renfrew Street, just a few steps from Caldwell's. A pudding supper for me—a deep-fried battered black pudding served with chips and processed peas, dark sweet tea, and bread spread with something that claims to be butter but obviously is not. Unrequited love may be disturbing my rest but it isn't affecting my appetite.

Shirley has fish and chips and a coffee.

"How do you mean, Shirley? I definitely get the impression that he likes me, Nicky, that he enjoys spending time with me. I'm sure I'm not wrong—so how come?"

Shirley looks at me.

"Sure, he likes you. Nicky likes everybody. And he *is* a fascinating character—Ah really don't think he does it on purpose, it's just the way he is. You're not the first. He's mad for queens, adores the camp, loves the scene, the more outrageous it is, the more he likes it—he's always been that way, ever since Ah've known him, which is a couple of years now. But as far as sex is concerned, that's no' his thing at all."

I wonder. No, surely not. That kiss…

"No sex? You don't mean—you mean he isn't—isn't *gay*?"

Shirley laughs, loudly, openly, delightedly.

"Och, he's gay all right—as gay as you or me. Gayer, maybe, if that's possible. No, what Ah mean is, the type Nicky goes for is lads like hisself. A couple of years younger, maybe. Wee feelie homies, seventeen, eighteen, nae mair."

She sits back and lights a cigarette.

"Ah know he likes ye, Audrey. Likes ye for yer personality, and for the fact that he wis the one that discovered ye in the first place." She blows out a cloud of smoke. "But for anything more than that, forget it. He knows ye now for who ye are. And he likes who ye are. But likes is where it stops."

I understand what she is saying. That Nicky's type is the young lad— the 'feelie homie', to use Shirley's expression, one of our private codes, denoting a straight or straight-looking young man in his teenage years.

I understand it. But do I believe it?

"But—I never see him with anybody, anybody special, that is. How come there's no boyfriend? It can't be lack of offers."

Shirley passes me a cigarette, which I take. As she lights it for me, she agrees. "No, it's been a wee while since Nicky was with anybody permanent, a good six months, maybe longer. But give it time, mark my words, before very long there'll be somebody new in his life."

She shouts over to the man behind the counter, "Another coffee here, please, pal?"

And registering my stricken look, she continues, "Audrey, let me give ye a wee bit of advice. Nicky's a good person tae have on yer side. He'll look out for you, make sure you're OK. If ye're in trouble, he'll be there for you. He's been a good friend tae me, and he'll be a good friend tae you. Don't spoil that by chasing after something that can never happen. Yil only end up falling out wi' him. Yer a young thing—whit is it, seventeen? There'll be plenty of fellas after *you*."

She smiles and winks. "An' Ah know one that is, for a fact. Enjoy yersel' while ye can."

Logically, I understand what my friend is saying, and that the advice is sound. I will, I decide, try to follow it.

But a burning love is not to be extinguished so easily.

"Thanks, Shirley, I suppose you're right. I'll try."

Uncomfortable, I change the subject. "So—who is this fella who's got his eye on me? The one you mentioned?"

Shirley's coffee arrives. Her smile develops a touch of malice.

"Yiv no' noticed? It's Alec, Alec McGowan. Aye, he's definitely got you in his sights, Miss Hepburn. He told me that hisself."

I burst out laughing. "Alec? You're kidding me, Shirley!"

I have come to know Alec since Connie knocked him unconscious in the *El Guero*. While I find him agreeable enough, I have absolutely no interest in taking our acquaintance any further.

I stub out my cigarette, not even half-smoked.

"No, Audrey, it's right enough. You're just his type. Trust me on this." And with a '*Shame tae waste that*', she picks up my dog end from the ashtray and tucks it behind her ear.

"Oh, I do, Shirley. But Alec McGowan... Not exactly love's young dream, is he? And anyway, he's got his hands full already between Olivia and Connie."

Shirley pushes her plate aside. "Oh, he has, aye. But there's always room for one more in Alec's love boat."

Her expression becomes serious. "But look out, hen—if she found out, Connie would murder ye."

Yes, indeed she would. Alec must, I reflect, have *something* going for him, to attract such bilateral devotion. A wicked desire to know what that might be enters my mind. And disappears as quickly.

"Naw, yil stay away from Alec if you're smart. But don't worry. Next thing ye know, there'll be someone new along just for you. Ah'll keep ma eyes open, Ah promise. But bear in mind what I said aboot Nicky, eh?"

"I will, Shirley, I will." I glance at my watch and stand up. "Shit, I'm going to be late back for work."

I squeeze her shoulder. "Thanks for the advice, Shirley. Let me get that coffee."

"Thanks, hen, that's nice of ye. Ah'll be seeing ye around. Don't forget Ah'm still waiting tae introduce ye tae the lassies up the brothel. Gie's a call."

I say I will, and dash back to work, where the afternoon rush will be building up.

I try to follow Shirley's instructions. But it makes no difference, I just can't get him out of my head. '*To know, know, know him*' is nearly worn out, and it will be difficult getting another copy, even with my record connections—the song is four years old.

'*Maybe Shirley is wrong,*' I think. '*Maybe she has other reasons for trying to put me off. Maybe she is after him herself...*'

Ridiculous thoughts.

May 1962.

It is a Friday night, warm summer is in the air. I am standing chatting with Wilma in the Central Station, near the bookstall. The Railway Police have been hanging around our usual spot by the buffet, so we are staying out of their way. They rarely cause us any difficulties, despite the anti-loitering signs, but there's no point in pushing our luck. I have asked Wilma if she wants to go up to *Guy's* for a drink, but it seems she has an appointment later down at the docks, where, she tells me, she spends a lot of time these days.

"It's a right laugh down there, a whole different scene. Ah get pissed off hanging roon here. Ah don't fit in. Nothin' up here for me, Ah'm just too outrageous for this lot. But it's something else doon at the docks. All sorts goin' on, sailors off the ships ready for a bit of shore leave. Me and ma friend Bridget dae real well—even make a few bob from time tae time. Ye know whit sailors are."

She nudges me and giggles. "Aye, *Betty's Bar*'s the place. Till closing time. Then it's aff tae a party oan wan o' the boats. Great laugh, we huv. Maybe a wee bit rough fer you, hen, but ye should gie it a go some time. Don't worry, Ah'll look out for ye."

I say I will think about it.

Looking at Wilma, I notice that she is not exaggerating when she describes her appearance as 'too outrageous'. She is obviously made-up, her tightly curled hair is tortured into a semi-beehive, and she is wearing what are basically women's clothes—purple ski pants, the kind that have a strap that goes under the instep, a pastel lavender twin-set and flat mauve mules with a discreet sequin *appliqué*. She draws a lot of stares, but her intimidating size discourages any further boldness.

I notice Alec McGowan has just arrived in the station from the Gordon Street entrance. He saunters over, does a double take at Wilma, and steps back.

"Fer fuck's sake, William, whit huv *you* come as? Ye need tae tone it down a bit—dae ye want tae get yersel' arrested?"

Wilma is riled.

"And whit's it goat tae dae wi' you, McGowan? Ah'll dress any way Ah want—and if you don't like it, ye can fuck off. Audrey here's no' bothered—are ye Audrey?—so why should you be?"

Her head goes back and her chin goes up.

"Worried somebody might think yer queer?"

This hits home, judging from Alec's expression, and Wilma presses her advantage.

"Still shaggin' big Olivia these days?"

"Sorry, Wilma... Nae offence..." Alec mumbles, backing away slightly.

He is intimidated, but for some reason doesn't want to leave. "Ah'm just sayin'... It's fer yer ane sake... Well, never mind."

Wilma turns her back on him.

Alec is dressed in one of his typical 'hard man' outfits; today it's 'early teddy-boy'. In his way he looks as peculiar as Wilma. Particularly when I think of how this tough guy was decisively flattened by my friend Connie Stevens a few short months ago.

He turns to me. "How's it goin' Audrey?"

He smiles ingratiatingly, showing off his best feature, his teeth. I wonder how long he will have them all if he continues to take the lovely Miss Stevens for granted.

"Ah must say, yer lookin' good the night. Mind, ye always dae."

I have realised that Shirley's suggestion that Alec has something of a *tendresse* for me is probably right. Certainly, he is forever making oblique suggestions that we take our acquaintance further, suggestions that I choose to ignore for the most part, realising what a dangerous situation might arise if I were to become any more friendly with him.

He moves in for the kill.

"Fancy comin' for a drink?" he asks me. "Ah've got a few bob, enough for wan or two each."

I am a bit bored. "Maybe I will, Alec, in a wee while. We'll see."

"Aw, come on—ye know Ah've always wanted tae get tae know ye better."

Though Wilma's back is to us, she has been paying close attention to our conversation.

"Yoo-hoo, Connie!" she cries suddenly, waving. "Yer husband's contemplating adultery. Over here."

One or two passers-by look over in our direction.

The colour drains from Alec's face, and he turns round to follow Wilma's gaze.

Wilma smiles and turns back. "Relax, Alec, it's OK. Just kidding."

"Ya *bastard*! Christ, ye nearly stoapped ma heart, Wilma. Gie it a rest, there's a guid lassie."

Conversation falters. Alec gives me what he no doubt considers a devastating smile. It must work on Olivia, but it is wasted on me. Anyway, the effect is rather spoiled when, without even turning away, he hawks noisily, and lets fly a solid-looking wad of phlegm that lands at Wilma's feet, missing her left slipper by about an inch.

She jumps back, glaring down at Alec's *ejecta*. "Fuck's sake, Alec, watch where yer firin' yer goggolites. They shoes are new!"

Goggolites? I've never heard that one before. The word sounds about as disgusting as the result looks, though suitably expressive. I must remember it. Moving in the circle I now inhabit is an education in vocabulary as much as in anything else.

Alec's tone is placatory. "Aw, sorry hen, Ah wisnae thinkin'. Sorry, an' aw that."

"Hmph!" Wilma looks at him, looks at her shoes, looks at her watch, then turns to me. "Time Ah wis aff, Audrey. *Betty's Bar* will just be warming up. Want tae come doon wi' me and see how the other half lives?"

"Thanks, not tonight Wilma. Some other time maybe."

Alec has something to add. "Afore ye go Wilma—huv ye heard? Elaine Stewart's back in town."

The name means nothing to me.

But Wilma stops in her tracks. "Naw! Is she? Ah thought she had went doon tae London. For good."

"Aye, she did; but she's back."

Wilma looks at her watch again. "Well, there'll be a few worried faces when *that* news gets about. Don't know why, Ah've always liked Miss Stewart masel'."

And she shuffles off into the night trailing a cloud of perfume and the stares of a good fifty per cent of the customers in the station.

"Ah'm no' sorry she's gone," says Alec, caressing his quiff and looking after her. "Ah like Wilma, Ah really do, always huv, but the way she goes around…"

He turns back. "Anyway, it gie's me mair time tae spend wi' you, Audrey, 's that no' right? How aboot that drink?"

Alec and I make our way up Hope Street to the *Strand*. Friday night, and it is heaving. It's the little bar on the ground floor that is the recognised gay hang out, the large downstairs room plays host to the rest of the world. This place could comfortably accommodate twenty or thirty. At the moment there are fifty people crowded into it, pressed against the narrow bar, against each other, against a wall, each clutching a drink in one hand and a cigarette in the other.

I see a good many familiar faces. I have a quick word with Judy Garland and Susan Strasberg—otherwise Ronnie and Peter—while Alec fights his way to the bar to get me my lager and lime.

Suddenly I spot Nicky squeezed into a table in the far corner, and, excusing myself to my friends, push my way through the mob. He is looking as desirable as ever, and I guess that the outfit he is wearing is new. I certainly haven't seen it before.

"Nicky, darling," I coo. I lean over the table and plant a kiss on his lips.

"OK, Audrey? How's it going?"

He seems slightly cool and unresponsive. Does he squirm just a little?

"Fine thanks—just having a drink with Alec, he's gone to the bar."

Maybe I can arouse a little enthusiasm if he thinks I am interested in someone else.

"And how are you?" I say.

"Oh, smashing, Audrey, really well. Here, let me introduce you to Paul. Audrey, this is Paul, Paul Doyle. Paul—meet Audrey. Paul's my new boyfriend."

The world tips. Did he say 'boyfriend'?

An attractive young man stands up and stretches out a hand. Blond hair, blue eyes, good-looking, slim, no more than seventeen, about my own age.

"Hello, Audrey," he says.

Amid the turmoil of my feelings, I am aware that he is vaguely familiar. Perhaps I have seen him round the town in the past.

As I take the proffered hand, I think that I would rather like to punch him hard in that pretty face.

"Paul's on the Corporation buses too, he's training to be a conductor."

Nicky has something of a proprietorial air, and I shudder inwardly when I see him gently touch the hair of his new friend as the latter sits down.

With an enormous effort I pull myself together. I smile. It is a struggle. "Nice to meet you, Paul. So—how long have you two been together?"

Paul blushes. He has that high colour to which a blush comes easily.

"Oh, not long—a couple of weeks," says Nicky. "Hopin' tae get him taken on at my garage, maybe even get him on ma bus. We can be a team, eh?"

"Well—I hope you'll be very happy."

Yes, I actually say that.

"Thanks, Audrey," Nicky smiles. Does he look slightly embarrassed?

Just at that moment, I am aware of someone behind me. Alec with my drink, I guess.

"Ah—and here's the big man back from the bar at last," says Nicky. "What kept you, Jakey? Audrey, meet Jake, a friend of Paul's. Jake—this is Audrey."

I turn around. The very tall, dark-haired young man carrying the drinks looks at me. I look at him. He smiles.

Oh shit!

'*God—I know him.*'

And he knows me. His name is Jake Quinn, and he works at a garage which is about five minutes' walk from my home in Rutherglen.

He looks surprised. He's no more surprised than I am.

He sets the drinks down and looks at me.

"Oh? Audrey, is it, these days? Well, well. And here Ah always thought your name was George."

It has happened. I've been spotted. The possible consequences don't bear thinking about. I wonder if it is possible to faint on demand?

I find it isn't.

"Och, there ye are, Audrey. Ah wondered where ye'd disappeared tae. No' tryin' tae gie me the slip, are ye? Awright, Nicky?"

Alec McGowan squeezes past me, grins, and passes me a lager and lime.

What an utter, utter mess!

It was bound to happen, I realise. Sooner or later I was going to run into someone who knows me, someone I was at school with, maybe, someone from my home town, perhaps, or even a member of my family, the worst possibility.

But that it should be him! Not that I know him well, or know anything specific to his discredit. However, the garage where he is employed is but a stone's throw from my home. In fact, I have occasionally admired through the open double doors the odd husky male, shirt off in the summer heat, attending to whatever it is they do in garages.

I console myself with the thought that, since this Jake is apparently involved in the gay scene in Glasgow, he will have as much interest in avoiding exposure as do I. More, perhaps. I don't know anything about his background, but his work environment teams with solidly heterosexual types, and I imagine any such revelations would cause him considerable problems.

I resolve simply to avoid him as much as possible, without being obviously disagreeable or unfriendly—that might rouse his ire, and the vague and unfocussed resentment I sense simmering in him.

That could lead to who knows what.

7. Learning the Game

Hearts that are broken and love that's untrue
These go with learning the game
When you love her and she doesn't love you
You're only learning the game
Buddy Holly, 1960

June 1962.

End of year examinations are on my mind throughout the month of June, and I succeed in passing respectably Music I and French. Next year it will be Music II, English I and Psychology. My degree is basically Music/English, but you have to take a one-year course in a few other subjects. Psychology appeals to me—perhaps because in my private life I have recently got to know so many cases in desperate need of urgent analysis, myself not the least among them. My third and final year will be English II and either Logic or Moral Philosophy, one or the other of which is compulsory. Since I am not too sure what either is, I haven't made a choice as yet.

I enjoy a major triumph in my appearance in *Le Malade Imaginaire*. I have a tiny part, only a few lines, but am shot to sudden celebrity by an incident worthy of Hollywood itself. Professor Kenneth Brown, of the Music Department, has arranged for our production of the play to feature the music originally composed for its première in 1673. A few hours before curtain-up, Prof. Brown is—yes, really!—stricken down with some mysterious bug or other, and after a brief rehearsal, I find myself in the pit, in my costume, seated at the harpsichord alongside two violins and a 'cello, virtually sight-reading the score. Between the musical interludes which end each act, I have just time to nip backstage, deliver my lines, and rush back to the pit for the grand finale. I am a sensation—and actually make the newspapers.

Then it's end of term, and I am looking forward to an exciting summer. I will be working at Caldwell's three afternoons a week as well as my regular Saturday stint, and thus I will have every excuse I need to be in town virtually permanently. And no classes. Plenty of time to investigate further my new world, and rather more money than usual to spend in it.

Though everyone on the scene knows pretty much everyone else, it's a fact that apart from a few determined loners, most of us 'girls' have a 'sister', someone with whom they are usually seen around. Queens, it seems, like French horns, prefer to hunt in couples. Thus Julie London and Shirley Temple are generally together. Wilma Flintstone and Lena

Martell are best friends.

Or, rather, they were. Wilma, these days, spends more time with her new companion, the mysterious Bridget, someone who is never seen around the usual haunts in town, but is spoken of with some awe. Luckily, Wilma's ex-sister, Lena, has recently acquired a boyfriend by the name of Charlie, who now takes up most of her time. A fact of which I am slightly envious, as Charlie is attractive—small, dark and handsome. I console myself with the fact that, unfortunately, he has a very feminine and high-pitched speaking voice, and by his side dainty little Lena sounds like Jim Reeves. But, safe in the arms of conjugal bliss, Lena has virtually retired from society. One sees her rarely, as she now spends most of her days as a Shettleston housewife.

Maggie Wilde and Dora Doll are bosom buddies. Dora, a very tall, slim queen, is usually referred to as Big Dora Doll. Glaswegians generally tend to be short in stature. Indeed, in our particular society, anyone over five feet eight is regularly described as 'big'. Olivia is always Big Olivia (Olivia is big in every direction), and at six feet, I am Big Audrey as often as not.

As far as names are concerned, one of the most unusual of we Big People is Little Egypt. Because he is tall and well-built, this particular 'Jim' is regularly referred to as Big Egypt; I suppose Big Little Egypt would be rather confusing. Little Egypt (or Big Egypt) has not one but two sisters—there is Claudia Cardinale, and the trio is completed by the delightfully named Vanessa the Undresser.

I have no sister. I certainly spend a fair amount of time with Shirley, but at heart the latter is a loner. Shirley is likely to disappear from time to time, off on some mysterious errand, connected possibly with her place of employment, the famous brothel; she is always vague on details. But she turns up eventually, usually in a new *ensemble*, as if she had never been gone, and with no explanation for her temporary absence. It would be bad form to enquire too closely. We all have our private corners.

I did attempt to introduce my school friend, Ian, to the delights of Glasgow-by-night, but with little success. After a brief season as Natalie Wood, Ian decided that the wild life was not for him, and disappears from these pages never to be encountered again.

I do become very friendly with a certain Dorothy Provine. Named for the star of the TV show *The Roaring Twenties*, she confides in me that Alec McGowan had once suggested that, in view of her youth, Mandy Miller might be a good choice of name. She shudders in horror.

"Well, Audrey, I know Alec lusts after me, that's a given. But the idea that he sees me as Mandy Miller—who was a *child* star—is just a little worrying."

In fact Mandy Miller is by now grown up, and is exactly the same age as Dorothy and I. But of course, who could forget the deathless lyrics of *Nellie the Elephant*, vintage 1956?

We become friends. But not sisters. Dorothy, although intrigued by the Wild Bunch, finds her natural place on the side of the angels. The debutantes' bar and its denizens welcome her gratefully.

Being young and attractive, Dorothy is known to occasionally exploit the commercial possibilities of her position. And Shirley Temple (who, when between profitable 'dates' of her own, acts as something of a part-time procuress) is able to steer her now and then in the direction of a hungry gentleman whose means exceed his personal appeal. After my own first reluctant venture into the flesh trade I am certainly not inclined to criticise. But my few exploits in that area thereafter are strictly for cash (and on one desperate occasion for forty cigarettes, details in due course), whereas the likes of Dorothy and Shirley Temple barter for trips through to Edinburgh, holidays, dinners and presents.

I remember Dorothy telling me about a visit she had made to a very up-market restaurant in the company of one of her panting swains.

"Well, I picked up the menu. Scottish smoked salmon, three pounds. Can you imagine? So I said, '*Come along, Douglas, I refuse to eat here. These prices are reasonable.*' "

Dorothy and I remain close friends, and will form a surprising partnership on one or two occasions. But for the most part we operate in different areas.

So here I am, nearly eighteen, no boyfriend, no husband. No best friend, no 'sister'.

But that is about to change.

The gents' toilets at Queen Street, Glasgow's second railway station, are notorious. Particularly for the 'glory holes', great gaping voids in the tile work separating adjacent cubicles; no doubt the product of some very determined nail file fiddling over a very long period by generations of avid queens. Highly popular, these, with the 'undercover Marys' who commute homeward from the busy station; that is, those of our persuasion who choose to keep their secret to themselves, and who go home to an ostensibly straight life. We seasoned queens don't tend to patronise these particular premises. Imagine one's horror if one made a move and found oneself adjacent to Maggie Wilde or Susan Hayward—

my dear, the *scandal*! Tootsie trade in spades!

However, on this occasion I happen to find myself *in extremis* while passing the station, and am compelled to avail myself of the facilities. After entering the cubicle, I carefully cover the fist-size holes either side of me with sheets of toilet paper attached with spit (the accepted indication of *not interested*), sit down, and proceed to business. I pass the time by reading the various scrawls left by previous patrons. I am vaguely aware of the comings and goings around me, the banging of cubicle doors, the attendant grunts, farts, splashings and other less identifiable noises. I am amused by one particular *bon mot*. Apparently, '*It's no use standing on the seat, the crabs in here can jump six feet.*'

Just as I prepare to leave, I hear the person in the cubicle on my left flush the toilet, open the door and presumably depart. As the door bangs behind, something rolls under the gap between the wall and the tiled floor. I look down and am amused and delighted to see that it is a tube of make-up—Max Factor's *Sheer Genius* cream foundation. And it's my shade, too—*Tempting Touch*. I quickly scoop it up and pocket it. What a find.

Just in time, as I hear the adjacent door bang open again, and a distinctly ladylike voice exclaim, "Oh bugger it! Three and six that cost me!" I snigger quietly to myself.

It is the evening of the same day, and I am in *Guy's*. This is a place where two worlds collide. Though on the surface a hangout for the bolder queens, it is a big bar, and the area immediately inside the door frequently accommodates those few of the debutantes who have the courage to leave the cosy confines of the *Royal*. The wilder element, with whom I generally associate, are on the other side, near the toilets. Due to my friendship with Dorothy, I am, to a limited extent, accepted by the debutante *coterie*, and I stop to say 'hello' to lovely Ava Gardner and her 'sister', Lana Turner. These two also tend to cross the social boundaries now and then, and I know them fairly well.

"Good evening, Audrey, dear," Ava greets me. "Do you know Gordon, Angie Dickinson?"

Jim Bowse, aka Ava Gardner, is one of the handsomest men imaginable; film star face, hair immaculately arranged, maybe twenty-four or twenty-five. His 'sister', Alan, or 'Lana Turner', a hairdresser from Irving, is shorter and rather older, with a gammy leg but a sweet nature. These two are often to be seen in the company of a certain Vicky Lester, a queen I know only slightly. Dark and good-looking, Vicky's main claim to notice is that she has a habit of bursting into tears at the slightest provocation. And no, not just a few discreet sobs. When Vicky is off on a jag, the tears positively roll down her face and drip on the floor. There seems to be no really compelling reason for these exhibitions most of the time. It's just her thing, it appears.

But Vicky is not in evidence tonight. I take a look at the person standing between Ava and Lana. My age, maybe a little older, tall, but shorter than me, lovely grey eyes, with fine brown hair and a smooth complexion; the agreeable impression rather spoilt by an unattractively shark-like mouth. Thin lips and crooked front teeth. The last time I saw a mouth like that, it had a hook in it.

"No, I don't think we've met," I say. "Hi Gordon, nice to meet you."

"Oh," he drawls, in a rather affected voice. "So you're Audrey Hepburn. Oh yes, I've heard all about *you*."

To my ear, the implication is that, whatever he heard, it wasn't to my credit. I am about to respond in the approved manner—something bitchy is on the tip of my tongue—when I realise that in fact this 'Angie Dickinson' is smiling in a friendly way, and possibly didn't mean any offence. Well, for now, at least, I decide to accept that interpretation.

"Oh—really?" I say, in a non-committal tone.

"Oh yes, Audrey," he breathes. "You're a *lay-gend* in Glasgow."

'Angie' has redeemed himself. I'm not sure how I achieved legendary status in Glasgow in a few short months, but am flattered by the compliment.

Somehow or other we get into conversation, and end up spending the rest of the evening together chatting away. I learn that this Angie works in McLaren's, a Gents' Outfitters in Gordon Street. In 'display', apparently—I translate that as 'window-dresser'. It's an up-market shop, but Angie confides that she actually hails from Drumchapel, a rather working class area of Glasgow. Not one of the worst, but a little on the rough side. I find it hard to equate these plebeian origins with the cultured voice and manner of my new friend. When I point this out, Angie explains frankly that she comes from a very ordinary background (although Daddy is a banker), but intends to better herself, and move up the social scale by cultivating the debutante element. Her occasional upper-class inflections and carefully rounded vowels are a first step on the ladder.

"Please don't mention to anyone that I'm from Drumchapel, Audrey. When people *awsk*, I always say 'Drumry'."

Drumry is a rather more affluent suburb, one further stop on the train

109

beyond Drumchapel. I am happy to assist in Angie's subterfuge, and say so.

I enjoy her company, and when ten o' clock rolls around, I ask her if she fancies a coffee at the *El Guero*.

"Love to, Audrey, but I *cawn't* tonight. Work tomorrow. Got to get the next train home."

"To Drumry, of course," I say.

"*Netch-erly*," replies a delighted Angie.

I suggest we meet again at the weekend.

"Yes, that would be lovely—pop into the shop and we can make arrangements—where and when, all that."

I decide to walk to the station with her. Queen Street station.

It is only just before she leaves me that she says, "You must excuse the way I look, Audrey, by the way." In fact she is immaculate. "Dropped my make-up in the cottage there at lunch-time, it rolled under the wall, and some evil bitch nicked it."

It is some weeks into our friendship before I dare to confess to Angie that the evil bitch was me. We laugh a lot about it, and dine out on the story regularly.

It appears I have found a sister. Just need a boyfriend for the set.

Speaking of which, throughout the rest of the summer, Nicky is notable for his relative absence from the usual haunts. Occasionally he and the new love in his life turn up in *Guys* or the *Strand*, always together, and usually in the company of my nemesis, Jake, the garage mechanic. I learn from our few conversations that Paul, Nicky's boyfriend, is also from Rutherglen, which news gives me a few uneasy moments. However, both he and Jake are always pleasant and agreeable enough, and I begin to relax, thinking that I was right in my assumption that they would have just as much to lose as I would should the terrible truth of our private lives come out. Nevertheless, I maintain the distance—it's all just a bit too close to home for comfort.

Gradually, I come to accept that, as a couple, Nicky and I are simply not destined to be. Not for now, at any rate. I remember Shirley's advice, and realise that she was right, and that it is far better to have Nicky as my very good friend than to risk spoiling that by continuing to languish after him. *The Teddy Bears* go back in the record cabinet. Perhaps it is my imagination, but I seem to sense that Nicky is aware of my apparent change of heart, and our relationship settles down on the surface into a comfortable routine.

So I manage without too much difficulty to interest myself in some other prospects. I am young—not yet eighteen—and, so I am told, the world is my oyster. Time, maybe, to prise open its shell. Time I found a boyfriend.

July 1962.

One afternoon I manage to light on a candidate. I am passing the time with Gina Lollobrigida, in the waiting area of the bus station, the very spot where my rebirth took place six months earlier. We chat desultorily about this and that. Gina is definitely one of the loners, but she is affable enough and good company except when she has been drinking. Maybe twenty three, pretty in a slightly faded, washed out kind of way, with baby blue eyes and fine wavy blond hair, her most arresting feature is the very obviously artificial plastic ear she sports on one side. It nearly, but not quite, matches her complexion—it's just a shade too dark. I never learn the story behind this ear—whether it is a congenital defect or the result of a brawl. No-one else seems to know, and I am far too polite to ask. After a couple of meetings you stop noticing anyway. And her hearing is certainly sharp enough.

While we chat, out of the corner of my eye I am aware of a man mounting the stairs and going into the toilets. I don't really register anything beyond that, until he comes out and heads towards us; and, with an, '*Awright, Gina?*', sits down beside us.

"Andy, dear! Not seen you for a while," Gina greets him, eyelashes fluttering. "Not on the run, I hope?"

He grins. "Naw, Gee, nothin' like that. Just been a bit busy."

Gina does the Bette Davis eye-popping thing that is a common facial tick among the Glasgow girls.

"Oh, busy? Really? Yes, I can imagine. How long ago was it now? Two months? Three?"

"Aye, sorry about that. I had to…"

Andy is obviously about to proffer some apology, but Gina cuts him off in mid-flow. She turns to me.

"Audrey, do you know Andy? Don't suppose you would, he lies low most of the time. A bit of a mystery, our Andy, aren't you, dear?"

Once again the sheepish grin.

"No mystery, Gina, an open book, me."

"Hm—with a few of the pages stuck together, eh? Wonder how that happened? Still wanking your brains out?"

"Hey…" He colours, but doesn't answer beyond that. I wonder why

111

Gina is being so deliberately bitchy? I am guessing they have some kind of history.

She turns to me. "Not a town boy, our Andy," she goes on. "Oh, does the cottages now and then just to relieve his tensions, but not exactly sociable."

Taking pity on the newcomer, I say, "Pay no attention to Gina, she's a bit grouchy today. Missed her period, apparently."

"Miss *Hepburn*—if you don't mind!" cackles Gina.

He smiles gratefully and takes my hand. And doesn't let go.

"Och, Ah'm used tae Gina, don't you worry. Audrey, did you say?"

"Yes, Audrey Hepburn." I am so used to the name that I introduce myself thus without a second thought. Well, in appropriate situations, of course.

Eyebrows raised quizzically (another Hollywood mannerism), I look down at our joined hands. Seeing this, he lets go, a little reluctantly.

Gina looks around airily, then rises to her feet.

"Well, I've a feeling I ought to leave you two alone. Wouldn't want to be in the way, after all. Be seeing you, Audrey."

Just before she turns to leave, she bends over and whispers in my ear. "He's OK, Andy, just a bit weird."

Andy and I embark on one of the strangest relationships I can recall in my not inconsiderable experience. After refusing indignantly his suggestion that we repair to the nearby toilets to consummate our encounter—I have no problem picking up the occasional bit of excitement in such places but have no intention of allowing it to be the scene of an intimate moment—we eventually arrange a rendezvous. He will under no circumstances consider meeting in one of the bars in Glasgow. He explains that he has no interest in the gay scene in town, and only occasionally visits the city in search of an adventure, as Gina had implied. So, after much to-ing and fro-ing, we arrange to meet near Spittal—dreadful name!—a housing estate not too far from where I live, later in the week. He knows the area, he tells me, and promises he will get a bus from Glasgow on the following Wednesday and meet me, nine o'clock, at a spot we both know, outside the cemetery gates. I can walk there from home in ten minutes.

Andy has no car, apparently—I can hear my friend Dorothy Provine now.

'No car? Are you mad, Audrey?'.

But there is something indefinably attractive about him. No, not

112

attractive. Sexy. Not especially good looking, he is tall, slim and shabbily dressed, and, yes—a bit seedy and disreputable looking. Much older than me, he is about thirty. But there is a spark there, I sense it.

Wednesday the eighteenth rolls around. I have no strong expectation that he will actually turn up. But he does.

And so it begins. It is in no way an affair. Indeed, to dignify it as a relationship would be to exaggerate. It is a mutual need and attraction that brings us together. I never discovered Andy's surname. That says it all.

We meet up once a week over a period of about two months. Always in the same place, outside the cemetery gates. Funnily enough, with him I have no qualms about indulging this close to home. Some instinct tells me that Andy will never be a problem in that way.

We never go anywhere socially, nowhere at all. We meet up to have sex, that's it. Not that he isn't perfectly agreeable, we chat a bit, but he makes it clear that he has absolutely no interest in taking things into any other area. But he is an enthusiastic and expert kisser, which counts for a lot with me.

I never learn anything about him—where he lives, what he works at, his family. He is, as Gina had said, a mystery. I wonder if perhaps he is married? He denies it, but who knows? It would be one explanation.

Our intimate encounters take place among the trees, in a large wooded area on the road to Cathkin Braes, a rural spot a mile or two from my home town. It is high summer and the nights are light past ten o' clock, so we have to be careful. He is always extremely nervous, but extremely eager. It is exciting—in a way his edginess adds a piquancy. I am aware on some level that the whole thing is rather unhealthy; not normal, even by our standards. But I have just turned eighteen, and with nothing else of that nature in my life, it is irresistible.

"Can I call you 'Myra'?" he says one night out of the blue, in the throes of passion.

"Myra?" I reply. "What's wrong with 'Audrey'?"

"Oh, nothing, nothing. But I think you look like a 'Myra'."

I am not too sure what a Myra looks like. And it will be nineteen sixty-five before looking like a Myra becomes the last thing anybody would want.

So, for the moment, and just to him, once a week, I am not Audrey, I am Myra.

For some reason, one evening, as we stroll back after a strenuous bout, Andy decides to open up. I have continually tried to probe him for personal details, but, up till now, unsuccessfully. I still nurse hopes that perhaps our relationship, such as it is, may blossom into something more conventional. But what I hear is not what I want to hear.

I learn that, perhaps ten years previously, he had been caught *in flagrante* by the police. He had been charged and sent to prison for two years. While in prison, he was compelled under the terms of his sentence to undergo some kind of aversion therapy designed to cure him of his perverse habits. Unsuccessfully, obviously. Since then he has suffered from recurrent anxiety problems, paranoia, nightmares, and an inability to accept himself or to form relationships. He is awash with guilt and shame, but unable to resist the needs of his nature. He is terrified of being caught again. He is, in a sense, only half a person.

Poor man.

I never see him again. I simply can't. It is just too sad.

Angie and I are now recognised as *sisters*. We go everywhere together, share confidences (but not concerning Andy—that relationship, recently begun, is not one I am happy to discuss, it's just too weird, even shameful), drool over this one or that one, and swap hair and make-up tips, just like any pair of healthy teenage girls. In spite of Angie's original goal, to 'climb the ladder of success wrong by wrong', she comes to enjoy the company of the crowd I hang around with, and over time her middle-class aspirations crumble and fall by the wayside.

Angie is deeply enamoured of a certain Alan Taylor, a regular patron of the *Strand* bar, and a tall, handsome chap, a type that tends to be thin on the ground in our circle. Alan is never to be seen without his boon companion, Roger Christiansen, a Scandinavian import, if memory serves. If Angie and I are sisters, I suppose they are brothers. Or, more simply, pals. Tonight Angie and I are out drinking in the *Strand*—she can put away a remarkable amount of booze, I have come to realise, while I am still on the occasional lager and lime—and, returning from the toilet, she pushes her way through the crowd and confronts me with a smug, 'cat-that-got-the-cream' look on her face.

"Audrey, my *deah*—guess what? I've got a date! With Alan Taylor, tomorrow night."

Though I am a little surprised, I am happy for her.

"Well, you've been trying long enough," I say. "Well done, Angie. Hope he lives up to expectations. You can tell me all about it afterwards."

She shakes her head decisively. "But I won't have to—you've got to

114

be there too."

"Eh?" I ask. "I mean, I'm pleased for you and all that, but what would you want me along for?"

Angie, usually very articulate, can barely enunciate for her excitement. "Because Roger is coming too."

This date is sounding more and more peculiar.

"Why?" I ask.

Angie ponders for a moment.

Eventually, "I think Alan's a little nervous", she says.

The robust Mr Taylor looks as though he hasn't a nerve in his body. Although it's true that Angie in full flood could provoke a tremor in even the most stolid.

"So I thought," she goes on, "if you come along too, we could—you know—double date."

I have to admit to myself that the idea is oddly appealing.

However…

"But Angie—I've never even *spoken* to Roger Christiansen. I don't really fancy him."

Bringing her mouth close to my ear, she whispers, "Maybe not, Audrey—but he's admired *you*. From *a-fawr*. He told me."

Oh, really? I've never considered Roger as a potential partner. But he's far from hideous.

Foolishly, I think, '*Why not? At the worst it could be a laugh.*'

"OK, Angie, you're on. What time tomorrow?"

Angie and I sit in the bar in Exchange Square. I am having a gin and tonic—Dutch gin for Dutch courage—and Angie is on probably her third double vodka. This bar is called *The Gay Gordon*. A supreme irony, as Angie's real name is Gordon, and—well, you get the point.

It is half past eight. They are already half an hour late.

"What's keeping them, Ange? We've been here ages…"

"Oh, they'll be here—just got held up, probably. Another gin, Audrey?"

I shrug. "I'll have a lager and lime, thanks."

She hiccups. "Oh Audrey! And you used to be such a *fun* person!"

Angie trips a little unsteadily across to the bar.

We leave at ten o'clock, with still no sign of the gentlemen. I pour Angie into the late train for Drumchapel ('*No, no, Audrey—Drumry*', she slurs, with a silly giggle) and walk away from the station.

I have a shrewd suspicion that this 'double date' arrangement may have been all in her head. The fruit of a casual remark dropped by Alan or Roger. '*Oh yeah, we have a drink or two in the* Gay Gordon *now and then, nice bar, you should try it sometime.*'

Yes, something like that.

'*God, Angie,*' I think. '*You're a nightmare! What a waste of a Saturday night!*'

But there's still time for a coffee at the *El Guero*. Anything might happen.

August 1962.

I stretch into a *plié* or two at the barre. Ten in the morning, Miss Irene McKinley's *Academie de Danse*, ballet, tap, modern and everything in between. For some mad reason, I have decided I will be a ballet dancer. I know that to excel in the balletic art, one should start early; seven, eight, or even younger. I am eighteen, perhaps a little late, but I have boundless confidence and am convinced I can do anything at all. I am actually a reasonably competent dancer (Ballroom and Latin American Bronze Medal), and used to be a frequent visitor to the Albert ballroom in time gone by, with my 'girl-friend', Lorna; this in the days when I was still trying to fit the mold and the Green Door was firmly shut. But what has given me the idea that I can suddenly transform myself into Anna Pavlova, I cannot imagine. I am beyond terrible, and after about four weeks have to face that reality. But not before I have a memorable encounter at an evening Tap Class. Yes, not content with ballet slippers, the sequinned heels of Ginger Rogers are in my sights. I occasionally think now that I was perhaps a little unbalanced in my teens.

The class is a complete waste of time. I don't even possess a pair of tap shoes, and after struggling inexpertly through a dozen time-steps, decide to sit it out on the sidelines. I watch the dozen or so sturdy girls puffing and panting, and note the only other male in the class, a tiny youth with dark floppy hair and huge green eyes, who is obviously something of an expert.

Later he and I chat as we change back into our street clothes. Effeminate behaviour is hardly a novelty to me, indeed it is the air that I breathe, but this is an extreme case. Girlish in every detail, maybe seventeen but looking younger, I wonder that I haven't seen him in town before. He tells me he lives in Moss Park, a South Side suburb, and has been attending dance classes since he was a tot. He is certainly very competent, and he explains that he hopes to make a career in ballet. But the image of this slip of a thing partnering a ballerina defeats my imagination. This is in the early sixties, long before Wayne Sleep will make balletic shortness fashionable.

I ask if he has ever visited 'the town'. He says not, but we are both aware, without anything being said, that he understands what I am asking.

"Would you like to, Alan?" I ask. My new friend is definitely unusual and has a pleasant wit. I feel he might make an interesting addition to our society.

"Why not?" he says.

Coffee at the *El* Guero follows; and thus it is I who am responsible for introducing 'Dame Margot Fonteyn'—usually just *Margot*, and sometimes, amid the uncultured, just *Dame*—to the world.

Am I taking over Nicky's rôle in The Name Game? Or in this particular case, The Dame Game?

Not really. Given Alan's balletic skills, and the fact that his surname is Fountain, it really couldn't have been anything else.

Little Margot remains a casual friend, but is only an occasional visitor to the seamy side, and is rarely seen in the bars. She tends to hang around the fringes. But a year or two down the line, in the Locarno ballroom, and attired in 'a wee Cilla Black dress', wig and heels, she will expertly cha-cha the night away on the arm of 'Bat Lady', a good-looking queen who in the daytime works as a fashion model for Granite House.

But that's another story.

I run into Wilma one evening as I stand chatting to Angie in Central station. We're about to head off to the pub, and I can tell Angie has already had a couple of heart-starters to fortify herself for the hours ahead. She is just launching into a description of her latest outfit, when Wilma trots up the stairs from Union Street, pausing to say hello to the little man who sells newspapers at the station entrance. '*Laate Fine-awl*,' he bawls every five seconds or so. It is a minor oddity that if the lovely Dorothy Provine happens to pass him, he manages to insert a '*Hello, Blondie*'in between his cries. Only to Dorothy, no-one else. I've no idea why.

Wilma, for once, and for a miracle, is dressed as a man. Indeed I hardly recognise her for a moment. The three of us stand and chat about everything and nothing.

Suddenly, out of the blue, Wilma says, "Audrey—Ah wis wondering—are ye doing anything the morra? In the morning?"

"Me? No, nothing in particular, Wilma. Why?" I am in the record shop

117

in the afternoon, but my morning is unengaged.

Wilma drops her voice.

"Well, ye see, Ah'm up in court the morn's morn, and Ah'm a bit nervous aboot going on ma own. Bridget would come wi' me, but she's goat a couple of fines outstanding and is feart tae show her face in case she gets nicked. Only if ye want, mind. It'd be nice tae see a friendly face."

I am very fond of Wilma. In spite of her oddities, and her attention-grabbing dress-sense, she's one of the nicest people around, and I have no hesitation in agreeing. Anyway, I have never been inside a court in my life, it will be a new experience.

"Sure, Wilma—what time and where?"

"Oh—can I come too?" Angie chimes in, "I've got a morning off owed me."

Wilma laughs. "Aye, Angie, welcome—the mair the merrier. We'll make a party of it."

I really thought I had seen everything. How wrong I was.

We had arranged to rendezvous in front of the court the next morning at ten. Angie and I met up earlier for some breakfast in the *El Guero*, Angie has made arrangements with her work, and we are well on time. But there is as yet no sign of the defendant, Miss Flintstone, Wilma.

Angie and I share a cigarette, and take in the comings and goings up and down the steps of the small court building. There are an astonishing number of people around. Criminality is obviously even bigger business in Glasgow than I had imagined. This is the Sheriff Court, not the High Court, and tends to deal with the multitude of minor infringements, both civil and criminal.

Angie treads on the end of our cigarette vigorously. "I hope she's going to appear, Audrey. I could have had a lie-in if I'd thought she might not show-up."

Just at that moment, Wilma turns the corner. And she is not alone.

"Hi, girls. Bridget here decided tae come along as well, and take a chance on not being recognised."

Looking at the newcomer, I think that is extremely unlikely. While Wilma is in male mode, her friend is like something from another world. I can see from where Wilma has got her ideas of fashion. But this has been carried to an infinitely higher level.

Bridget is shorter than Wilma, but still fairly tall and broad. Her hair is bleached a paper white, and back-combed and lacquered to a gravity-defying height—perhaps six inches at its tallest point. Her face, what one can see of it under its coating, is handsome, although marred (or perhaps, made) by a long and vicious-looking scar on the right cheek.

The make-up simply screams. The heavily painted eyes feature eye-shadow, eye-liner and mascara. The face is plastered in a mask-like base, the cheeks are rouged. There is no lipstick—the creamy foundation is spread over the lips, and they are of a pallor that would in an older person indicate a terminal heart condition. Her clothes are Wilma to the power of *X*. Scarlet toreador pants, skin-tight, hug her legs, matching scarlet mules with low heels are on her feet, and under the close-fitting rose-pink sweater, I'm certain I can detect a hint of breasts. But for all this, she is in no way disguised as a woman. It is obvious that she does not attempt to convince. She is out to shock.

Bridget is *bold*. In our world that means confrontational. And particularly, confrontational with the straight world. Of course, when in groups, we queens tend to be just that, especially if facing down a minority; a revenge for the cries of *Jessie, Pansy,* and *Nancy* we have all been subjected to at some time. But 'bold' also implies something more than that. It is used of a person who confronts straight society single-handedly and demands to be accepted on their own terms, defying the norm openly, refusing to compromise. It is always a compliment. Wilma is bold. Bridget is ultra-bold.

She greets us languidly and disinterestedly. I think at first that she has some kind of mild speech impediment, but then realise that is because she is not Scots—she is English. Poor Angie's rat-trap mouth hangs open in amazement. I have an insane urge to raise my hand up to close it.

As the four of us turn to make our way into the court, the crowd parts like the Red Sea. Every eye is on us. But not one word is said, not one remark is made. This is beyond comment. Bridget is terrifying.

Wilma receives a small fine for her offence, whatever it was. I am far too interested in taking in Bridget to pay much attention to the proceedings. The latter obviously has succeeded in avoiding recognition by the authorities—how, I can't imagine. Maybe because no-one dares to come within yards of her.

When we leave the court, Bridget suddenly becomes more affable, and proposes that we all go and have some lunch together. Both Angie and I mumble something to the effect that we have to get back to work. I frankly wouldn't have the courage to sit at a table in a restaurant with

Bridget. There is a limit. And that is something I thought I would never admit. For boldness, I have certainly met my match.

Her look at us, mingled amusement and contempt, conveys perfectly her attitude. She knows exactly why we refuse the invitation, and her lip curls.

"Fine, just as you like."

Wilma says, "Aye, Bridget, they two are working lassies."

She smiles at us. "Thanks for coming along, girls, Ah really appreciate it."

She turns back to her friend. "Oh, did Ah tell ye, Bridget, whit that sailor said tae me? The German one? Hans something?"

"Knees and boomps-a-daisy?" says Bridget, as they move off arm-in-arm.

"Aye, could be," says Wilma. "He asked me whit Ah did for a living, and Ah told him Ah worked on the streets in the evenings. '*Oh,*' he says, '*Are you a traffic warden?*'"

Amid roars of laughter, the two disappear.

Angie and I are silent as we head back towards the town centre.

8. Devil Woman

Devil woman, devil woman.
Let go of me. devil woman,
Let me be, and leave me alone
I want to go home.
Marty Robbins, 1962

So. That's the picture, the backdrop. Have I limned it adequately? Do you see it in your mind's eye at all? Do you feel you know a few of these museum specimens just a little? Do you begin to know *me*? Words can be inadequate, I understand, and I'm sure mine frequently are. No matter. This is as good as it gets, I'm afraid.

But one of the most important exhibits of all is still waiting in the storage area, just about to be wheeled into public view. Actually, you, gentle reader, have seen this one already. In a darkened cinema, on an evening when she was not quite herself. Or perhaps, when she was entirely herself.

Elaine Stewart.

"Oh, Ah love that song. '*Devil woman, devil woman, let go of me*'. That's me, Audrey—devil woman."

A few notes are sung and the little figure strikes a theatrical pose, with a small self-deprecating smile.

I smile too. Anything less like a *devil woman* than Elaine would be hard to imagine.

"And isn't it terrible about Marilyn? Poor soul."

The news of the death of the Hollywood legend has recently reached us. Though never a huge fan of the world's most famous blonde—her appeal somehow passed me by—I agree that it is indeed tragic.

I first met Elaine a month or so back. It was Maggie Wilde who introduced us. In, naturally, Central Station.

July 1962.

I haven't really registered the short, ordinary-looking person standing innocently by the reservations office, just a few yards from where I loiter in my usual spot, by the weighing machine next to the buffet. But I see Maggie make her entrance from the Hope Street side of the station, instantly recognisable. The tight white trench coat is her inevitable trade mark, visible from miles away, rather as the Great Wall of China is

121

said to be visible from space. As she shimmies towards me I raise a hand in greeting. She gets about halfway across the concourse, and I am surprised when, instead of heading in my direction—Maggie loves a gossip, and the possibility of a free cigarette—she executes a smart half turn and, instead, hails someone ecstatically.

"Miss *Stewart*! Thought ye were still in London."

I don't hear the response, but, deciding that I am not going to be left out of the loop, make my way towards the pair, by now deep in chat.

"Oh, hi Audrey," says Maggie, barely looking round. "Didn't see you over there."

Her attention is on the other. "Ah must say, the change has done ye good, Elaine. Yer lookin' well."

She finally turns to me. "Got a fag, hen?"

"I see *you've* no' changed, Maggie," smiles the stranger. "Still smoking Freemans?"

"Ah've just run oot…"

The unknown one continues, "Sorry Maggie, I cannae help you. I've only got rollups, and I know you wouldnae lower yourself to roll your own."

"Och, Ah can make an exception jist this once," says Maggie, unabashed.

"No need, ladies."

I take a pack of ten Bristol from my pocket and pass them round.

Maggie takes my lighter, a brand new gold-coloured Colibri.

"Thanks, Audrey, yer a star," she says, sparking up. Then, with a "Here, Elaine", she passes the lighter on to her friend.

"So, who's this, Maggie?" says this 'Elaine', firing up in turn and handing it back.

"Oh—huv yiz no' met? Jeez, ma manners…"

Maggie is about to deftly pocket my lighter instead of returning it, but I manage to intercept her.

"Oh, sorry Audrey, whit am Ah daein'?" she fakes unblushingly. "Sorry. Elaine, this is Audrey, Audrey Hepburn. Audrey, meet Elaine Stewart."

The newcomer looks me up and down critically, but not unkindly.

"Audrey Hepburn?" She hesitates. "Hmm. Well, I suppose that's all right. The old one's dead, after all."

I am a bit confused by this remark, but decide to let it go for the moment.

I will learn later that there was another Audrey Hepburn on the

Glaswegian streets a few years ago, one who is no longer with us. And I will come to realise that 'Elaine Stewart' is in a sense the record-keeper and historian of gay Glasgow; and that, although effectively you can call yourself whatever you want, and it will be accepted by the majority, you might be made aware of Elaine's subtle disapproval if she considered your choice inappropriate.

I understand the problem. Currently we have two Elizabeth Taylors. This possible head-on clash is resolved by referring to one of them simply as *Liz Taylor*, and the other as *Liz Taylor fae Greenock*. (The latter's 'sister' is Princess Margaret Rose, who manages to look uncannily like both the American comedian, George Burns, and my Aunt Minnie, that fanatical devourer of the *News of the World*.)

It is round about now that I realise I have seen this Elaine Stewart before. Here is the person, I suddenly recall, who put on that devastating exhibition of derring-do and ultra-boldness during the showing of *The Tattered Dress* which I attended months ago.

Yes, I remember. Michael Feeley. '*He danced under the lights...*'

But... that scene at the cinema had featured someone who appeared to be suffering from some sort of mental affliction. I recall that even the other queens present had been astonished, even shocked, at the proceedings. But Elaine Stewart, as I see her for the second time, is obviously completely sane; straightforward, bright and amusing. It is a bit of a conundrum.

August 1962.

I come to know Elaine very well. No, we don't tend to do the social scene together—Elaine is thoroughly and permanently unwelcome in all the usual bars, for reasons which will become clear later. But I am due to start back at University in another month, and am determined to spend as much time as possible in town, in my brave new world, while I have the chance, before the shades of the prison house close round me once again. Elaine is always around, usually in the station, and if not, in one of the other recognised meeting places. Thus, we spend hours in each other's company, chatting, gossiping and laughing; sometimes in the *El Guero*; sometimes along with others of our ilk; more often just the two of us. I treat her to a tea or a coffee, maybe a sandwich, now and then—Elaine is permanently penniless, but never scrounges or borrows in the manner of Maggie Wilde. If she does happen to have anything, it's yours without a question and without asking.

Her history, it turns out, is a sad and curious one. Through our long chats I learn that she was raised Michael Feeley, in an orphanage in, of all places, Rutherglen, my home town. I know St Columbkille's, the Roman Catholic-run place in question, although it's use as an orphanage was discontinued some years ago. But I remember from my childhood the crowds of sad-looking children I would pass on my way to school in the extensive grounds of the building, and how grateful and thankful I was not to be of their number.

This is where Elaine grew up. Maybe I even saw her there, all unaware.

She has worked from time to time, she tells me, in low-paying jobs. But not currently. She explains frankly that she has a weakness for drink, and that when heavily under the influence she becomes another personality altogether; the personality I first saw when 'the *real* Elaine Stewart' enthralled the world with her impromptu and compelling performance in the cinema.

Fortunately she is not in a position to regularly over-indulge. She lives exclusively on her dole money, and gets around four pounds a week from the government. In addition she is provided with accommodation, paid to her in vouchers. She explains that she resides in *The Pop. The Popular Hotel* (ironic name) is a model lodging house in nearby Holm Street. I visit it once or twice in her company; it is the saddest of places. The tiny cubicles, the upper parts of the walls composed of heavy wire mesh, have the bare minimum of furnishing; a hard, uncomfortable bed; a small table scarred, scored, and covered in cigarette burns; a couple of hooks on which to hang the few clothes most of the residents possess. There is a kitchen providing tea or coffee and sandwiches, charged for.

With my relatively privileged upbringing, I had no idea such places existed. But they do, oh they do. This one is ghastly. It reeks of despair, poverty and misery. But it serves its purpose. Elaine would be living on the streets were it not for *The Popular Hotel*. And at least it's warm.

"If you see me on a Thursday evening, please, George, don't speak to me. Ah'm not myself when I've had a drink, and I would *hate* to fall out with you because I said or did something to upset you. Remember—on Thursday, Miss Stewart is to be *avoided*. That's the day I get paid, and I'm straight round to the off-licence for a bottle or two of wine. Treat myself to some slap from *Woolies*, and hit the town, made-up like a candy ball."

She smiles ruefully. "I sometimes end up getting arrested, of course, but I enjoy it while it lasts. Remember—Thursday night, Elaine is on a spree, so keep away from her."

The appalling tragedy is that this is a person who is intelligent, warm-hearted, decent, honest, kind, witty and loyal. Among all my Glasgow acquaintances, Elaine is probably the best of the bunch. Yes, she will bitch along with the rest of us about this one or that one, but her remarks are filled with humour, and devoid of any real malice. And she knows everything and everybody. She is a walking directory of the Glasgow gay scene, and is always happy to advise me should a question arise.

September 1962.

"Aye, glamorous guy, that Shug Nelson," Elaine remarks out of the side of her mouth, in reference to a brooding presence nearby in the station; somewhat in the Alec McGowan mold, though slim and infinitely better-looking, high cheek-boned, rough and alluring. He is a regular feature around here, and one I have noted with some interest, though we have never spoken. He is rather intimidating. I wonder if the Elvis quiff will ever go out of fashion in Glasgow?

Elaine goes on. "Ah've seen you looking at him, Miss Hepburn, don't think ye can fool me. But steer clear, Audrey, Shug Nelson's mad, bad and dangerous to know."

Yes, I have definitely been eyeing up the gentleman in question. My strange fling with the unhappy Andy recently came to an end. I finished it by the simple expedient of not turning up for our regular dates, and assume he has got the message. Certainly, I haven't seen hide nor hair of him since. So, boyfriend-less, I am open to every and any opportunity for a little excitement in that area.

Elaine is giving me the whole lowdown.

"Now his brother Benny is a lovely guy—do you know him, Benny Nelson?" I shake my head. "Aye, chalk and cheese these two. I'll introduce you to him if he's around, Benny. But that one, Shug—to be avoided."

She smiles, a little maliciously. "He picks up desperate old queens, charges them for his services, and then, while they're carried away with his looks and his rough masculine charms, he thieves off them on the sly. Nicks a wallet here, cash or a watch there, jewellery, maybe, whatever he can lay his hands on."

I wonder fleetingly how much this Shug Nelson charges for his services. I have nothing worth stealing. He stands there, glowering gloriously, not far from us, and Elaine lowers her voice, not wanting to be overheard. I bend down a little so I can make out what she's saying.

"Know what he did just a week or two ago? You'll never believe it." She takes a breath before continuing. "*Promise* me you'll keep this to yourself, Audrey. If he found out Ah'd been putting it around, he'd murder me. Promise?"

"Yes."

"Well. You know the photo booths around the town? For passports and that? There's one just up the road, in *R.S. McColl's*."

"Yes."

"Well, Shug there went inside one of the booths, put his money in, dropped his trousers and took photos of…"

She stops.

"Of what? His knees?"

"No, you know—of his cock…"

I am reminded that Elaine is exceptional in Glasgow for the fastidiousness of her language and her reluctance to use vulgar terms. 'Cock' is unusually blunt for her.

Nevertheless, as if determined, despite her qualms, to be accurate at any cost, she forces out, "…and his balls."

Yes, it would be tricky, I think to myself, to capture the one without the other two.

"No!" I say. "You're kidding!"

"No, no, it's right enough. I've seen them, he's got two strips of them, four photos on each."

She is whispering. "In them he's, you know—exposing himself, and—er—tossing himself off. And other things."

Other things? Elaine is obviously highly embarrassed at this necessity for verbal frankness.

Meantime, the subject of our conversation, unaware of our interest, continues to scowl attractively, hands thrust deep into his pockets. I, on the other hand, am wondering what these 'other things' may be. So I ask.

Elaine is becoming more and more uncomfortable. She is actually blushing.

Her voice drops near to inaudibility. "Well, in the second lot he's showing off his—well—his *arse*. Stop now, Audrey, don't ask me any more."

I am mystified.

Is this nice-looking young man's passion for photographic indulgence just a rather original way of passing an otherwise unoccupied half-hour? Is he simply an enthusiastic narcissist? If so, I have to admire his inventiveness. The instant camera is still some years in the future.

But I have to know more.

"So—what did he want them for, these photos? I mean, if he's turned on by his own personal attractions, he could have a wank in front of a mirror."

Elaine shudders at the bluntness of my language, tuts and shakes her head. "No, no, you don't understand, Audrey. They weren't for him. They were to *sell*—five bob a time. To potential customers."

I suddenly understand that these photographs are effectively publicity shots.

But something is puzzling me. "OK. But tell me, Elaine—how could anybody be sure that it was actually *him* in the photos? I mean—these booths are tiny."

I am trying to picture how the necessary contortions might be achieved.

She considers this. "Mm, yes. Well, you couldn't be certain it was him, not really. Could be anybody. He stood on the seat. I mean, you can only see the—well, the area. But it's him, all right. Or at least, so he told me."

I think this over, and say nothing for a moment.

"Get the picture, Audrey?" says Elaine, nudging me and winking.

"I'd love to. He's gorgeous. But I haven't got five bob."

Elaine draws in her breath sharply. "Oh no, you stay away from him, Audrey. He's a glamorous guy, sure enough, but he's not a very nice person."

Then she giggles, and adds after a pause, "But it *is* a very nice arse."

I see the enterprising Mr Nelson in quite a different light after Elaine's revelations about his unusual hobby. But, having been well-warned, I stay well clear.

I have not completely given up my interest in the entertainment business, in spite of having had my eyes thoroughly opened to real life, and my options enlarged. Glasgow's beautiful *Alhambra* theatre is currently staging its summer spectacular, the *Five Past Eight* show, starring Stanley Baxter and Una McLean. And Miss Dorothy Provine and I attend one of the performances together. A dancer in the show, Peter Griffin, is an acquaintance of Dorothy's, and we are invited round backstage to meet him afterwards. A tall slim Australian, witty and amusing, and as camp as Christmas, Peter is charm itself, and he suggests generously that Dorothy and I might like to attend his birthday party in a few days' time—a fancy dress affair—at the flat he shares with three of the other boys in the production. We are thrilled to be considered, and absolutely determined to be there. So we immediately fall to discussing what we will wear.

Dorothy has made her mind up to appear as a French courtesan. She hasn't quite decided yet which one—after all, appearance-wise they are much of a muchness—but she swears me to secrecy. I have not the least idea who I might go as—my options are limited by both a lack of funds and a lack of imagination. Eventually, I settle on disguising myself as a kind of cat character. Cat Woman, maybe. I still have my ballet tights and slippers, and manage to find a tight black top that fits me like a second skin. Make-up and an elaborate cat mask do the rest.

On the whole, I suppose I don't look too out-of-place. Anyway, I'm only eighteen, how bad can it be? Dorothy, no doubt having exerted a gentle pressure on whoever is paying her expenses these days, is stunning. Immaculately gowned (red and silver, hired), be-wigged (white and powdered, hired) and made-up (perfectly applied, her own), she is Madame de Pompadour.

Unfortunately, our host, Peter, has come as Marie-Antoinette, and it is a little hard to tell them apart. Or would be, if we had the chance to see them side by side. But Peter's wig is made from cotton wool, and his home-made crinoline is largely contrived from a cage of chicken wire festooned with pink net and white paper doilies. And unfortunately, this construction is so wide that, when it has been erected around him, he is unable to make a grand entrance into the *salon*, as the doorway is too narrow. Consequently, he spends most of the evening, fully attired, in the kitchen. We all take turns to go in and admire him.

The party is illuminating. It is the first really adult affair I have ever attended, and Dorothy and I, between us, are indubitably one of the hits of the evening. Due, as much as anything, to our extreme youth. I am heavily propositioned at one point by an older gentleman. I'm not quite sure who he is, and am not at all interested.

'*Still*,' I think, with Mae West, '*better to be looked over than overlooked.*'

It is when the party has finished, and we are sitting around having coffee, and chatting with Peter and two of the other boys in the show, that the suggestion is first mooted.

"You look fabulous, you two. So young, so feminine. Why don't you come along and see the show again? But this time—as girls! Wouldn't that be *marvelous*?"

Dorothy needs no second bidding. By the time we leave, midnight, after changing out of our costumes, she is already planning her outfit. I am at first a little reluctant—what on earth would I wear? I'm six feet tall, not a common height for a Glasgow lassie out for an evening at the theatre. But I am eventually persuaded. By a stroke of good fortune, it turns out that my parents and my sister Jennifer will be away on holiday, leaving me in the house on my own. I realise that I will be able to raid my mother's wardrobe for the necessary. The fact that she is five feet three doesn't occur to me until I actually start trying on some of her things.

Jennifer would be a much better source of attire; like me she is tall and slim. However, she is only fifteen, and I don't really think that 'white blouse and gym slip' would be an appropriate look.

'*This is not going to be easy,*' I realise.

It's the end of summer, a Thursday evening. Angie and I leave *Guy's* at closing time, and she decides that she has got time for a coffee before heading for the station and home. As we descend Hope Street, she is nattering non-stop as usual.

"So he comes into the *shawp*, this fella, twenty-five, maybe twenty-six, smartly dressed, suited and booted, umbrella with a whangee handle. Nice wee Robin Hood hat with a feather—you know the type of hat, Audrey? Tyrolean's the word, I suppose, although of course Robin Hood was English...

"Anyway, this guy buys *seex* shirts. Top of the range too, five quid each, lovely pastel shades, they're a new line, I'll see if I can nick one for you—fifteen collar, isn't it? Consider it done. Violet OK?

"Anyway, then, as he's going out, this guy, he gives me the eye—and no, I'm *not* imagining it, Audrey. I'm in the window, doing an arrangement of sportswear, and as he passes, he actually *weenks* and—you'll never guess—he blows me a *keess*!"

She pauses for breath. "Here, are you *listening* to me, you?"

In truth I am not. Except for wondering momentarily what a whangee handle might be, I have been paying little attention.

"Sorry, Ange," I say. Angie is *Ange* these days, as often as not. Some people rather unkindly call her *Ange la Flange*, which may be a reference to her mouth. Or maybe not.

"I've been thinking about this trip to the theatre. You know, me and Dorothy. Supposed to be going in drag, I told you about it. I'm not sure it's a good idea. I don't know what I'm going to wear. Nothing fits me, I'm too tall. And what about wigs?"

Angie takes a moment to answer.

129

"Hm, *yer-rs*, I can see the problem," she says.

Suddenly she brightens, "I've got it. The sack is the answer."

"The what is the what?"

"The sack, Audrey—the sack dress. You remember the style?"

Certainly I do. The loose-fitting and un-tailored 'sack' dress had a brief vogue a few years back.

"Mind you, it's *very* fifties," goes on Angie. "*Très démodé* these days. But Glasgow is hardly the *dernier cri* in the fashion stakes, I daresay you'd get away with it. Maybe your mother has one in the back of the wardrobe? No?"

"No," I say, "she doesn't. Definitely."

I've been through everything my mother possesses, right to the back of the wardrobe.

"Hm, pity, that," says Angie. "But, thinking on the same lines, if you could find a wee straight dress in maybe a moygashel print, that might serve. You know the style I mean, hangs straight from the shoulder, no tailoring to speak of. They've something on those lines in Grafton's window, saw them the other day, all sizes, not expensive. Your legs are fine."

Angie is on a roll. "And for your hair—forget a wig, so artificial-looking—how about a headscarf? Very trendy these days. Look at the Queen."

'*Yes,*' I think. '*For the races, maybe. Hardly for the theatre. She'll be suggesting a tiara next.*'

My face must be saying it all. Angie defends her corner.

"You could do worse, Audrey, think about it. You know—stick a couple of rollers in the front of your own hair, put a wee bend in it, take them out, then back-comb it a bit, some lacquer, a couple of hair grips, a bit of padding underneath the headscarf, on the crown. That would do it."

I consider her suggestion. Maybe there's something in it.

We arrive at Central Station.

"The *El Guero*, Angie?" I say.

"Oh, must we, Audrey? It's *sew* common in there. All the scruffs. How about *R.S. McColl's*? So much *smah-ter*."

The latter is another late night coffee joint, only a baby step up the social ladder from the *El Guero*. But dear Angie still cherishes every little class distinction, her society pretensions haven't quite crumbled as yet. *R.S. McColl's* is OK, it's just deadly dull compared with the rowdy delights of the *El Guero*, where, on a good night, you might see a queen decisively flatten her husband.

But as Angie is happy to go along with my whims most of the time, tonight I decide to humour her.

"OK."

'*Yes,*' I think, '*a head scarf. Maybe...*'

We enter the station and cross the busy concourse.

"Now, Audrey—have you got jewelry? You'll need jewelry."

"Oh yes, Angie, that's no problem. My mother has some nice bits and pieces."

As we approach the exit leading to Union Street, I suddenly notice Elaine, leaning against the window of the booking office. I'm about to approach her when I realise that she is definitely drunk. And I remember that it's Thursday, pay day.

I recall her warning. But I have had a few myself (three lager and limes, probably, I'm still not much of a drinker), and Angie is half-cut, though as usual she holds her booze well.

"Oh look," she says. "There's Elaine. Let's go over and say *hello.*"

Elaine is patently more than a little under the influence. She lounges against the window, casting contemptuous glances at the passing crowd. But for the moment, silently. Her face runs through her customary gamut of film star expressions. Rebellious Bette Davis in *Jezebel,* suffering Joan Crawford in *Mildred Pierce,* sultry Barbara Stanwyck in *Double Indemnity.*

Occasionally she mutters to herself. There is no bottle visible, but she will have something tucked away in her jacket, I'm sure. She knows that if the Railway Police spot her drinking in public, it will mean ejection from the station.

'*Maybe,*' I think, '*she's not too far gone.*'

Despite her admonition—'*Never speak to me on a Thursday night*'—I decide to risk it.

"Hello, Elaine," I say, Angie trailing behind me. "Any gossip?"

I immediately realise that I have misjudged the situation. This is a stranger, who glares at me menacingly.

"Miss Hepburn, you *slut*! What do you want? Don't you *dare* touch Fury! Who do you think you are?"

Her tone changes to a low hiss. She indicates with a vague gesture an innocent and anonymous gentleman commuter who is hurrying by.

"That man is not for *you,* Vida."

The person in question passes on, unaware that he is the object of discussion.

"He's *mine, mine,* I tell you! Get your *own* man, you little tramp."

I make a vaguely pacifying gesture. But it has no effect.

"And that *mink*!" She takes the lapel of my jacket between finger and thumb. "I know how you earned that, Vida—*on your back.*"

I remove her hand, look at Angie, shrug, and turn again towards Elaine. "OK, Elaine, we're going, sorry to have bothered you."

I make to leave, but before I can, Elaine again grabs me by my lapel.

"Well, you *whore,* before you do—wear *this* for luck!"

And she draws back her other hand and slaps me hard across the face. My glasses shoot off.

"Oh, for God's sake, Elaine," I say, more angry than anything else. "What…"

My cheek stings. And suddenly everything changes.

Elaine puts both hands up to her mouth, a look of genuine shock and horror on her face.

"Oh, Audrey," she whispers. "I'm sorry. So sorry. Forgive me."

She turns, and races down the stairs that lead to the gents' toilets.

"Come on, Audrey, let's go," sighs Angie, handing me my glasses. "She's out of it. A waste of time talking to her. Is your face all right?"

"Yes, yes, it's fine, Angie, don't worry. And it's really not Elaine's fault—if she's warned me once, she's warned me a dozen times. I should have listened."

Is it a forewarning of impending drama that restrains me, or simply a genuine concern? A bit of both I suppose.

"Look, you go on Angie. I'll wait here for a bit just to make sure she's OK. Get us a table, I'll be along in a minute."

"Are you sure, Audrey? I can wait too, if you like."

"No need, no need. Go on, I'll see you shortly. Ten minutes at the most, OK?"

"OK," she replies with some reluctance, turning to go, "don't be long."

I head downstairs in pursuit of Elaine.

The layout of the Central Station toilets is a rather unusual one. The urinals, instead of being set out in lines, are arranged in groups of four round the massive pillars which support the ceiling and the concourse above. On the right as you reach the bottom of the stairs is a row of cubicles. On the left a set of hand basins.

The stalls are busy. I circle carefully round each group, but can see no sign of Elaine. However, two of the cubicles are occupied and I suppose that she must be in one of those.

"Elaine," I call gently, standing equidistant from the two closed doors.

"Elaine."

There is no response. I wait a moment before trying again.

"Elaine!" I repeat, slightly louder. A few heads turn in my direction. "Elaine!"

The door of one of the two cubicles opens and disgorges a gentleman who looks at me in some surprise as he makes his way in the direction of the wash basins.

I head for the cubicle whose door is still closed. I wonder for a moment if she has somehow managed to slip past me. But I can't see how that would be possible.

I knock on the door. *Engaged*, reads the sign on the lock.

Still there is no response.

I bang harder, almost bruising my knuckles on the cold metal.

"Michael! Michael! Open the door," I shout. "It's me, Audrey."

By this time most of the gentlemen in the throes of release are looking at me curiously. I couldn't care less. I sense something is wrong.

I bang on the door again, several times, using my fist.

"Michael! Michael!" I yell.

I look down, and see a thin red stream issuing from under the door.

I draw my fist to my mouth. "Ohgodohgod," I whisper.

Then I turn and fly for the stairs, past the gentlemen holding it, shaking it dry, or buttoning it away.

The Railway Police. They will know what to do, they will help.

But naturally, when I arrive at the head of the stairs, they are nowhere in sight. I can't believe it—there are always one or two of them strolling around officiously, doing nothing at all. I look over towards the far side of the station, where their office is, hoping to catch a glimpse of a uniform, the glint of a button. Nothing.

I look around. There must be *someone* I know here, someone who can help, someone who will know what to do. There are always at least one or two of our crowd around the station. The pubs have just closed, where are they all?

The only familiar face I see is Mental Gillian, a strange, demented creature, a little fat queen who is eternally in the station, waiting for her 'date' to turn up. He never does. But she waits quietly, always alone, speaking to no-one. It is no good approaching Gillian, she is feeble-minded. Maybe a stranger...?

Then, with a surge of relief, I spot Shug Nelson, Mr Photoplay himself, just coming out of the station bar. I've never spoken to him, but without hesitation, I run towards him and grab his hand.

"Shug, Shug, help me. It's Elaine."

As I look at him, I realise that he is slightly drunk.

He shakes my hand off, takes a step back, frowns, and looks me up and down, confused.

"Eh? Whit's the matter? Who're you? An' how come ye know ma name?"

"Never mind that, come on, come on." I seize his hand again in a death grip.

"Whit the fuck?"

He drags me towards him as I continue to babble.

He raises his other hand. "Hang oan, hang oan, calm doon. Now—start again."

I am close to tears. "It's Elaine, she's downstairs, there's been an accident, I don't know… Please, you've got to help me."

"Elaine Stewart, ye mean? Michael? Where?"

I gulp and point in the direction of the toilets.

He squares his shoulders. "OK, OK. Lead the way."

Grateful, I turn and head back, dragging him after me.

"An' ye can let go of my haun now, you're givin' me pins an' needles."

"Oh, sorry…"

Together we clatter down the staircase, and I point towards the cubicle in question. Not necessary, really, as there are already two or three people gathered round it looking at the blood, now a small pool, that continues to puddle. They examine it carefully, intently, rather as if there will be questions to follow.

"Right, OK, shift it, you lot."

Shug elbows his way between them, pulling them away from the door, one by his shoulder, one by his coat. They huddle back, relieved that someone finally seems to be in charge.

Shug looks down at the bloody patch. "Michael! Mick!" he bellows, battering the door with the flat of his palm. "Come *oan*, oot o' there, enough of yer nonsense, dae ye hear me? Open this door right now! Or else!"

'Or else what?' I wonder.

There is no response at all. Shug grits his teeth.

"Christ!"

He turns to me. "Here, haud this fer me, you. It's new, mind ye don't drap it in the piss," he says, stripping off his jacket and handing it over.

"Staun back, the rest of yiz."

The spectators take several steps back. Shug takes a deep breath, moves away from the door, turns sideways on, and shoulders it. It vibrates a bit, but doesn't budge. He repeats the manoeuvre twice more, but with the same result.

Meanwhile I have a sudden image of the door flying open to reveal— nothing at all. Wouldn't that be funny?

"Aw, fuck it, ya bastard," Shug mutters under his breath. He takes another step back, raises his foot, and crashes it into the lock. And the door flies wide.

Elaine is stretchered into the ambulance that someone has finally had the sense to call. Her left wrist is bandaged; her face is paper white; her make-up stands out starkly. She looks very small. She is either unconscious or sleeping, I am hoping the latter.

As the crew manoeuvre the stretcher up the ambulance steps, a half-full wine bottle falls from her clothing and smashes on the ground by the rear wheels.

"Shit," says the driver mechanically.

I stand next to Shug, on the pavement, still clutching his jacket as if my life depended on it.

He shakes his head. "She's no' right, that Elaine. No' right in the heid. Whit wis aw that aboot, fer fuck's sake?"

I don't know what to say to that. I hand him his jacket.

"You awright, you?" he says, glancing at me, as he takes it.

"Yes, I'm fine, thanks. And thank you for your help. If you hadn't…"

"Aw, forget it, forget it. Ah jist hope Ah've no' ruined ma shoes."

He looks down at them, and slips an arm into his jacket.

As he stretches round to insert the other arm, I move to help him, and notice a small square of cardboard flutter to the ground at my feet. While his back is to me, I stoop quickly, and pick it up.

He shrugs into the jacket, and turns to me.

"OK, Ah'm aff. Great night, eh? Ah don't fuckin' think! See ya."

He turns and heads off down Union Street, with his customary bouncing, cocky walk.

I look after him. I sigh and shake my head. You're my hero, Mr Nelson. If only…

I glance down at the piece of cardboard in my hand. I smile, and tuck it in my pocket.

'Not a very nice person,' Elaine had insisted.

But it *is* a very nice arse.

In the ambulance I sit holding Elaine's hand. Just for a moment she opens her eyes.

"Well, devil woman," I say, "You've given us quite a show tonight."

She smiles hazily. I suppose they've given her something.

"Oh, Miss Hepburn… you *are* funny."

And she drifts off again.

In the Western Infirmary's Casualty Department, I sit in Recovery with Elaine, who is still on her stretcher. They have stitched up her badly gashed wrist, and have left us here until whatever they gave her wears off. Then she can go home.

To the comfort of *The Popular Hotel*.

If they *have* given her something, it was strong. Even now she drifts in and out of consciousness, not always making sense.

At one point, she opens her eyes and looks at me. She whispers.

"Do you know what they said, Audrey? The nuns? Do you know what they said to me?"

"No."

"They said, '*Naebody wants ye, Michael, because you're made of shite. You're all made of shite, every bit of you.*' Is that a way to talk to a child?"

She screws up her eyes and two tears trickle down her face.

The very stones should weep.

That is not quite the last shock I will have that evening. I have deposited Elaine at *The Pop*, and managed to get home to Rutherglen via the all night bus service that runs from George Square. I will be in trouble for being late home, but, as I am only a little late, it will only be a little trouble. It's all relative. Though after the night I've had I could do without it.

As I turn the corner into Greenhill Road, a figure moves away from the wall against which he has been leaning. I see with a shock that it is Jake Quinn. What is he doing here? I know he lives in Rutherglen, but what is he doing *here*? Practically on my doorstep? At this time of night?

"Hello, George. Ah've been waiting for ye. Saw ye in the town earlier, and hung around here hoping to catch you on your way home."

"Oh yes?" I attempt a casual tone. But I'm not feeling at all casual, really. There is something about this man that scares me. And I don't really know why. It's more than the fact that he is practically a neighbour, although that is bad enough. There is something cold and cruel about

136

his face, especially around the eyes. Objectively, he is not bad looking, being very tall, slim and with thick dark floppy hair. His features are sharp, aquiline, even distinguished looking.

But those eyes... I bet he tortured animals when he was a kid.

"Yeah. It's about your pal Nicky. Bridgeton Nicky."

Nicky?

"What about him?"

"Yeah. The famous Nicky. Well, he's upset ma friend Paul."

Paul Doyle, Nicky's boyfriend.

"Oh—how did he do that? Upset him, I mean?"

Jake pulls out his cigarettes and offers me one. I don't take it. I never want to owe this guy anything.

He leans against the wall again, relaxed, and lights up.

"Well..." He pauses. "You know they were going out together? Yeah? Well, Nicky's packed him in, told him to get lost."

"Oh? Well—I'm sorry to hear that."

In fact, I am delighted. But I will fake sympathy for a bit.

"Shame, they seemed so well suited, didn't they?"

"Not sure about that. Maybe." He puffs on his cigarette. "Anyway, Nicky caught Paul thieving oot his maw's purse, and so he slung him out."

Good for Nicky. High time.

"Oh, I see. Well, you can't blame him for that, really, can you?"

"No, no, you're right, I don't blame him for that. What I blame him for is beating Paul up, breaking his nose and two ribs. He's a mess, Paul. And he's only a kid."

Actually, he's the same age as me.

"Well, that does sound a bit extreme, I suppose."

Nicky should have broken his neck, the little rat bastard.

"Right. And, ye see, as far as young Paul's concerned... Ah look out for him, sort of."

Yes. I get the picture. No doubt longing to do everything Nicky was doing with him, but terrified of a refusal.

I wait. When nothing further is added, I say, "So—what is it you wanted from me?"

He draws once more on his cigarette.

"Here it is, George. I want you to tell your pal Nicky that Ah'll be watching out for him. Tell him tae be a bit careful where he goes and who with. That's all. OK?"

"OK. I will when I see him."

Nicky, I think, is perfectly capable of looking after himself, and this long streak of piss will have to get up very early in the morning to get one over on *him*.

All the same, I will warn him, just in case.

"OK, thanks," he says. I turn to go.

He treads out his cigarette. "Dae Ah no' get a wee good night kiss, then?"

I look at him, and affect a coy reluctance.

"Not tonight, Jake. It's late and I'm already in trouble."

"Mummy and Daddy waitin' up for ye? OK, some other time then. Ye don't know what yer missing, George. But maybe yil find out, eh?"

He winks lewdly as he ambles off.

October 1962.

It's the night of our theatre visit. Dorothy and I *en femme*.

"Two to Gorbals Cross, please," I say, pushing my voice up into a higher than normal register, as I hand the conductor a shilling.

He takes the money, removes two tickets from the stack he carries, and franks them in his machine. He passes them back to me along with my change.

"There ye are, hen." He moves off up the bus. "Fares please!"

I hand a ticket to Dorothy, and we smile at each other. So far so good.

We have just left the boys' flat, pulling the door hard behind us so it locks automatically. They had already headed off for the theatre and their Friday night show, and we had been left to ourselves to arrange our disguises. To get to the *Alhambra* theatre, we knew, we would need to take two buses. One from the flat, in Moss Park, to Gorbals Cross, and then a further one from there into the town centre and Waterloo Street.

We seem to be carrying it off so far. Certainly we don't appear to be drawing any unwelcome attention. While we waited for the bus, Dorothy engaged in a short conversation with a fellow passenger, without any untoward result. I purchased ten cigarettes from the newsagent's next to the bus stop, ditto.

After we get off the Corporation bus at Gorbals' Cross, and wait for the SMT bus that will take us onwards to our destination, we check each other out.

The headscarf trick suggested by Angie has proved remarkably successful. So much so that Dorothy has adopted it too. She, being rather shorter than I, has had less trouble in outfitting herself. She is in a smart two-piece *ensemble*, and what she refers to as *Aunty Betty's sling-back shoes*. I imagine her underwear is contrived much as mine is; foundation garment, and lots of padding. I am also in a two piece, but frankly, it fits where it touches, and even there, not too well. It is just a completely different shape from me. I have used a bit of hand tacking on the top to encourage its waistline to coincide with my own. The skirt is less trouble, although it is much wider in the hips than I am, a problem I have solved by adding bits and pieces to fill me out, rather than attempting to persuade the skirt to conform to my shape. The over-generous waist line is kept tight with a couple of well-concealed bulldog clips.

My main problem has been shoes. The only pair I could squeeze into (my size eight into the shoes' size seven) are white satin court shoes. Desperately inappropriate, and desperately uncomfortable, but I have no choice. There is simply nothing else that comes close.

We are lightly made-up and discreetly jeweled. Not for us the excesses of the likes of Bridget. We have discussed the matter, and both feel that in these areas, less is definitely plenty.

We arrive at the theatre without further incident, now considerably more relaxed, fairly sure that we are going to get away with this masquerade. In an excess of confidence, we purchase tickets in the left hand 'jury box', a long single row of seats that projects from the end of the circle tier towards the stage boxes and the proscenium. We realise that our friends in the show will be able to spot us more readily in this exposed position—as indeed they do. It's difficult to be absolutely certain, but we do not appear as yet to be attracting undue scrutiny from anywhere. We settle down to enjoy the first half of the show.

Comes the intermission, and I decide that though it is fun, this game is not sufficiently exciting, not challenging enough. Leaving Dorothy in the theatre, I head down Waterloo Street, cross Hope Street and enter Central Station. I am sure that some of my cronies will be in their usual places, and look forward to astonishing them with my boldness and my beauty. I should have arranged to meet up with Angie or Elaine at the appropriate time, but I hadn't considered it.

But the station is deserted. The pubs are still open, so that probably explains it. Still, I give it a minute or two, hoping a familiar face will appear.

Nothing.

I descend the stairs into Union Street (*'La-ate Fine-awl'*) and have a quick look in the *El Guero*, just in case some acquaintance is enjoying a bun and a tea, but with no result. Eventually, I decide I had better head back to the theatre, where the second half of the show will be about to start.

As I walk down the side of the building towards the entrance, all appears quiet and calm. Dorothy will be waiting; probably in her seat by now, I suppose.

Just as I am about to turn in, however, an arm appears, a hand grabs my elbow and a rough masculine voice says, "And here's the other one!"

Oh dear! We have been captured!

Later, we learn from our friends in the cast that word of our impending visit had somehow percolated innocently enough, through the boyfriend of one of the girls in the show, directly to the theatre management. And, quaking, we are led into a well-appointed office, and brought before the imposing person of none other than Mr Herbert Lumsden himself, the general manager.

Herbert is a large gentleman, probably in his fifties, with the figure of a regular *bon vivant*, but with little sign of the worldly, tolerant attitude that sort of lifestyle might be expected to engender. Herbert explains to us that we are very naughty boys, and that the two other gentlemen present, those who made the 'arrest', are friends of his and police officers.

I am dubious. They look more like a couple of his pals from a gentlemen's club. And I suppose there is no reason that they may not be both.

A sort of lecture follows. Dorothy is producing a Niagara of penitence, quite deliberately playing the sympathy card. I sit relatively stony-faced, on the surface unmoved, although inside I am in turmoil. I avoid saying anything at all, beyond the fact that our escapade is a joke, a bit of fun, a dare, nothing more. I appear quite calm, I imagine, but in fact I am terrified; terrified that word of this exploit may get back to my family, and of the repercussions that will follow if it does. But I am determined not to give in and show my concern. I am aware that we are being bullied by these so-called adults, and I have been taught that bullies must be faced down. So despite my qualms, I keep cool, at least outwardly.

Eventually, inevitably, Mr Lumsden runs out of steam, if not out of breath, though he will run out of the latter permanently in a few years. It gradually becomes apparent to me that, for all their bluster, these people simply don't know what to do with or about us.

Melodrama becomes comedy, when Mr Lumsden suggests, completely serious, that we consider taking up golf. Ah, Herbert, if only all the world's problems were so readily solved! A few swings of the club, maybe a pair of boxing gloves, a kick at a football, perhaps? And every poof automatically becomes a model of heterosexuality. We are obviously something completely outside Mr Lumsden's experience. And yet this is a man who runs a major theatre. Half of his staff are gay, as are half of the people on his stage. Does he walk around with his eyes closed?

Comedy descends to farce when we are told to leave and advised to go straight home. On the bus, no less. The bus we came here on. I am almost tempted to ask for a refund, as we have missed the second half of the show. But I restrain myself, glad to have got out of the situation intact.

Many years later, a friend will tell me how, at a dinner party he attended, Mr Stanley Baxter himself recounted the story of the two queens who had attended one of his performances in drag, and of the consequences that ensued.

Dorothy and I have become, in a small way, a showbiz legend.

9. *Little Town Flirt*

Here she comes, just look at that style;
She's looking at you, giving you that smile;
'Cause you can get hurt,
Yeah, you can get hurt
Foolin' around with that little town flirt
Del Shannon, 1963

Early afternoon. I am standing in the station, chatting to Elaine, who is apparently none the worse for her failed suicide attempt—not, she tells me, her first. Although she admits frankly that she remembers very little of the evening, or indeed, of the other evenings when similar events have occurred.

"But I didnae actually mean tae kill myself, Audrey. It was more of a—well, a dramatic gesture, really."

"A cry for help?" I ask.

"No, no. Just wanting some attention, I suppose."

"Well, you certainly got that, Elaine. But can I suggest that the next time you want to attract attention, you wave a flag or hold up your hand?"

I notice a trio of people coming across from the direction of the Central Hotel, from the exit that leads directly into the station.

In the lead I recognise Dame Margot Fonteyn, my former dance school colleague. The other two are strangers to me. One is a tall good-looking young man, maybe nineteen, and the other a dark-complexioned queen I have never seen before.

I wave.

"Margot, hi," I call out, and they head towards us.

Margot smiles. "Hello, Audrey, not seen you for a while. Hi, Elaine."
She looks back over her shoulder.

"We've just been having lunch at the Central Hotel. Petula here treated us; nice of her."

I am definitely more intrigued by Margot's *other* friend, but I glance at the dark-haired queen.

"Hello, Petula. Don't think we've met," I say. She shakes hands with both myself and Elaine.

"Oh, call me 'Pet', please—everybody does," she gushes enthusiastically.

"OK, Pet," I say, sounding like a jolly Geordie housewife.

I will, I think, stick with *Petula*. Petula Clark, I imagine. I can't recall any other Petula.

Knowing Margot as I do, and having by now some experience in these matters, I recognise this Petula for what she is. She is not Margot's sister, she is a hand-maiden. She is not an equal partner, she's an insignificant nobody whom Margot tolerates when there is no other company. Possibly because she doesn't mind spending money on Margot and her entourage. She certainly looks fairly affluent. Margot is nobody's fool, and such arrangements are not unknown to me.

"And who is *this*?" I say, referring to the lanky Adonis on Margot's other side.

Margot smiles. A shrewd customer, she has no doubt registered that my interest is not entirely—well—disinterested.

"This is Bobby, my boyfriend. He's Canadian."

"Good afternoon, Bobby," I say, shaking his hand.

"Good afternoon, ma'am," he responds with a little bow, which nearly has me on the floor.

We decide to head across to the *El Guero* for some coffee. Petula is paying, apparently. Yes, as I had imagined, paying is one of her functions. Cappuccinos for us ladies, a Coke for Bobby. Elaine orders a cake, too. I wish I'd thought of that.

Bobby heads for the toilets after finishing his drink. Elaine has gone off to chat to her friend Kay Kendall. Petula seems to have little to say.

"*He's* nice, Margot." I look after Bobby, and add some sugar to my coffee. "Known him long?"

"No, not long. Do you like him?"

I know how crafty she can be, and I scent an ulterior motive.

"Well, yes—he's not bad-looking, and he seems nice."

She looks up from her coffee.

"Do you want him?" she says.

"Eh?"

"You can have him if you want him. It's up to you."

It is on the tip of my tongue to ridicule this strange suggestion. But I don't.

Instead I say, "What do you mean? That is—he's your boyfriend, you said so."

"Yes, he is," she replies, quite unmoved. "But you can have him, if you like. I'm a bit bored with him."

I am not generally one to examine a gift horse too closely. But I give

143

Bobby a thorough once-over when he returns from the toilet. As far as I can see, he is a fine, upstanding young man. Attractive, tall, well-mannered. How bad can it be? What, I wonder, is wrong with him?

I am still a bit baffled by Margot's question. Surely it was some kind of joke? But I should have realised that the Dame always knows what she's about.

She turns to her escort.

"Bobby dear, you like Audrey, don't you? She's nice, isn't she?"

Bobby smiles, revealing perfect Canadian teeth. "Oh, yes, Margot. She's lovely, Audrey."

"Well, you're hers now, dear. She'll look after you."

Bobby's expression barely alters.

"OK." He smiles some more. At Margot. At me.

I wonder if perhaps he is marginally defective?

Margot stands up.

"Sorry Audrey, got to go. Bye, Elaine," she calls over. "Coming, Pet?"

The hand-maiden also rises to her feet.

Just before they leave, Margot bends down to pick up her bag.

"Have fun, Audrey," she whispers. "Don't worry, he's nice. You don't mind me passing him on to you, do you?"

I shake my head, '*No.*'

"Good. That's how I got him."

Bobby is indeed nice. Perhaps a nicer person has never existed. He is relentlessly polite, well-mannered, considerate and kind.

I learn that he is not just some random Canadian ex-pat who wound up in Glasgow by chance. He has family here. In fact his relative is a certain Charlie (Chuck) Springfield, a Glasgow face on the butch side, whom I know quite well. My new boyfriend, Bobby Springfield, is Chuck's nephew.

I have described Uncle Chuck correctly, I think, as being from the butch, or masculine, side of our society. It is probably just simple bitchiness that causes Dorothy to wonder if, at an earlier period, Uncle Chuck Springfield might have been *Dusty* Springfield.

But sweet Bobby continues to be endlessly nice. I even introduce him to my family, in the guise of a friend. They also find him nice. Bobby and I have sex now and then, usually at his uncle's place. That, too, is fairly nice.

November 1962.

A few weeks later, we are sitting in the *Vol* cafeteria, Jamaica Street. Just Bobby and I, along with Vera Ellen, a queen I only know slightly, but occasionally chat to. Bobby has gone to the counter to get us our coffees and his Coke.

"Well, *he's* a new face, Audrey." Vera settles herself in her seat. "Not seen him before. You're boyfriend, I take it?"

I nod in agreement.

She pauses.

"Seems very pleasant."

"Oh, he is, Vera. Extremely. A nice boy; well-mannered, polite, always agreeable. We've only been together a short while."

"Good looking, too," she goes on, glancing over at him and moistening her lips.

"Yes, isn't he?"

I allow a moment to go by before saying, "Do you want him?"

I am delighted to say that sweet Bobby has at last found someone who will never tire of his niceness. He and Vera Ellen remain a couple for as long as I know them.

I am being haunted, there is no other word for it, by Jake Quinn. I have passed on his message to Nicky, warning of the dire fate awaiting him for his rough treatment of Paul. Nicky receives the information with just the contempt I would have expected. There is never any further consequence. As I had imagined, Mr Quinn is as full of shit as he is of hot air.

Nevertheless, once or twice a week, when I am walking home, he is waiting there, at Greenhill Road. Occasionally I take a different route home to try to avoid him. But when he realises what I am up to, he moves his loitering point to Main Street, where all the buses terminate, and he can't miss me.

"Ah'll just see ye home safe, OK?"

Eventually, I simply have to accept him as a regular obstacle.

I am anxious not to offend him. I sense he is awaiting the opportunity to get his own back, though I'm not sure what for, or on whom. He only rarely mentions Nicky or Paul, but often continues his suggestions, couched in a jokey, heavy-handed, flirty style, that he and I should get to know each other better. I wish I could figure out what is going on there, because I know he doesn't really fancy me. On the contrary, he would, I think, quite like to hurt me in some way. He is resentful, my existence offends him. To him I am privileged, well educated, with good prospects; yet I'm still able to have my fun on the wild side without paying any price.

I know that he is gay. But he is gay in some strange, twisted way that is incapable of finding satisfaction or fulfilment. He is, too, I understand, deeply unhappy and angry; and for some reason, I am to blame for this. Or rather, the world is to blame, and I am the world's elected representative. Not that he ever says so directly. But it clangs between the lines of our conversations.

All I can do for now is put up with the situation, and hope he finds someone else to take his bitterness and rage out on before too long.

December 1962.

There is some interesting news on the theatre front. The musical *Carnival* is about to open at the *King's* theatre over the Christmas period before transferring to the West End of London. The show has enjoyed a considerable success in the States, and the backers hope it will meet with a similar reception in the UK.

Based on the 1953 film *Lili,* which starred Leslie Caron, it tells the story of a naïve French girl who falls in love with a crippled, tormented, tortured puppeteer. Eventually their differences are resolved, and they all live happily... etcetera. But what gets my attention is the fact that the leading rôle will be played by one of my cousins, Sally Logan, who is a few years older than me. This will be Sally's big chance. She has already enjoyed considerable success in the Scottish variety theatre as a singer, but this is in quite another league, and may lead to who knows what?

Naturally the Logan family are in attendance *en masse* on the first night.

It has to be said that the gentle, sentimental show is no more than agreeable. Pleasant if unmemorable songs, a fine performance from Sally (though they have dyed her lovely red-gold hair a flat, dead, black for the part) and a generally expert cast, but after *West Side Story, Carnival* is pretty thin beer. It will sadly flop in London, closing after only thirty-four performances. But its star, Sally, will return to Glasgow and her family, and continue her career successfully for many years to come.

December also sees my first—and, sadly, only—appearance as a soloist with the Glasgow University orchestra. I play a Mozart piano concerto—the A major, K. 414—and have, I think, a fair success. The reviews in the Glasgow papers say that my concerto performances will benefit when I learn to take a more dominant rôle in the proceedings, but compliment me on my fluent technique and my understanding of Mozartian style.

This university year will be my last year of music study, and I take full advantage. For the music society, which offers students public performances in an intimate setting, I perform a Couperin *ordre* on the harpsichord, join a violinist and a 'cellist in trios by Schubert and Tchaikovsky, and give an all-Schumann piano recital.

I am seconded into the percussion department of the University Orchestra for a performance of Honegger's *Le Roi David* in the large concert hall, where I happily clash cymbals and thump the bass drum at the right moments. But I have a dreadful mishap in *The Invocation of the Witch of Endor*. My job is to keep up a continuous roll on the tam-tam, or gong, throughout, starting almost inaudibly and gradually increasing in volume to a *fortissimo* climax. The tam-tam is a large heavy metal disc with an upturned edge, suspended in a wooden frame. Unfortunately, such is my enthusiasm, that, at the ultimate moment, I whack the tam-tam so hard that the sponge head of the stick flies off, and the thing itself falls over among the trombones in front. But it makes a glorious and appropriate noise.

Things in other areas are not quite so positive. Oh, Psychology, which I am studying for just a year, I very much enjoy. It is fairly straightforward, and I learn all about colour-blindness, Rorschach ink blots, the mechanism of the inner ear, and phototropism. But English, my first year of two, I detest. I can't say why—I used to find English interesting.

University is not school, and attendance at classes is not compulsory, checked, or recorded. As a result, at English lectures, I tend to be noticeable by my absence half the time. Not good, I know, but the temptation to spend an hour or two with my cronies, drinking coffee, smoking and chatting, rather than struggling with Milton or John Donne, is irresistible. On one level I know I am building up problems for the future. On another, I manage to convince myself that I can surely get through my English exam if I just cram for a month or so before the day itself.

It is Nicky who extends the invitation. An acquaintance of his, a certain Beanie (Bill) McColl, who owns a café on the South Side, is apparently in the habit, once or twice a year, of hosting a rather grand party in his mansion flat in Nithsdale Road, Queen's Park, a high-class and affluent suburb. Yes, seedy old Glasgow does have a few upmarket areas.

It is to be on New Year's Eve. And my attendance, it appears, has been requested. These invitations, Nicky tells me, are like gold dust, and much sought after by every queen nursing even the slightest of social ambitions. He tells me, too, that it is his recommendation that has secured this priceless gift especially for me and a friend, and I see no reason to doubt it. I suspect that Nicky's relations with Mr McColl may at one time have been of an intimate nature, even though the latter is hardly Nicky's usual type. He is middle aged, and, though an agreeable and charming person, no Young Lochinvar. I have come to realise that Nicky, like most of us, is not entirely averse to profiting from his youth and looks from time to time, and that his preferences are a little more elastic than I had previously been led to believe. Maybe there is still hope?

The invitation is for myself, Angie, and Dorothy.

Our reactions are rather different.

Dorothy accepts it as no more than her due—after all, she is one of the brightest stars in the Glasgow firmament, is she not? Young, beautiful and smart. Angie is enthralled, convinced that at last, here, finally, her social qualifications have been recognised. I don't tell her that she was not actually mentioned on the original guest list; it was my influence with Nicky that persuaded him to include my sister among God's elect.

I don't say anything to Angie about this, it would be a cruelty to disillusion her. So I will save that pleasure for a time when I feel a little cruelty is justified.

As for myself, I am not too concerned one way or the other. I imagine it will be a rather staid, pretentious and high-toned affair, not my sort of thing at all. There will be no Wilma, Elaine, or Connie there, of that I am sure; and no men of the type that I go for. I cannot decide whether to bother or not, and it's only Angie's relentless pressure that finally persuades me.

Nicky tells me too that Beanie has a piano in the apartment, and would be delighted if I would deign to run my fingers over the keys, 'if I feel so inclined'. I am never averse to a little showing-off, and it is this that finally convinces me.

In fact, contrary to my expectations, it turns out to be an enjoyable evening. The company is certainly not my usual one, but I come to think I have perhaps been a bit hasty in dismissing out of hand the debutante side of our society. I meet a number of intelligent and charming people, and realise that it is pleasant from time to time to chat to others who actually share some of my less obvious interests.

We don't see a great deal of Dorothy. She is busy socialising, and no doubt arranging for some gentleman of mature years but youthful ambitions to succumb to her charms and open his cheque book.

Angie, however, has a wonderful time. I have warned her on pain of death to behave, and to go easy on the booze, and though by the time we leave she is feeling no pain, she is far from the only guest to over-indulge. The drink flows like water, the food is minimal but delicious, and the large apartment itself is splendid, beautifully decorated and furnished.

There are perhaps forty people present, a few of whom I know, though the majority are strangers to me. Lovely Ava Gardner is there, along with Lana Turner. She introduces me to a very good-looking young friend of hers called Jimmy Reddoch. I can't quite work out if he is Ava's latest flame, or just a friend—Ava is a bit of an expert in giving a little information but not quite enough. Then there is Trevor, a lecturer from the Glasgow Art School, a very upper-class gent indeed, with his cravat, English accent and slightly arty attire.

Dorothy introduces me to some of her set. Others come and go. I can't register all the names, though some of the faces are familiar. Nicky floats around, quite 'mine host', ensuring that everyone has a drink in his hand. I have to give Angie the odd meaningful look from time to time, but by and large she behaves herself.

Suddenly, it's cabaret time! We are all encouraged to find a seat, some on chairs, some on the floor, others perched on the furniture. The lights are adjusted—indeed, a portable spotlight is switched on. The music on the record-player starts—Marilyn's *Diamonds are a girl's best friend*. And into the circle thus created struts someone who is called, apparently, 'Shushie Reid'. Or it may be 'Shooshie', or even 'Sushi'. Silver lamé dress, blond wig and heels. Miss Reid (George Reid, I will discover later) proceeds to mime convincingly to the well-known and beloved number, and takes a bow to a tumultuous reception. A couple of other songs follow, much in the same vein, and then the star leaves the stage.

I am a little less than impressed. Though it is carried off efficiently, I don't consider the idea of someone miming to a record to represent *real* entertainment. But it's enjoyable enough in its way, makes a change, and the debutantes love it.

Then it is my moment. I play a few pieces on the piano, and am gratified to receive an enthusiastic reaction.

"George, I'd no idea you could play so beautifully, dear, really great," says Ava.

Finally, it is the turn of Trevor, the Art Lecturer. He seats himself at the keyboard, and proceeds to give us a selection of The Best of Noël Coward.

And he is surprisingly good. He obviously plays by ear, and his voice is nothing special, but he captures the manner to perfection and his clipped diction and coy stresses bring the house down.

Angie is in heaven. I overhear her say to him, in her most affected and cut-glass accent, "Oh Trevor, dear, that was *wahn-der-fool*! Do give us *Terribly House and Garden*, Flanders and Swann. If you know it. Or what about that lovely Hermione Gingold number, what is it again? Oh yes—*The Borgias are Having an Orgy*."

Trevor is happy to oblige.

Later I overhear handsome Jimmy Reddoch murmur to Angie, "Well, Angie, what sophisticated tastes you have! You've been hiding your light under a bushel!"

I think she is going to faint at his feet in ecstasy after this sign of recognition. Indeed, she will continue to repeat the remark *ad nauseam* to anyone within earshot for years afterwards, till you could just about scream.

We leave the party in the early hours having passed a surprisingly pleasant evening.

I belong to Glasgow, and Glasgow belongs to me. Or rather, Glasgow belongs to us. We queens flit hither and yon through the city streets day and night in our little packs, behaving for the most part pretty outrageously. We pose and preen, we shriek and giggle, we flaunt ourselves shamelessly before all and sundry.

And we get away with it. Hardly anyone dares to criticise or even to comment. Those few who do are likely to end up being roundly abused themselves, and made to look foolish. We know just how and whom to target, having been so often targets ourselves. We don't hold back, and we have an ample stock of devastating rejoinders, the fruit of long practice in deflecting criticism with wit. It is a brave man or woman (or a foolish one) who dares to take us on.

But though it's not obvious, we select our victims very carefully. Glasgow may no longer be the *No Mean City* of the '30s, but even now, in the '60s, it is regarded as one of the roughest and most dangerous towns in Britain. Probably only Liverpool has an equally daunting reputation. Fights in the street or in bars are commonplace, razor-slashing hasn't quite died out, and knives are carried by some of the rowdier element, the ones who go out looking for trouble, and there are not a few of those. In default of any other weapon, a glass or bottle is a favourite means of evening the odds, and in the pubs these are always to hand.

Cautionary tales abound in our secret society of the fates of this one or that one, the queen who said or did the wrong thing in the wrong place, or at the wrong time, or to the wrong person. Who was attacked and injured, who was beaten up and left for dead. So though we may appear to be completely impartial in our choice of quarry, this is not in fact the case. By dint of long practice, our instincts and reflexes are honed to an almost supernatural sensitivity. We know when to let it out, and when to hold it in.

Or most of us do, most of the time.

January 1963.

On an otherwise dead-end Friday, Angie and I decide to try something different. The town-centre bars tend to be less busy as the winter temperatures start to drop; the station is cold and draughty; many of our crowd seem to be in hibernation. The *El Guero* is warm and cosy, but on a Friday night we are looking for adventure, not coffee.

Both of us are currently unattached. It is Angie who proposes that we take a trip to *Betty's Bar*, the regular hang-out of Bridget and Wilma, down by the docks. Wilma is forever suggesting we give it a go, and we had certainly planned to try it out some time. So why not tonight, Angie asks? Though the pub has a dangerous reputation, I agree that it might be worth a look, if only for an hour or so, just to satisfy our curiosity.

It is also Angie who suggests that it might be wise to fortify ourselves with something bracing before we venture into the lair of the slightly scary Bridget and her *entourage*. But instead of a couple of swift ones in the pub, she proposes we each buy a bottle of wine from the off-licence, find a quiet spot, and down it before we set out.

I am not sure. My only experience of wine up till now has been the occasional glass with a meal, and that was taken for form's sake—I don't actually care for the taste at all. But I allow myself to be persuaded. After all, I am in search of new experiences, is that not so?

We head for an off-licence where they seem to know Angie quite well, and each buy a bottle of something called *Barchester Ruby*, four shillings. Angie warns me off the cheaper *Three Six Five* at three shillings and sixpence.

"No, Audrey, that stuff is terrible. Winos drink it—we mustn't insult our palates, after all."

Well, all I can say is that, to be worse than the wine we actually buy, *Three Six Five—A wine for every day of the year*, it says helpfully on the label—must be truly dreadful. Unlike anything alcoholic I have tasted up till now, *Barchester Ruby* is as sweet as cough syrup and about as much fun to drink.

After our purchase, and at Angie's suggestion, we head towards a line of telephone kiosks in George Square, and enter neighbouring boxes. I undo the screw top on my bottle and sniff it gingerly. It smells a bit like sherry, or port. Not totally unpleasant at first. I try a sip. It is very sweet. But not too nasty. I turn to look at my sister, and am amazed to see that she has finished nearly a quarter of her bottle already. She is necking it like lemonade.

I try another mouthful. Yes, maybe I can manage this.

Angie has finished the entire contents by the time we emerge, and has ditched the empty bottle in the phone box. I have consumed about a third of mine, and can feel the effects. They are not unpleasant. My sister seems quite *compos mentis*, however, and looks at me in amazement as I clutch the bottle.

"Good God, Audrey, is that all you're having?"

I enunciate very carefully. "No, Angie. It's all I'm having for now."

She frowns.

"Audrey, you can hardly walk down the road clutching a half-empty bottle of wine—it's simply not done."

I suspect that she is hoping I will offer the remains to her.

Instead, I wither her.

"Oh excuse me, Miss Dickinson. Silly of me. Knocking back wine straight from the bottle in a public phone box is perfectly acceptable behaviour. But walking down the road carrying a bottle of wine is beyond the pale. Beyond the Pale Ale, in fact. Is that what you are saying?"

She glares at me. "No, Audrey, it's *not* what I'm saying. But out *heah* your public can *see* you with it. In the phone box, they *cawn't*."

Her completely unwarranted pretensions occasionally irritate me. "Oh, shut up, for fuck's sake, Ange."

The point becomes moot anyway when I trip over the kerb crossing Argyle Street, and drop the bottle. It smashes in the gutter, and the blood red stream heads off in the direction of Partick.

"Oh no, Audrey... What a *waste!*"

I think for a moment Angie is going to cry. Or maybe get down on her knees and lap it up. However, she simply sniffs, and we continue on our way.

Betty's Bar is rough, dog rough.

No, that doesn't really cover it at all. Most of the customers are male (sailors, international, judging from the selection of languages that assault my ear), but there are more than a few ladies present whose profession is not at all difficult to divine. Sat in one corner is, of all the unlikely people, Dame Margot Fonteyn, along with a queen I know as Brenda Lee. The latter has a bad reputation as a disputative character, although personally I have never had any trouble with her. Anyway, I have been told that her favourite targets for attack, when in belligerent mood, are policemen.

Over in another corner sits Wilma, queen of all she surveys, surrounded by a bevy of admiring males. At least, I assume they are admiring—maybe they are just hypnotised. She has moved even closer to the Bridget ideal in dress and make-up. But underneath all that she is still Wilma. She spots us and waves.

"Audrey, Angie—over here, over here. C'moan fellas, make some room for ma friends."

A couple of her courtiers stand up, and usher Miss Dickinson and myself into the company. We sit down in the seats they have vacated, and they lounge attentively behind us.

"Drinks for these lassies," Wilma demands imperiously. "Cider and wine OK, girls?"

Angie smiles and nods.

Cider and wine?

I am hoping I have misunderstood.

But I haven't. And after the third cider and wine cocktail—you pour the wine into the cider, I discover—I am feeling no pain. So this is what *drunk* feels like, is it? I think I like it. And it's the first time in my life. It's not that the room is spinning round, or anything that obvious. But I feel surprisingly mellow. Even happy and relaxed in this den, this notorious thieves' kitchen.

I am being chatted up by a young sailor—so young that maybe he's a cabin boy—who is, I think he says, American. But no, I have misheard— the bar is *very* noisy—he is Armenian. Or maybe Albanian. I don't get his name at all, though he repeats it several times. And he has some difficulty with mine.

"Oradray," he tries.

After the third go round, I say, "OK—leave it there, it's close enough."

Someone puts Roy Orbison's *Running scared* on the jukebox, and during the introductory vamp Bridget appears from behind the bar where she has been serving. She proceeds to sing along with the record, start to finish. And her voice is surprisingly good. Even the final ascent to the climactic high note is solidly there and bang in tune:

> *'My heart was breaking, which one would it be?*
> *You turned around and walked away with me.'*

There is a burst of enthusiastic applause at the conclusion. Bridget smiles somewhat condescendingly, accepting a homage that is no more than her due, and retires once more to her position behind the bar.

As I look after Bridget, something I had noticed before and wondered about strikes me again. I lean across the table and speak quietly.

"Wilma," I say. "Don't think I'm just being nosey, but—has Bridget got—well—breasts? It certainly looks as if she has. Small, but definitely there. Unless she's just a bit overweight?"

Wilma purses her lips.

"Well—don't say anything to her, mind, but—aye, she's on the hormone tablets. For a year or so now."

"Hormone tablets? What's that?"

"Well, ye asked me if she's got breasts, Bridget. That's whit they dae, the tablets, develop yer breasts."

"Oh, I see," I say, although I don't, really.

"Aye, an' keep it tae yersel', Audrey, but Ah've just started on them too."

"You?"

Wilma smiles. "Aye. A year, maybe two, an' Ah'll be ready for the operation."

As the jukebox continues to churn out the hits of the day, a few people get up to dance. There is no dance floor as such. They just manoeuvre round the tables and between the drunks. My Jack Tar asks me if I would like to take a turn round the floor, but I decline. Leandros (I have finally found out his name, and the fact that he is actually Greek, *Ellinikos* in his own language, apparently) is young and charming, and has been paying for my drinks all night, but I am not sure I could do justice to a slow foxtrot. Angie, who is being mauled in a genteel fashion by someone who closely resembles Popeye's rival, Bluto, is keen to trip a measure. But after she receives a warning look from me—she is even more pissed than I am—she decides that, dance-wise, discretion is probably the way to go. At least on this, our first visit.

Wilma has no such reservations, and the floor is cleared for her big moment. A beefy, heavily made-up prostitute, Marion—Big Marion, inevitably—joins her in their own interpretation of *The Locomotion*.

It is obviously a well-rehearsed routine, and I remember from previous occasions that, in spite of her size, Wilma is a great dancer. She swivels to and fro, leaning over her partner, who leans back, their shoulders shaking in time to the music; side by side they do the locomotion thing, arms miming the action of the pistons; Wilma adds the traditional moves from *The Twist*, rising on tiptoe and then descending to a crouch, knees bent; rotates her hips suggestively; and ends with a cartwheel that only just avoids taking her through the window. The reaction is ecstatic.

The evening continues agreeably enough. My admirer is anxious that we get to know each other better.

"You come wi' me on my sheep? Is no' far, Oradray. I make love to you all night, if you want it. We make party. Your friend, my friend, too."

I don't commit myself, but think, '*Well, why not? This place is fun, what on earth was I worried about? All those prophets of doom, those Cassandras who warned me how dangerous and rough this bar is—they were wrong.*'

I am obviously too pissed to take account of the fact that although Cassandra's prophecies were never believed, they were right on the money.

I look around. '*The people are fun, the atmosphere is great, and as for this cider and wine... it's delicious.*'

I'm just on the point of leaning over to ask Angie if she fancies entertaining Bluto for the night, and suggesting that, if so, we should stick together, when there comes, over the music, an ear-splitting shriek from the direction of the toilets. Wilma is immediately on her feet.

"Whit wis that? Turn that jukebox down, Phyllis!" she yells.

She surveys the room. "Where's Bridget? Onybody seen Bridget?"

There is a second scream. Wilma pushes past her immediate company, and forces her way through the crowded bar towards the toilets. As she reaches them, the door flies open, and a broad-shouldered and muscular sailor emerges, doing up the front of his trousers. He is obviously

German, and equally obviously, far from happy.

"*Verflüchte diebe!* Tries to fuckin' rip me off! *Schwein* tries to take my wallet. *Verdammte schwüle…*"

Just behind him staggers Bridget. She is all but unrecognisable. Her blouse is ripped down the front. She is not wearing a bra, but I can see that before too long she is going to need one. Her beehive is no longer sheet-white, but scarlet, her face is a mask of blood. It runs into her eyes, and drips from her chin. A piece of glass is embedded in her cheek. She sways forward and back, puts one hand to her face, then sinks to her knees.

Wilma pushes through the crowd.

"Right, ya bastard! Ah warned her! Ah *knew* you wis bad news. Glass ma friend, wid ye? Come oan, ya cunt!"

She launches herself at Bridget's assailant and tackles him to the floor.

And within seconds the entire place is in an uproar. Two of the sailor's mates pile on top of Wilma. Big Marion cracks a bottle over the head of one of them, then grabs the other by the hair, trying to pull him off. Glassware flies, conversations have turned to screams and curses, sporadic fights break out among people who up till a moment ago were laughing and chatting together. Everyone, it seems, is partisan. I would guess that many old scores are settled during the carnage.

I am utterly horrified. I have never seen anything like this in my life, and never expected to. I feel sick. Quite literally.

Amid the chaos are unexpected oases of calm.

Dame Margot is back-combing her hair while Brenda Lee holds up a small mirror for her.

Leandros is still whispering, "Say you come, Oradray, please, for me. I am loving you."

Angie surfaces briefly from Bluto's embrace to glance over and intone, "Oh, I *se-ay*, look. Poor Bridget. And her hair was looking *sew* lovely."

I rise to my feet, reach over and grab Angie's hand and jerk her unceremoniously from her admirer's ample lap.

"Come on, Miss Dickinson, we are *not* staying here. Come along. Right now."

"Oh, but *Audrey*… What about…?"

"*Now*, Angie, *now.*"

I pull her by the hand—indeed, almost yank her off her feet—and drag her in the direction of the door. I hope someone has had the sense to telephone for an ambulance.

As we cross the heaving floor, stepping carefully over bodies, Angie turns briefly back, picks up a handy bottle and cracks it hard over the head of Bridget's attacker.

"There, take *thet*, you *nar-sty* creature."

"Oradray, Oradray, wait for me, please. I come for you."

Leandros gets up.

Bluto, too, is on his feet.

"Angela, my lovely girl, come back," he calls.

"*Sew* sorry, boys, have to go—my friend here insists. And she used to be such a *fun* person…"

I give her hand a tug, we reach the door, and fall through it into the freezing January night.

We are walking quickly up the road that leads to Anderston Cross. I hear the sound of sirens—police, and, hopefully, an ambulance.

And I also hear behind me, "Oradray, Oradray, wait, I am coming for you."

It is Leandros. Puffing and out of breath he reaches us.

"It's OK, it's OK. You come with me now to sheep? Why you run away, Oradray, do you no' love me?"

"No, no, it's nothing like that, Leandros, I love you very much."

Indeed, he is very nice-looking, and not more than twenty-one. It wouldn't be at all hard to love him a little.

"But—that fight, it was awful, I couldn't stay."

He doesn't understand.

"What you mean, Oradray? Just a fight, a wee fight. Happens all the time there. In that place, every night. So—you come now?—to sheep? With me?"

To the ship? I shudder. Anything might happen to me alone on a Greek ship. I could end up miles out to sea, used and abused, passed around like a parcel, and sold into white slavery in the Dardanelles. Yes, I remember that film. So no, I've pushed my luck enough for one evening.

"I'm sorry, I couldn't face it tonight, not after that. Maybe another night?"

He actually looks broken-hearted.

"No, not another night. I must go back tomorrow morning, back to Piraeus. No' know when I back in Glasgow."

In spite of my distress at the scene I have just witnessed, and my roiling stomach where the wine and the cider seem to be vying for supremacy…

"Look, Leandros—why do you not come with us? I have a friend…"

Maybe I can find someone willing to put the two of us up for the night, it's only nine o' clock.

Angie grasps my shoulder and spins me round, enraged, indignant.

"Oh? I see! Well *thank you*, Miss Hepburn! Thank you so very much. You drag me away from *my* boyfriend. '*Oh,*' you say, '*come on, we have to go.*' It's OK for you, you've already arranged to meet up with your man, this one. You are so utterly selfish. What about me? What about *my* man?"

I have had just about enough of her with one thing and another.

"Look Angie, if you want Bluto, go back and get him! Nobody is stopping you."

"What? Who is Bluto?" says Angie, mouth dropping open, stepping back.

"Oh, will you just shut the fuck up for a moment, *please?*"

Leandros intervenes. "Oh, you two girls, please, no' tae fight, is not nice. You both nice, stop tae fight, please."

He turns and gazes into my eyes.

"Oradray, I cannae come with you. I would like, but I cannae. I must be back on the sheep by eleven o'clock. If not, I get murdered, it's the rules."

This is obviously not meant to be. Probably just as well.

I explain to Leandros as best I can, and he wanders off, disconsolate, back in the direction of the bar we have just left.

"Remember—I love you forever," he calls over his shoulder, as he makes his way a little unsteadily toward the docks. "I never forget you."

I wonder if he ever did? Oh dear. It's a world of missed opportunities.

Angie has recovered her composure, and is checking her face in her hand mirror.

"Never mind, eh, Audrey, we've still time for a couple in the *Strand*. Up for it?"

But my stomach is definitely saying 'No' to the thought of any more booze.

"Sorry, Angie. Can't face it. I'll call you tomorrow."

And I head for the bus station and home.

To round off the evening perfectly, who is waiting on the corner of Main Street and Mill Street? Waiting for me. Yes, Jake Quinn.

I am feeling truly dreadful. The bumpy bus ride home has put the final touches to my stomach's revolt and my misery. I only just managed to hold it in.

'*If I can just make it home…*' I think. I picture the lovely welcoming toilet bowl, the pleasure of simply letting this lot go, the technicolour yawn.

Of course, my mother has to be outflanked somehow, but I am used to carrying that off. I am actually even drunker than I realise.

And now this.

Jake smiles.

"Oh, Ah see. Well, hey, look at you! A bit pissed are we tonight, young George? Tut-tut. Yer green. Here, you need tae be sick, yil feel better."

He is right, spot on. I don't reply; as always when I am with him I am aware that I have to be careful what I say. But right now I would happily see him in hell.

"Come in here," he says. We are passing the Odeon cinema car park.

"Eh? What for?" I ask.

"So's ye can be sick."

"No, it's OK, I'll be fine when I get home. Just need to get up the road."

"Nonsense, not at all. Get in here."

And he grabs me by the arm and drags me after him into the large car park, then propels me toward a dark corner, under some trees. There are plenty of people around in the street, but no-one seems to pay any attention to us. I feel so weak and dreadful that I simply let myself be taken, unresisting.

'*Maybe he's right,*' I think. I certainly can't hold out much longer.

He faces me. "OK. Want me to turn my back?"

"Yes, please."

There can't be many things more embarrassing than spewing in public. Or even in front of him.

He turns away. I lean over and wait. I stick an experimental finger down my throat. But nothing happens. Nothing at all. I manage a burp once or twice, but that is the extent of it. I actually begin to feel slightly better. Oh, just to get *home*…

"Er—I don't think I'm going to be sick after all," I say. "I feel nearly OK."

"Sure?" he says, turning back.

"Yes. It seems to have settled down. Thanks. I'll get off home now."

I turn to leave, but he grabs me by the shoulders.

"Well, that's good. But while we're here… Ah've been waiting a long time for this."

And the next thing I know, before I can even think of anything to say, or can pull away, his mouth is on mine and his tongue is half-way down my throat.

And that does it.

Immediately, everything I have drunk on this dreadful evening comes back for an encore. I vomit copiously over him, into his mouth, down his clothes. And over myself, nearly choking in the process.

He leaps clear, his face contorted with rage.

"Ya bastard, ye did that on purpose!"

Of course I didn't. It was simply uncontrollable. He pulls out a handkerchief and tries to wipe himself down. But it is a vain effort, there was never a handkerchief big enough. He is coated from head to foot. He stinks. So do I.

"Shit, look at the state of me. Fuck!"

I start to apologise, but cut it short. Still gasping, but suddenly incandescent with rage, I push past him and turn. The habitual expletives that I have learned so well from my usual company pour forth, I sputter through the traces of vomit clinging to the inside of my mouth, and my accent metamorphoses effortlessly and appropriately.

"Serves you right, you sleazy fucker. It's just what you deserve, you cunt, grabbing me like that. You know I hate you, I always have. You scummy wanker, if I never see you again it will be too soon. I wish I'd done that months ago."

His jaw tightens, and he draws back his fist to punch me. But suddenly, it drops to his side. His rage seems to dissipate. He comes up to me and speaks right in my face.

In a low and reasonable tone, and with a death's head grin, he says, "Oh dear, George, you've done it this time, you really have. You'll pay for that. You wait."

He pushes past me and is gone.

I finally reach home. Too worn and stressed to attempt subterfuge, I just ring the doorbell. My mother answers the door immediately.

She takes one look at me. "Oh George. You're drunk!"

"Yes, I'm afraid I am," I say politely. And throw up once again, all over the pristine doorstep.

It is only a few days later that the phone call comes. Quite late at night, maybe ten o'clock. I'm at home, for once. It's my father who answers. I have heard the phone ring, but know it's not going to be anyone for me.

My father looks serious when he comes into my room. "I've just had a phone call from someone who claims he knows you."

"Oh yes?" I say, looking up from my book, suspecting nothing.

"Yes. Didn't give his name. But he says—this is difficult—he says he knows you well, and that you're... a homosexual. That wasn't the word he used."

I am horrified, panic-stricken. My stomach convulses; I could actually be sick.

But on one level, I realise I have always known that, one of these days, sooner or later, this matter would have to be confronted.

My poor father is finding the situation very tricky.

"Should we just ignore this, George? Is it just someone being malicious, someone who doesn't like you? I'll accept it, whatever you say. If it's not true, if it's just some kind of a joke, we won't mention it again."

So here it is, the moment of truth. What do I do? Do I deny it, and take my father's word that it will be forgotten? I could try that tack. But I know that it won't be forgotten. It may not be mentioned, but it will always be there, waiting in the background, ever on my parents' mind. They will be looking for signs, wondering. I will have to live a lie, and live it very carefully, as some others I know do.

Or do I admit the truth? Try to explain how things are, and hope that they are able to accept it? Live with the fact that I know they will be permanently unsettled and concerned for my safety?

The awful thing is that, either way, my parents' tranquillity is gone forever. Whichever course I take, that is inevitable. But if I tell the truth, at least my own life will be easier, to some extent. I will no longer have to lie constantly, and maybe, in time, my parents will be able to accept that I am sensible enough to thread the maze of my own world safely.

The lie is the obvious, instinctive response. But who knows whether other things may not arise in the future? Another phone call, a letter, simple gossip? Someone has seriously got it in for me, that's obvious— and I have no doubts at all as to who that someone is.

In the few seconds before I reply, I weigh up the two options available to me. It doesn't take any longer than that to come to a decision. This is because somewhere in the recesses of my mind, I have already confronted this dilemma and made a choice.

We're all going to suffer, whatever my response. Selfishly, I pick the option that will make my own life simpler in the long term.

"No, Dad. I'm afraid it's true."

10. Where the Boys Are

Where the boys are
Someone waits for me
A smiling face, a warm embrace
Two arms to hold me tenderly
Connie Francis, 1961

A dreadful time ensues. My parents and I walk on eggshells round each other. Nothing is mentioned, nothing said out loud. But I know that every time I walk out the door, they are worrying. In particular, my mother. My father could be considered a man of the world. He travelled to the States in his youth, and returned from America to the UK as a stowaway. I know this to be no family legend, I have seen the newspaper clipping giving details of the charges he and his two friends faced when they were caught disembarking. Many members of his family are in the theatre, and I have no doubt that he has mixed with all types, in his youth and beyond. Thus, while it would be an over-simplification to say he accepts the situation, he certainly seems to be mainly concerned that I should be safe and happy, in whatever position in life I find myself. We have never been particularly close in the past, my father and I—I am the original Mummy's Boy—but I am appreciative of his understanding and lack of criticism.

But my mother, on the other hand, has seen all her illusions shattered. I was the Golden Child, pianist *extraordinaire*, successful at school, passing all my examinations with flying colours. Now studying at University, where great things are expected of me. She tries very hard to be non-judgemental, to comprehend, but it is easy to see in her eyes that she hasn't a clue, and her expression is as often reproachful as understanding. I have delivered the ultimate disappointment. This is hard, very hard, to deal with. My mother and I have always been close—my sister Jennifer is definitely Daddy's Girl—but this closeness slips away, leaving a space full of unvoiced questions and unspoken answers.

It is she, I imagine, who originates the suggestion that perhaps a visit to our family doctor might be helpful. It devastates me to think of my mother, who is no fool, clutching at such straws—I am sure that nothing could be more pointless than discussing one's sexual orientation with dear old Doctor James. I am perfectly aware that the problem is in no sense a medical one, it's not something that can be treated and cured.

Quite apart from my own instinctive understanding of this, I have to look no further than the experiences of the unfortunate Andy, my former lover, at the hands of the judicial system, to be confirmed in my opinion.

However, aware of the huge blow I have delivered, I agree. Perhaps, I think, a doctor will be able to offer some insights into the situation, insights that I am just too close to the whole issue to see. Insights that may help my family to come to terms with recent events.

And indeed, to an extent, this proves to be the case. Doctor James is about sixty—to me he seems ancient—and confirms my own diagnosis.

"There's nothing wrong with you, nothing at all."

"No, I know there isn't," I say. "This wasn't my idea. It's my parents who thought it might help."

He looks at me.

"Are you happy?" he asks.

I wonder if I am?

"Well—let me put it this way. The only thing I am particularly *unhappy* about right now is the grief all this is causing my parents. Aside from that... Yes, I suppose so."

He writes something down, then looks up.

"I think perhaps it's them I should be talking to, not you."

"Yes," I breathe, feeling a surge of relief. And surprise—I would never have expected this white-haired and elderly gentleman to be so perceptive.

Matters do improve marginally after that. But I continue to feel guilty, and to feel that I am somehow blameworthy. And I know perfectly well that, logically, I shouldn't. I have done nothing wrong, I have not deliberately hurt anyone, I have merely followed my natural instincts in the private areas of my life. If I had been born with mental problems or physically handicapped, both of which situations would no doubt have caused my parents untold grief, no-one would have considered this to be in any way my fault. But this particular situation is seen very differently—it's as if I have made a bad choice deliberately, then pig-headedly refused to consider changing it when I am given the opportunity.

Almost worse is the fact that I know that my parents are questioning themselves. Are they somehow responsible? Did they do something wrong? Are they being somehow punished for—well—whatever? It is not logical, but it is inevitable.

I spend as much time as possible away from home; the atmosphere there is increasingly unbearable. I am not sure how long I can stand it.

February 1963.

Afternoon. Passing through the station, I spot Elaine, and head over towards her for a chat. She is, I note, in rather intriguing company. Not one, not two, but three young men whom I don't know surround her, and none of them is unattractive.

I hesitate at first. Maybe these are just some straight guys asking for directions or something. I don't want to put Elaine in an awkward position. Then I hear a burst of laughter, and see Elaine dig one of the guys in the ribs in an unmistakably familiar manner. So I walk over and position myself next to her.

"Hi," I say. "Any gossip?"

Elaine is in fine form.

"Miss Hepburn, star of stars," she greets me. "Come along, join the fun. Meet my friends here, all nice boys. We were in the jail together a while back, me and these two, Billy and George. A miscarriage of justice in my case, as you will appreciate. But not in theirs. These are thoroughly *bad* boys."

The trio shuffle their feet from side to side and grin rather inanely.

"Boys, meet Audrey. Audrey—this is George, Billy, and—what was your name, son? Oh aye, Brian."

The introductions are made. Unusually, with surnames included. I look over the selection on offer.

George Cooper is tall, with dirty-blonde hair, a pale complexion, sad hazel eyes, and a long, good-looking face. Perhaps twenty three or thereabouts.

'*He's nice,*' I think.

Bill Donaldson is shorter and stocky. Tight jeans, reddish hair in a crew cut, regular, handsome features, brilliant blue eyes. About the same age as the other.

'*Mm. He's nice, too.*'

Brian Campbell is younger, maybe nineteen or twenty, of medium height, and probably the least immediately striking of the three. His soft brown hair is parted on the right, and he has pale eyes that are neither quite blue nor grey. His other facial features are undistinguished, except for his mouth, which is beautiful. Full lips, perfectly shaped.

'*Nice mouth,*' I think

All three are, to my eyes, and in their different ways, desirable. And they are all *men*, there is no mistaking that. They are what might be described as crossovers—boys who are for the most part straight. Maybe

164

married, certainly seen by their peers as 'one of the lads'. But they have another side. Somewhere—and often, it seems, in prison—they have run up against a queen or two, and a whole new side of life has opened up for them. They are not strictly gay. But, as we say, they help out when we're busy.

I suppose that, technically, 'bisexual' is the word. But the few true bisexuals I have come across lead a hidden double life—they pose as 'straight' to the world at large, but sneak off for the occasional adventure on the naughty side. In contrast, these lads are in the main unconcerned and unashamed. They are just as likely to express interest in a girl as in a queen, and just as likely to go off with one or the other at the end of an evening. They are not strictly homosexual, heterosexual or bisexual. They are just, well, sexual. Many of the male customers in *Betty's Bar* are from the same mould—as Wilma put it, '*You know what sailors are.*' And this is the type that appeals to me above all others.

Even so, I don't anticipate at this stage that I will before very long get to know all three of these young men rather more than casually.

Elaine has explained to me many times that her own heart is already given irrevocably and eternally to a certain Donnie—yet another prison acquaintance, it appears. Donnie is not at liberty currently, but Elaine awaits the day of his release eagerly.

"Oh aye, Donnie. A right bastard, a bad bugger, but a chopper tae his knees."

Naturally that doesn't prevent her from casting her bread upon the waters from time to time. And today her catch is exceptional. Elaine is the original Fisher of Men.

I am welcomed into the company warmly.

I am not, in my own view, in any way good-looking. I am tall, thin, and bespectacled. I am, however, young, eighteen, and I have already learned the advantages of this, that it has its own particular appeal. And I have developed a personality that is individual. Oh, I have added bits and pieces from here and there to my mix, but in the main, I am an original.

Elaine herself is ordinary looking. She is on the short side, five seven, maybe, thick wavy brown hair, solid build. In spite of her difficult circumstances, she is nearly always shaved and tidy. Her clothes, though old and sometimes shabby, are clean. Her character and her dialogue are witty, amusing and all her own. We make a good team.

But in the end, when it comes down to the battle of the pseudo-sexes, I have learned that, however friendly us girls may be, and however

165

genuinely fond of one another, where men are concerned we are in competition. I am ready to compete.

But clever Elaine simply does not join in. I realise after a while that she is bright enough to understand that, whichever of these potential Romeos I end up with, assuming I manage to spark an interest in even one of them, there are still two left.

She is, as usual, much wiser than me.

Not that our conversation so far has even touched the fringes of these matters. It remains general, superficial, the lads responding with laughter to Elaine's more outrageous remarks. It is light-hearted and it is fun, a commodity that has been in short supply for me over the last week or two. I relish it and relax for the first time in quite a while.

I take in the three boys' cocky, self-confident behaviour—jostling each other one minute, laughing and sparring the next.

'*Well, well—is it the Three Musketeers?*' I think. '*Or the Three Stooges?*'

Eventually, I do become aware that the one called George is paying me particular attention. George Cooper, I remember. Of the three, he would probably be my first choice. I catch his eye on me more than once. I feel a warm tingle to know that I have possibly scored. Whether it leads to anything or not is less important. Nice if it does, but if not, it does me good to be for a while the centre of amorous interest instead of the focus of mistrust and concern.

Eventually all five of us head over to the *El Guero*—the pubs won't open for hours yet. Stocky, handsome Bill is flush, and pays for all our teas. He seems to be the nicest of the three. He contributes more than his friends to the conversation—George is pleasant, but appealingly monosyllabic, and Brian, it appears, is simply shy.

Bill asks if any of us wants a sandwich. But Elaine pooh-poohs that suggestion; and I know why. Elaine has a speciality. She 'wheechles' expertly—her own word for it.

As we pass down parallel with the counter to select our choice of food or drinks, it is my job to distract whoever is serving by making some enquiry about the price of this or that, or the availability of something or other, leaning forward to mask Elaine, who is behind me. While the server handles my enquiry, Elaine will have managed to extract a selection of goodies from the clear plastic bins that hold sandwiches and cakes. Her jacket seems to have about a dozen pockets, as the prizes disappear in a split second. It is dishonest, of course, and a little dangerous, certainly, but it is exciting, and we have never been caught at it yet.

166

The rest of the afternoon passes pleasantly enough. At five o'clock, Bill says he has to leave to go to work.

"Where do you work?" I ask.

"On the shows. The fairground. Travel round wi' them from place to place maist o' the time. Here, there and everywhere. But for the next month we're at the Kelvin Hall. Drop by the Waltzer if ye like, Ah'll see ye get a free ride. Oh, hey, don't take that the wrong way," he adds, laughing. "You too, Elaine."

Elaine smiles coyly. "Oh, no, Ah think it's Miss Hepburn's company you're after, Billy, no' mine. Ah wouldn't want to be in the way."

"Don't be daft, Elaine, maybe we'll go together," I smile.

"Ye ready, Brian?" says Bill, rising to his feet.

"Aye, OK Billy."

"You going too, then, Brian?" I ask. I am sorry that the party seems to be breaking up.

He gets up. "Aye. Ah work wi' Billy. On the Dodgems. Look me up if ye fancy a bit of fun."

Surprisingly, he winks at us both. I am astonished. This is about the first complete sentence he has managed all day.

The two boys head off.

Elaine, never slow to realise when she is *de trop*, makes an excuse and leaves me and Mr Cooper alone together. This one doesn't have a job, it seems.

I offer him a cigarette.

"No job? Why's that?"

He takes it and lights up.

"Ah'm oan the sick; problem wi' ma heart. Bill could get me a job along wi' him but it wid be too stressful, ma doctor says. Got somethin' called a valvular lesion. Had it since Ah wis a kid, had rheumatic fever."

"Oh—sorry to hear that, George."

I just hope his heart is up to the stresses I'm hoping to place on it. He puffs on his cigarette. "Och, it's nae problem, just have tae have a check-up now and then. Disnae bother me day-to-day."

'*Good,*' I think.

Conversation flags. Elaine was the catalyst, but now that myself and this man are alone together, I am suddenly tongue-tied and shy.

'*Damn! And I really fancy him.*'

When we reach the point where the silence is becoming embarrassing, I get up.

167

"Right," I say, stretching. "I'd better get off home too. Going out later. Nice to meet you, George."

"OK, see you around," he says.

I gather my bits and pieces together and prepare to leave.

Just before I do, he looks up.

"Do you want me to see you home or anything?"

I am reminded of an old joke. The Glasgow expression for a gentleman who sees a lady home after an evening out is a *lumber*, the verb being *to lumber*. The scene is a dance hall, eleven PM.

Man: *Hey, hen, can Ah lumber ye hame?*

Girl: *Aye, sure ye can.*

Man: *Righto. Where dae ye live, then?*

Girl: *Ah live in Riddrie.*

Man: (horrified) *Riddrie? It's no' a lumber ye want, hen, it's a pen-pal!*

Rutherglen is not quite as inaccessible as exotic Riddrie, and Mr Cooper and I share our first intimate moment in Stonelaw Woods, just fifteen minutes from where I live. Six-thirty, cold February, and the woods are pretty much in darkness. They abound in quiet and sheltered corners. The encounter is agreeable, but only covers the preliminaries. Nothing beyond heavy petting. This guy is a bit nervous of discovery, though the heart seems to be coping adequately.

I am not nervous. Why would I worry about exposure? That ship has sailed.

I walk this other George back to the bus-stop, holding onto his arm, my boldness half-embarrassing, half-pleasing him, and we make an arrangement to meet up again on Sunday.

I head for home. Some tensions have been relieved. It would be accurate to describe myself as lightly smitten. Have I, I wonder, maybe found a new boyfriend?

If so, what to do about it? A regular encounter in some park or other is hardly what I am looking for. So I put into effect a plan I have been meditating for a little while, ever since the day of judgement, now a couple of weeks in the past.

I will leave home, move out, run away.

My parents are not at all keen on this idea. Perhaps they imagine that they retain some control over me as long as I am living at home. In truth, they don't. I contrive to do pretty much as I please, counting on their reluctance to broach the subject to avoid any confrontations or disagreements.

But I need to get away. The constant strain of pretending and the curtailment of my personal liberty that results from my having to tiptoe round them is unbearable. The last thing I wish is to cause them pain.

'*So,*' I think, selfishly, '*if I'm not there, I can't hurt them, isn't that so?*'

In my utter self-absorption, I do not take into account that the most hurtful thing I can do is not to be there.

I lie shamelessly, and explain that I will be moving into a flat with a couple of other University students.

"After all," I say, "there are loads of them, my age and younger, who live in digs. People who are not from Glasgow. Don't worry, I'll be home every Sunday, maybe in the week too, now and then."

Yes, I have yet another part-time job. On Sundays I play the organ in one of our local churches. Total sceptic and unbeliever though I am, I am happy to take the church's money. After all, they have been living off the rest of us for centuries.

Eventually, my parents agree. There is really not much else they can do. I am eighteen, and not technically under their control any longer. They also generously consent to let me have my student grant paid directly into my own bank account. This comes to about four pounds a week. That plus my record shop money, now two pounds, and the pound I get from the church will bring my weekly income up to seven pounds. A sum I mistakenly imagine will allow me to live in some comfort.

Of course, the fable about moving in with other students is just that. I mean to find myself a place in the centre of Glasgow; a place of my own; a place where I can do exactly as I please.

It isn't difficult. I move into a bed-sit in St George's Road. Up a close, first floor front. It's not too bad, reasonably big and clean enough. True, the awful second- or third-hand furniture is depressing and the carpet is threadbare. But the bed is surprisingly comfortable, and though the enormous wardrobe swallows the few clothes I have brought with me, and looks at me as if hungry for more, on the whole I think I can just about put up with it. It's a place of my own.

George Cooper moves in with me two days later, and we become a couple.

But not for long. Disenchantment follows swiftly. After our first week together, he is rarely around. When he is, he borrows my clothes, smokes my cigarettes, cadges money (as if I don't have little enough of the latter) and makes love to me slightly absent-mindedly now and then. You might say that his damaged heart wasn't really in it.

And before long, I realise that my feelings for him were as fleeting as his for me. Aside from his fly-by-night behaviour and his incessant sponging, I find he has some less-than-attractive personal habits. And though I don't actually throw him out, I come to enjoy the days when he's away more than the days when he's around. Perhaps Elaine or Angie will pop in for a cup of tea and a gossip. Agnes of God, a strange queen who lives just round the corner, occasionally joins me for a bite to eat.

Small and thin, but with the largest hands and feet I have ever seen, maybe thirty, usually smartly and conservatively dressed, Agnes is religiously inclined. Indeed, she is devout to the point of eccentricity. Though she has no official connection with the church, her outfits frequently feature a vicar-style dog-collar, no doubt home-contrived, and clanking beads and rosaries.

In bizarre contrast, her language is excessively crude and vulgar, and 'fuck' and 'cunt' pepper her conversation as regularly and as thoughtlessly as do 'by the holy Virgin' and 'in the words of Our Lord'. Even in our world of the weird, she is exceptionally odd. But I find her strangely fascinating.

Particularly after she confides one day, over pie and peas, that she is planning to break into show business.

"Aye, Audrey," she says, putting her fork down, "it's aboot time gay people saw somethin' decent at their parties, dae ye know think?"

I manage to convey by a shrug that I may or may not agree. Not that Agnes cares, this is a monologue, not a discussion.

"Ah mean, Ah avoid they gatherings like the plague, masel', they're Satan's work, them, aw sex an' drugs an' strong drink. An' Ah'm no' usually invited anyway, thank the Good Shepherd. But you go tae them, don't ye, Audrey? Been tae a few gay dos, anyway, so Ah've heard?"

I indicate that, yes, I have now and then dared to show my face at some scandalous assemblage or other.

"Aye," says Agnes, "Ah thought so."

She waxes ruminative.

"Aye. Always some queen there, actin' the cunt in drag, singin' some shite, whorin' around the room, showin' off. Is that no' right?"

I nod, remembering Miss Shushie Reid's performance at the New Year party I attended recently.

"It's fuckin' disgustin', by the Blessed Sacrament. Ah mean, Our Saviour made us this way, the way we are, but yon is jist takin' the fuckin' piss. God forgive them, the dirty bastards."

I have to admire Agnes's enlightened attitude to the Creator and all

170

his works.

"So Ah wis thinkin'… Ah mean, Ah enjoy throwin' a wee frock on now an' then as much as the next one."

Yes, I know that Agnes is occasionally to be seen in public in full drag, usually in clothes that are about thirty years out of style, possibly left to her by her mother. She contrives to look very feminine for the most part. Aside from her spade-like hands, and her feet, which are each the size of a small dinghy.

"There's nae herm in it, it's no' a fuckin' sin—Ah mean, look at the Holy Father himself, the cardinals and bishops and aw they cunts— well, that's practically drag, isn't it?"

Well, yes, I can see where she gets her ideas from.

"Aye. So Ah wis thinkin', why not drag, but drag with a difference? Ah mean, a bit of a laugh, nothin' vulgar or suggestive, a song or two, sure, but done respectfully, in good taste."

She nods in satisfaction. "Aye, done wi' a bit of fuckin' reverence."

I say nothing. Indeed, there is nothing to say.

She pauses for breath. "What dae ye think? Can ye see it, Audrey?"

"Oh, yes, Angus," I say.

Yes,'Agnes of God' is 'Angus' in everyday life. Angus Todd.

In fact I can't see it at all, my imagination is just not up to the job. But I would love to see it some time in the future. It sounds in equal parts hysterical and excruciating.

We chat away some more. I am reluctant to leave, as the café is warm and cosy. Glasgow, outside, is still deep in winter. And I simply can't believe the amount of money the gas meter is capable of swallowing to maintain a relatively comfortable temperature.

So I find a way to supplement my income.

I have now been working at my Saturday job in the record shop for two years. During the University summer break, I also work there two or three afternoons in the week. I am well liked in Caldwell's, part of the regular team. And I am trusted, completely. So I set up what comes to be known among my friends as *Audrey's Disco*, or *Audrey's Orders*.

This is a simple scheme. Saturday afternoon, when we are rushed off our feet, one of my cronies will come into the shop, contrive to be served by me, and request one of the current crop of hits. I deliver it in a bag, and take the money. Already inside the bag will be another half-dozen discs. These will be sold off among my crowd at reduced price. I can make a pound or more per bag, and sometimes I can arrange two visits

171

on any given Saturday. This scam helps my household budget a little.

Later, I will devise a much more direct method of profiting from my unfortunate employers.

March 1963.

In March, the streets of Glasgow are dreary, cold and often wet.

In fact Glasgow is fairly colourless all the year round. Although a settlement since prehistoric times, today it is essentially a Victorian city, a product of the Industrial Revolution and the ship-building industry, and its structures, however notable architecturally, are universally masked in a coating of the soot and grime of two hundred years.

But things are changing slowly. Here and there, particularly in the city centre, sand blasting and jet-washing have begun to reveal the underlying character of the buildings. Red and yellow sandstone, terra cotta and rose pink, beige and golden, are the main materials, warm and beautiful when their carapace of muck is removed. George Square and the City Chambers, the seat of local government, gleam with fine quality marble. The Art Gallery in Kelvinside is a striking and lovely building when it is finally made presentable, cleaned, brushed, scraped and manicured. The cinemas and theatres, many of the former in the Art Deco style, and of the latter in Victorian Gothic, have always been comparatively well maintained. The granite-built University buildings, originally grand mansions laid out in terraces and crescents, are pale grey and silver in the winter light. These once private houses were taken over when the original University structure burst its banks and overflowed into the neighbouring streets

And these renovations are beginning to spread out into the suburbs. Even in scorned slums like the Gorbals or Govan, despite some ill-advised demolition and reconstruction, the original buildings are coming to be admired and even sought after. Today, fifty years further on, they command prices that would have seemed inconceivable when they were first built.

Good for shopping, Glasgow city centre. The higher class emporia are in Buchanan Street and Sauchiehall Street, broad and imposing. It is there one finds the grand department stores, *Pettigrew and Stephen, Wylie Hills, McDonalds* and *Tréron et Cie.*, the fashion houses and the best restaurants. Argyle Street to the south, and Renfield Street to the east tend to house the less up-market outlets, selling the mass-produced and lower quality to those who cannot afford to patronise the better class establishments. There, one may shop for *What Every Woman Wants*. If

172

you are wondering what that might be, you have only to step a few yards further west to discover that *Slick Chicks Dig Dicks*. Though it sounds like a sex shop, they actually sell wallpapers and paints.

In the summer months, as in most places, the gloom is less evident. We often have warm and sunny summers. Thanks, I was taught in school, to the tail-end flowings of the Gulf Stream. And a little sunshine manages to make even Glasgow brighter and gayer, in every sense of the word.

But for now, March, 1963, in winter, Glasgow is not gay, it's grey.

Remembering the lads' invitation, I suggest to Angie one evening that she and I should pay a visit to the fair, which is the current attraction at the Kelvin Hall, an enormous venue just opposite the Glasgow Art Gallery and the Western Infirmary. Not at all far, either, from the University, where my attendance has become sporadic since I attained domestic independence. I am regularly seen in the Department of Music, and still appear at my Psychology classes, because I continue to find these subjects interesting. But I doubt I have attended more than half a dozen English lectures, and indeed, have only a hazy idea what the English syllabus is supposed to cover.

In July the fair will be on Glasgow Green, outside in the warm summer nights. But for now, in winter (it's nearly spring, I suppose, though one would never know it) it is held indoors.

The Kelvin Hall is a huge space, covering I don't know how many acres. But the enormous fair fills it completely.

Angie quickly gets over her disappointment that there is no licensed bar—she has no choice, it is a legal requirement. The general mayhem, the possible accidents and emergencies, the damage to life and limb that might result from a crowd of inebriated Glaswegians venturing to sample the Chair o' Planes or the Dive Bomber don't bear thinking about.

Of course there's nothing at all to stop the determined from getting half-cut before they arrive, and not everyone in the enormous crowd is sober. But my sister and I content ourselves with wandering around, intoxicated only by the blaring music, the screams, the smells, and the heady atmosphere of joy tinged with terror.

I give her a nudge. "We need to find the Waltzer. That's the ride Billy said he worked on."

"Oh, yes, that's right," Angie nods. "I remember you said. The Waltzer. Shall we have a look?"

We only have to follow the shrieks. And sure enough, there he is,

Mr Donaldson of the copper hair and the tight jeans. He is currently impressing a group of young girls who are sharing a car. He jumps on the back of it and uses his weight to make it spin harder and faster; then, jumping off, he turns smartly and slaps the back of the car with his palm, and it careens dizzily in the other direction, impossibly quick. While he performs these athletic manoeuvres, the floor of the ride rises and falls regularly, and he balances himself effortlessly on the balls of his feet, like Captain Ahab in the teeth of a force nine gale. The girls screech satisfyingly.

This is a type of spectacle I have seen many times. As a youngster, I remember thrilling to the antics of the rough boys who flirted shamelessly, spun the cars back and forth, and diced with death jumping on and off the ride. How I wished then that I could be one of the girls who drew such attention.

Bill is a professional. His performance in this rather weird mating ritual is extraordinary, and the young ladies he is currently favouring are appropriately impressed. As the ride slows down, and the squeals diminish, he helps them out of the car. They simper and thank him coyly, flirting with him.

God, I hate them, and the effortless way they manage to engage male interest. It seems so unfair that I can't do that.

But common sense intrudes, and I consider my own advantages philosophically. I don't have to have periods, get pregnant, or give birth. And men know that, unlike these young things, if asked The Question, my '*Yes*' won't be hedged round with conditions.

"Come on, Angie," I say, grabbing her hand and pulling her up the steps. "We're going to have some of that." And we tumble into the just-vacated carriage.

Bill takes a moment to recognise me.

"A tanner each, please," he says, before his face breaks into a grin.

"Audrey, yeah? So ye made it? Great!" he yells.

And, "Naw, naw, nae need," he says, holding his palm up, as I proffer a shilling. "Cannae huv ladies payin'."

I'm loving it.

After I introduce Angie to him, he pushes over the metal barrier which is the only thing that is going to stop my sister and I taking to the air when the ride is in full swing. The music starts up—Del Shannon is singing *Don't gild the lily, Lily*—and everything starts into motion.

"OK, girls," says Bill with a smile. "Prepare yerselves for the ride of your life."

Angie decides to essay a sophisticated *bon mot*. "Oh, it'll have to be…" she starts.

And that is as far as she gets; the breath is knocked out of her. For the next three minutes, neither of us is able to produce a sensible word. But we manage, both of us, to shriek our heads off in the approved girly manner. Bill excels himself, and I doubt a car has ever been more spun, twirled and gyrated in the long history of the fairground.

When we eventually descend, cork-legged, Bill comes with us.

As we pass the group of four young girls who had preceded us, they call out to him beseechingly, "Aw, gawn mister, gie's a birl like yon—we're goin' oan again."

I am delighted beyond measure when Bill replies, "Sorry girls, just off oan ma break."

He puts his arm around Angie's shoulder. "Gawn tae share a toffee apple wi' ma girl-friend here."

Angie is close to fainting with delight. The three of us head off laughing and chatting.

'*Wow!*' I think to myself as we thread through the crowds. '*This Bill is a bit special. He doesn't flaunt it, but neither does he hide it. He is utterly comfortable in his own skin.*'

"Just through here," says Bill.

'*Where was my head that day in the El Guero?*' I wonder as we pass the rifle range. '*This is the guy I should have been making a play for, not boring old George.*'

Maybe, I think, it's not too late.

We have a toffee apple each. Bill knows everyone, and there is no payment asked for or offered.

"You still George's girl, Audrey?"

I smile at him guilelessly. "Well, I'm not *Bobby's Girl*, certainly."

Ever the smart mouth.

He laughs, showing white even teeth. "Not *Bobby's Girl*, eh? Nice one, like it."

I consider his question.

"Seriously, Bill, I'm not sure these days. I suppose so."

"Well, good luck wi' Big George, you'll need it."

"Yeah, thanks," I say.

'*Bobby's Girl?*' I think to myself. '*No. But I wouldn't mind being Billy's girl.*'

He turns to my friend.

"And whit aboot you, Angie? You a single girl? Surely not, a doll like

175

you?"

She is so devastated by the compliment, and so enthralled to find this vision is giving her his undivided attention, that she is at first unable to reply coherently.

"I'm between men at the moment," she eventually manages to mumble, blushing to the roots of her hair.

"But I'm open to offers," she goes on, recovering some confidence.

"Open? Whit, yer legs, dae ye mean?" he asks with a smile.

"Oh, Billy, stop, don't be so rude, you're *embarrassing* me," she shrills, giving him a flirtatious little slap on the back of his arm.

He roars with laughter. "Embarrassing you? Wid ye mebbe prefer it if Ah wis *embracing* you?"

He obviously thinks he's quite the wit, this one.

As for Sister Angie, she is in transports of delight at being briefly the centre of attention.

We chat for a few more minutes, and I endeavour to put a little encouraging flirtation into my tone. But it is either not recognised, or deliberately ignored. Perhaps because Bill is so used to being pursued that he simply takes the admiration for granted.

Just before he heads off back to work, he turns to me.

"Drop by the Dodgems and say hello tae wee Brian, Audrey. Ah widnae be surprised if there's another free ride in it for ye, if yer interested."

I realise he enjoys this fairly feeble *double entendre* enormously, as he trots it out regularly. I don't find it particularly funny myself, but his obvious delight in his own wit is engaging.

And with a wink, and a hitch at the belt of his jeans, he is gone. Both Angie and I look after him rather wistfully.

"A fine boy, Audrey," she sighs.

The Dodgems are only a step away, but I don't spot Brian at first. When I do, I realise it's because he looks very different from when we first met. He has lost the parting in his hair—it is now Brylcreemed and quiffed in the approved Glasgow style—and he has adopted something of the manner of the other two—jack-the lad, hard-case, don't-mess-with-me sort of style. But unlike Bill, Brian doesn't really carry it off with much aplomb. And the Waltzer gives far more opportunity for posing and flirting than do the relatively staid Dodgems. The best Brian gets is to stand on the back of a car as it goes around, and disentangle the occasional snarl-up that occurs.

"Want to go on, Ange?" I ask her.

She wrinkles her nose. "No, I don't think so, Audrey. The Dodgems always give me a headache. All these roughs *creshing* into one's back… It's *so* uncamp."

'Uncamp' is her latest expression.

I am of the same mind. But I wave across at Brian, who waves back. He is standing by the cash desk talking to the hard-faced blonde supervisor. Then, as the cars slow down, stop, and disgorge their passengers, he comes over, smiling, hands in pockets.

"Awright, Audrey? Nice tae see ye. You too, hen. Yiz fer a ride?"

I introduce my friend to him. As I look at him I realise that I have over-estimated his age. He is probably no older than I am.

I explain that Angie and I are not huge fans of the Dodgems.

"They're a bit—well—bumpy. And Angie is very sensitive. She's worried about being rear-ended," I say.

"Rear-ended?" He looks at her with a smile. "Ah wid've thought that wis right up your street, Angie."

Then he is convulsed by his own drollness.

Miss Dickinson is not sure whether to be flattered or offended. She settles for something in the middle.

He cajoles us. "Aw, c'moan, Ah'll see yiz are OK, make sure none o' they big rough lads mess wi' ye."

Looking round, I notice one or two big rough lads I would be happy to allow to mess with me, just a little.

"Aw, go on, ye'll be fine, Ah guarantee it, trust me."

He seems particularly anxious that we accept. We've been on the Waltzer, and I understand that if we refuse his offer he will feel slighted. So eventually we agree to have just one go, and the beautiful mouth curves upwards in a smile.

'*Gosh,*' I think, '*in a year or two…*'

"Fine boy, Audrey," whispers Angie yet again, as she struggles in on the passenger side.

When his break comes round, Brian and I head off for a coffee, while Angie, bruised, battered, but unbowed and gagging for a drink, totters back in the direction of the Waltzer, no doubt intending to exercise her charms on the gorgeous Bill some more. This Brian seems considerably more chatty than he was on our first meeting; possibly because he doesn't have the other two around.

"So you an' George are a couple these days? 'S that right? No' seen

177

George for a while, but the word gets around," he says over his shoulder, as he carries two milky coffees over to our table, me trailing behind. "Ah'll be seein' him next Monday, though, we've a wee bit o' business on, the three of us."

When we sit down, I explain that, though George and I had our brief moment, we are no longer really an item. I tell Brian that George's marching orders are already drawn up. I feel very worldly, discussing my love life in this way, just like a real woman.

"He's a waste of time, that George," I say. "He keeps disappearing. And he's forever cadging off me. Then I don't see him for days on end."

"No, you won't," says Brian as he sips his coffee. "He'll be at hame wi' his wife."

I nearly drop my cup.

"Eh?" I say. "His *wife*?"

"Oh aye." He registers my reaction and looks up. "Did ye no' know he wis married? Did he no' tell ye?"

I am at something of a loss. "What? No, no, I didn't. He didn't."

"Oh aye," he repeats, setting down his cup. "Goat two kids, so he has."

I'm not sure why, but when I digest this, I realise that in fact I am not all that surprised. I had already suspected that George was draining his spuds elsewhere now and then.

"He lied to me, then," I mutter.

"Yes. And you're not the first, by a long way. A bit of a devious bugger, our George. Even if he *is* ma cousin."

"Oh?" I say. "You're cousins?"

"Yeah." He stretches out in his chair and takes out a cigarette. "Mind, he's a few years older than me, and a bit of the black sheep. Not that any of us is angels, not by any means. Our family, that is. Always a wee bit on the wrong side of the law."

The originator and manageress of *Audrey's Disco* is hardly in a position to criticise, I reflect. I ask him how old he is.

"Turned eighteen just last month." He puffs on his cigarette.

God, he's younger than me.

He passes me his packet.

"Aye, eighteen now. Going to have to watch it. If Ah get nicked again it's the jail for me this time. Done the Borstal thing already; it's the Bar-L next."

He gives me a light as I absorb all this. Then he returns to his previous topic.

"Aye," he goes on, "None o' ma business, really, but yer better off

178

wi'oot Georgie-boy. You could dae much better for yersel' than that."
I smile a little bitterly.
"Oh—do you think so? Well, I'm afraid the offers are a little thin on the ground right now. Any suggestions?"
I am thinking of red-haired Billy in those skin-tight jeans.
"Yeah. What aboot me?"

This is a whole different experience. "This is ma first time."
I misunderstand. "Your first time—ever?"
He laughs. "No, no. Ma first time wi'—well, you know…"
Yes, I know.
We are in my room. After sending Angie off in the direction of the nearest licensed premises, I hung around till he finished work, and we stopped off for fish and chips on the way back.
He kisses me gently, experimentally. And that is the keynote of the entire thing. I am gentle too, because I know he is shy and inexperienced. He is gentle because it is his nature.
But eventually there comes a point where gentleness gives way to something more urgent.
It was never any part of my plan when starting this memoir to cover sexual encounters in any detail. I lack the skill to paint them convincingly, and find my attempts at such effusions flat and lifeless.
And in truth sex was a secondary matter in the little world that is the subject of this story; of course, we had sex whenever we got the chance, just like every other male of our age.
However, exceptionally, I need to make it clear here, that, up till now, I have never done, or even considered, The Deed itself. It is rather less commonly indulged in than the 'straight' majority realise, and we queens pride ourselves on being expert in other methods of stimulation. The theory being that we leave the basic unimaginative shagging to people (i.e. women) who are not skilled at anything else.
That is not to say that The Deed doesn't happen in our society—it does, regularly. But it is far from the be-all and end-all it is sometimes considered.
However, it becomes clear that Brian is definitely anticipating The Deed. He manages to manoeuvre me into a position where his intention could not be clearer. Philosophically, I accept that the day has come when the gates of the citadel must be breached, and I'm happy that, if it is to occur, it should be at the hands—well, not quite the hands, naturally—of someone as innocent and inexperienced as this Brian.

But... Damn it! It simply won't work. Try as he may, he makes no headway at all. I'm not much help. On the few occasions when, grunting, he appears to gain some momentary advantage, the pain is so excruciating that I screech. To compound the problem, Brian was obviously near the front of the queue when the equipment was handed out, and is thus not really suitable for a debutant like myself.

Eventually he desists, realising that there is little likelihood of success. '*Oh no,*' I think. '*That has killed everything. That's it. He'll go now.*'

And the worst of it is that I really like him, despite his lack of experience, and my own.

But he seems unperturbed. He laughs as he rearranges himself, leans back and lights a cigarette.

"You should have told me you were a virgin. Ah must say, that was a wee bit unexpected."

I am not sure if I should be flattered by this—I suspect not.

"But I wish ye'd said. I'm sorry if I hurt you."

I am reminded yet again of a terrible joke.

Man: *You should've told me ye were a virgin—I wid've taken ma time.*
Girl: *You should've told me ye had time—I wid've have taken ma tights off.*

He dogs out his cigarette, leans over, and kisses me again, this time roughly and passionately.

As we disengage, I say, "There are still plenty of other things we can do, Brian."

I run my hand over his chest, and my tongue suggestively over my lips. I remember seeing Brigitte Bardot do that in a film called *En Cas de Malheur (Love is my Profession)*. With sub-titles.

His eyes nearly pop out of his head. "You mean?—I've never—"

I don't let him finish. "Well, it will depend. I mean, Brian, there's no such thing as a free lunch."

Such an apt turn of phrase under the circumstances; I am really very good.

"I will expect something in return."

He laughs, but with a little frown, unsure.

"Well... OK, you're on, you're on. One good turn... But—you first. You'll have to show me how."

And then? Well, let's just say that by three o'clock in the morning, we are just considering getting some sleep.

Angie is pea green when I tell her.

"Really! How do you *do* it, Audrey? I mean, you're all very well in your way, you have nice hair and lovely eyebrows, but I'm *much* prettier."

I smile. "Ah, Angie, that may be so."

In truth there's not much in it—neither of us is exactly gorgeous.

"But I'm something you're not, something men find irresistible."

"Oh? And what's that?"

"I'm available."

She snorts and chokes into her cup. "You're a *slag*, Audrey Hepburn, do you know that?"

We are coffee-ing in the *El Guero*. Brian's at work.

"Well, keep your hands off the other one, that Billy. He's for me. I'm saving myself for him."

'*Oh really, Miss Dickinson?*' I think. '*Better cash in these savings quickly, if you're hoping to beat me to the draw.*'

Brian is all very well. I really like him. He's easy to get on with, sweet-natured, kind, considerate, sexy, and delightfully naïve. However, we've only recently got together, and I am not thinking of closing off my options just yet. There's a big world out there, and I have bags of wild oats waiting to be sown.

Mr Ever Ready, as I call him for reasons that you can probably figure out, spends all his time with me when he's not at work. A couple of drinks in the evening, a bite to eat. Always bed, never bored.

We decide to have our photograph taken together to memorialise our acquaintance, and head for one of the ubiquitous photo booths. Our double shots come out rather well, although it's a tight squeeze.

Then a wicked, a perverse idea comes into my head. I suggest he emulate the legendary Shug Nelson, and attempt an intimate solo shot.

"For my private album, eh, Brian? Don't worry, I'll keep guard outside," I say, "in case anyone else wants to use the machine."

"What? You mean?..."

I put on my most appealing look. "Yes. Go on—I dare you to."

He is initially unsure. So I apply a little pressure.

"I bet Billy would do it without a second thought."

He still looks uncertain, but I can tell that the idea intrigues him.

"Aye, OK, OK. But mind you keep yer eyes open, Ah'm no' too sure aboot this."

"Aw, go on—what can happen? I'll be right here, it'll be fine."

He reddens slightly.

"And Ah'll need to get masel' a bit—well, you know—ready—in the mood."

"OK. Want a hand?" I ask.

He backs away slightly, worried in case I'm serious.

"No, no, it's fine." He grins. "Ye know me, got a hard-on half the time anyway. Never a problem, that."

He pulls back the curtain, and turns to me. "Now don't wander off, you, keep an eye out."

"Of course."

He goes into the booth and draws the curtain. I hear the clank as he undoes his belt, and when I see his feet disappear from the floor I understand that he has climbed onto the stool provided. There is a long pause—no doubt getting himself 'ready'. Then I hear the clunk of his coins, and a second later see the first flash of the camera.

It's only a moment, but I get briefly distracted by a display of books in the window of the shop next door. I turn back just in time to see an elderly lady in a beaver lamb coat and a feathered hat quickly bend down and peer under the concealing curtain. Presumably reassured at seeing no feet on the floor, she pulls it aside and ducks her head into the booth.

She gives a banshee shriek, and at the same instant the flash goes off. I rush over, hoping I can defuse the situation.

She whips the curtain closed and turns to me, her face a mask of horror.

"My God—did you see what he was doing? That young man? He's a—a *pervert*! I've never seen anything like it in my life."

No, I don't suppose she has—there aren't many like Brian's.

I'm not quite sure how to respond.

She grabs my arm and shakes it. "Did you see? Did you?"

She releases my arm and draws herself up indignantly. "You know what, I've a good mind to call a policeman. Do you think I should? *Somebody* should…"

I start to snigger—I just can't stop myself. She stares at me, realisation dawning.

"Good God—you mean—you're in on this too? Is this some kind of a joke? A student prank?"

She waggles her head from side to side, breathing hard. She fixes me with a gimlet gaze.

"What kind of people *are* you?"

I recover my composure and improvise.

182

"Oh, don't worry, madam, it's all official. He's the service engineer and I'm his assistant. He has to try a variety of poses to be sure the machine is working properly, that's all. We have to get in there together in a minute for the climax, and you can imagine how tricky that's going to be."

As she opens her mouth wide to reply, her upper denture drops down and forward, and hangs over her lower lip. She tries unsuccessfully to suck it in again, and waves an admonitory finger at me.

"I'm going to find a politheman right away," she hisses, still trying vainly to tongue the recalcitrant plastic back into place. "You and your thort thouldn't be allowed on the thtreetth."

I start to speak but she silences me. "Oh yeth, I know what you are. Jutht you wait."

No, I don't think we'll wait.

She strides off uphill towards Sauchiehall Street, her hand to her mouth, looking round her, muttering. "... a thimple pathport photo..."

"Come on Brian," I shout, "time to head for the hills."

He is already emerging from the photo booth, face crimson, rather flustered, and fastening his belt.

"Aw fuck, Ah thought you said you'd keep a look-out?"

"Sorry, she was too quick for me. But we'd better shift, Brian. The old cow has gone to find a policeman."

"Aw, come on," he pleads. "Can we no' wait just a wee minute to see how they've come oot?"

"No, we daren't. Don't want you arrested for an indecent exposure, do we?"

He sighs. "No, I suppose not. Mind, it seems a shame after all that effort."

Just at that second, the strip of photos tumbles from the machine. Brian grabs it, and we run off hand in hand in the opposite direction from our nemesis, towards Argyle Street. Arrived there we pause, and Brian examines his likenesses.

I peer over his shoulder. They have come out pretty well considering the complex contortions involved. Including the last one, with the lady's head and hat edging into the shot. It looks as if she's about to administer a very upper-class blow-job.

"Well, Brian," I say at length, "I never realised how photogenic you are."

He examines them critically. "Aye, Ah am, you're right. They certainly bring out ma best points, Ah think."

He smiles and winks at me. "Come on, let's go for a bite tae eat, eh? Got a wee bit of business on the night wi' the guys, so Ah'll no' be back till late. Don't worry, Ah'll see you aboot ten—the *El Guero*?"

But he isn't there.

It lasted three or four days. Then he vanished.

I can't understand it. Was it something I did, something I said?

I go to the fairground, hoping to see him. If not, then Bill will be around, and may have some news for me.

But Bill is nowhere to be found. And his boss tells me the police have been there just this morning, looking for him.

I realise that there is some serious problem.

A knock on my door. I open it. It is two days since Brian went missing.

Bill comes in. Unusually, he looks unkempt, unshaven and a bit scruffy. He makes a great play of looking over his shoulder, collar of his jacket turned up, and whispering hoarsely. He rather overdoes the '*Glasgow's Most Wanted*' act.

"Close the door, George, close it. Couple o' coppers in the street, gi'ed me a funny look. They're after me, cannae be too careful. Got a cup o' tea?"

I put on the kettle and he paces around.

"Oh, sit down, Billy, for Christ's sake, you're making me nervous."

"Sure, sure. Goat a fag?"

He sits down.

I give him a cigarette, make him a strong cup of tea and seat myself opposite him.

"Right," I say. "I want to hear all about it, whatever it is. Where's Brian?"

He sips his tea, and pulls a face—the tea is hot.

"In the jail, George an' all. Ah only just goat away masel'."

My jaw drops.

"Brian's in prison? What happened? What were you three up to?"

He puffs on his cigarette as though it's his first for days. Maybe it is.

"Och, nothing, jist a wee job, off-licence in Hillhead, piece of cake, should have gone smoothly, don't know whit happened. They two had jist goat inside the door, Brian and George, crowbar job, next thing the bizzies is everywhere. Must have been tipped off."

He blows on his tea.

"Ah wis roon the back wi' the van, fer the fags an' booze an' that.

Dumped the van and jist legged it."

All I can think about is Brian in prison. The rest doesn't bother me. Such minor criminal activities are commonplace in my current circle. George, I couldn't care less about. His wife can visit him. Take the kids, make a day of it.

"I need to go and see Brian," I say. "What do I do, how do I manage it?"

The mechanics of prison visiting are unknown to me.

He sips his tea, and doesn't say anything for a moment.

"Well, come on, Billy. How?"

"Naw, naw, ye cannae dae that. He'd no' want it, you goin' there."

"Why not? I could take him cigarettes, and..."

"Naw, ye don't understand," he interrupts.

He pauses again.

"Look—it's wan thing oot here, on the outside, you knockin' around wi' him. But the jail's different, he'll huv tae keep his wits aboot him, play the hard man. If any of the other cons saw him getting a visit from the likes of you, his life wid be hell in there. Ah'm tellin' ye, he' widnae want it."

I am utterly astonished. What does he mean, *the likes of me*? Am I some kind of freak?

"Nae offence, George. Yer great, ye know Ah like ye. But ye must know whit Ah mean. Oot here, fine, but... And a young lad like Brian—he'll have enough problems in there as it is."

Gradually, the sense of what he is saying penetrates. Brian will have to hide his soft nature in prison, and adopt the standard hard-bitten, don't-give-a-fuck attitude, just to survive. A visit from a flaunting, extravagant queen could dent his reputation beyond repair.

I hesitate. "Well—maybe I could write to him? No, wait. Maybe *Audrey* could?"

"Oh, sure, sure. Nae problem wi' ye writing tae him. Ah wid find oot his prison number for ye, but Ah'm no' goin' tae be around here much longer masel'. Ah'm off doon tae London, in a few days. Too hot fer me roon here."

"So how do I get this number, then?"

"If ye phone the nick they'll gie ye the info, ask for Brian Campbell's number, then ye can write."

I take this in. "OK, thanks."

Then I realise what he has just said.

"You're going to London? But—how will you get there? London, I

185

mean?"

I don't suppose he has any money to speak of.

"Hitch it. Ah'll hitch. Done it afore—nae problem."

We are quiet for a moment. Then he speaks.

"Aboot you writing tae Brian… Don't take this the wrong way, but…"

"Don't take what the wrong way?"

He seems to be having some difficulty.

"This is no' for the likes of you, all this. Mixing wi' scum like some of them in the toon. Boyfriend in the nick, writing, wanting tae visit,"

He pauses and looks around him. "Livin' in this dump."

I'm not sure I like hearing my lovely home described as 'a dump'.

OK, it's a dump.

He sips his tea before continuing. "It's easy tae see yiv goat a bit o' class. University an' aw that. Ah bet yer folks are worried aboot ye. Did they throw ye oot? Whatever it is, ye need tae get oot o' this, ye can dae better."

I am astonished at his penetration.

Well, perhaps that should be re-phrased, to avoid misunderstanding.

I am amazed at his perceptiveness.

I had imagined I was so assimilated that no-one would be readily able to detect any trace of my real background. Sure, people know I am a University student. Now and then. But most of them think of that as just a way of skiving, further education just a means of putting off the evil day when employment or unemployment becomes an issue. Nothing to do with intelligence or education.

How can I explain to this man that it is in this life that I have finally found the meaning of my own?

I don't try.

"It's nice of you to worry about me, Bill, but really—you'd be better off worrying about yourself. I'm fine, honestly. Just going through a bit of a wild phase."

"Och, Ah'm no' worried aboot ye. Ah jist don't understand ye."

I give him another cigarette. He takes it and sprawls back in his chair, knees wide apart. He smiles.

"Well, whatever this phase is, yiv certainly no' held back, Ah must say. Big George… Young Brian…"

He grins, lascivious.

"Fancy going for the full set?"

'*Well, who,*' I think, '*could resist an invitation so delicately framed?*'

Slut? Trollop? Tart?

You might think so, but sorry, I can't agree. Bear in mind, please, that these, my adventures with The Three Stooges, have only just doubled the total number of my sexual partners to date. When I say 'partners', I am not counting the furtive anonymous gropings and fumblings that take place in secret spots. These are meaningless, a kind of assisted self-gratification, nothing more.

I walk with Bill some way along London Road, just to give him a bit of company for a mile or so. We have spent the last three days together. I am oddly reluctant to separate. Something important is going out of my life with him. It's the end of an era, in a small way.

We stop.

"Ye'd better be heading back. It's a bit of a hike."

"Yes. But you know what they say—a girl's best friends are her legs."

The familiar, lewd grin. "Aye, but remember—there comes a time when even the best of friends huv tae part."

He roars with laughter at his own wit.

When it is time to go, he kisses me warmly and wishes me luck. I wish him the same, give him my last pound, and we prepare to separate.

At the last minute, he turns back.

"Come wi' me, if ye like. Ye'd soon find a job doon in London, you, ye're smart. Ah'll be oan the fairgrounds as usual, Battersea, mebbe."

He smiles. "Worst comes, Ah can pit ye oan the game, an' live off yer immoral earnings."

He sees my expression and laughs out loud. "Hold on, hold on—that was a *joke*."

Perhaps it was. But no, I'm not yet ready for a step like that. A toe in the water, a foot, maybe. But not in over my head. One thing at a time.

"Thanks, Billy, but no thanks. I have things going on here. But I hope I'll see you again, sometime."

"Aye, hope so too. Look after yersel'. Give ma best tae Brian when ye write."

"Yes, of course I will, Bill."

I hesitate, suddenly unsure. "If I *do* write, that is."

He looks at me, eyebrows raised. "Oh? Havin' second thoughts, then?"

I shrug. "No, not really, but... Well, maybe."

He nods. "It's up tae you, your choice. But don't go writin' an' raisin' his hopes if yer no' sure. That wid be the worst thing fer him. Think it through first, eh?"

187

I nod. I can see his point. "I will, yes."

"Good."

He looks round, shivering in the thin spring sunlight. "Ah'm off then."

He turns, and is gone.

I am alone. My room is cold and draughty.

I miss Brian. I miss Billy. I even miss George, the bastard.

The *married* bastard.

Billy's little lecture must have had some effect. Three days later, completely broke, I pack my few things, and am back in the bosom of my loving, if somewhat baffled, family.

II. Sittin' in the Back Seat

Keep your mind on your drivin',
Keep your hands on the wheel,
Keep your snoopy eyes on the road ahead.
We're havin' fun, sittin' in the back seat,
Kissin' and a-huggin' with Fred.
The Avons, 1959.

Things at home have settled down a little. I think my absence for even such a short while, four or five weeks, has helped. My parents and I seem to have reached a kind of pact, whereby I am allowed, though not encouraged, to discuss my lifestyle to a limited extent. This, however, does lead to a fair bit of lying, or at least whitewashing. I don't think my dear Mum and Dad are ready for a frank blow-by blow of my latest adventures. I speak vaguely of a boyfriend, a fellow student, whose offer of work has required him to move to London, whence my unexpected homecoming. I say we plan to keep in touch, but no more than that. I hate lying, not for moral reasons, but because it's just so much damned trouble. But what's the alternative?

And I decide that it is high time I took my own behaviour in hand. They are trying, so I must, too. I will go back to regular attendance at my courses, stay indoors at least three or four nights in the week; get involved with some music project at University; try as hard as I can to catch up on my English classes—if I fail the end of term exam, I will have to take the course again, and add a year onto my degree.

I try, I really do. I arrange to go and see my English tutor, who could not be more helpful. I gather I am far from the first student to let the freedom of University life go to his head. He suggests I immediately start attending lectures again; even though I will have fallen behind, he will give me some help, papers to peruse, books to consult. I agree. It all seems possible.

I try, too, to avoid lingering in Glasgow. For a month or so, I am absent from all the usual haunts. I don't make any attempt to contact Brian, who will be serving his sentence by this time, I suppose. I deliberately avoid finding out the details, although I could if I tried, no doubt. I am home on time, stay in for the most part, practise my piano, try to catch up on my English. I continue my job at Caldwell's, and close down *Audrey's Disco*.

But the addiction is simply too strong.

And it is just that, an addiction. It is a drug which I am completely helpless to resist. During my month's abstinence I become irritable and depressed. I lose weight, which is one thing I cannot afford to do—I am barely ten stone wringing wet as it is. I snap at everyone, even my sister, with whom I generally have a warm and close relationship. I am sadly horrible and horribly sad; tense and always close to tears. I smoke like a chimney. All the physical symptoms one would expect of someone trying to give up a drug on which they have become hooked. I am utterly miserable.

Eventually it all becomes too much for me. I feel I may actually have a breakdown. So I modify the terms of the deal I have made with myself. I will continue with classes as far as I can. I will live at home for as long as I can stand it. But if I don't have my freedom, I will simply go mad.

Because, despite my parents' best intentions, and my own, it is quite impossible for me to have any kind of open life at home. I see others of my age, school friends, relatives, involved in relationships, getting engaged, all in the bosom of their families; approved of, following the rules, perfect replicas of their elders. Oh, maybe the odd little straying from the primrose path, but—*"Oh, it's just youthful high spirits, you know boys... Wild oats... Youth must have its fling..."*

The girl-friend or boyfriend is introduced, parents are gratified or horrified as the case may be, family gatherings are enjoyed, parties are planned, rings are exchanged. Perhaps the occasional little unexpected pregnancy may shatter the calm momentarily, but that will all terminate happily at the end of the barrel of a shotgun.

At least that is one catastrophe I won't be visiting on my hapless parents.

I try to imagine what they would think if I turned up on the doorstep with, perhaps, Brian—*"Here, Mum, Dad, this is my boyfriend, Brian. He's just out of prison, small-time stuff, nothing violent, he's a decent lad. And oh, I've slept with both his pals as well, but that was just a bit of fun, and he doesn't mind."*

Desperate, I actually wonder about changing the style of the company I keep. Perhaps in the debutantes' *Royal* I may meet someone respectable enough to come up to standard. But I don't seriously consider this for more than a moment. I have a definite type, the slightly bad lad, rough round the edges, but good at heart; working class, masculine; cool with queens, but not one of them. In the *Royal*, that type is about as rare as a virgin in the Barrowland Ballroom.

There lies the true irony—*There's rosemary, that's for remembrance—*

because the ideal candidate exists. Nicky—despite my resolve, he still features in my imaginings now and then—could pull it off. He has all the necessary qualifications I require, but his enormous charm and likeability would, I am sure, win over anyone. Even my family. But that is never going to happen. He and I are now firmly defined as friends, the barrier that is the hardest to cross.

This situation is impossible.

And so it all starts up again. If anything it's worse than before.

April 1963.

I decide I must have emergency money. I realise that, inevitably, sooner or later I will be off the rails again, away from home. It is simply the only way I can live without suffocating. But next time I don't want to fall into the trap of permanently scraping around for the money to live.

So what should I do? Get a paper round?

No need, the means are already at hand. *Audrey's Disco* is back in business. Through all this turmoil, I am continuously present every Saturday in the record shop. I never miss a day. And I commence what is probably the most shameful scheme (or scam) I have ever devised.

It is often the case that a customer is looking for a record that we do not currently have in stock. The item is placed on order from a wholesaler, and a deposit of one pound is taken. The high end LPs are one pound nineteen shillings and eleven pence, the popular titles one pound thirteen and eleven. Details should then be entered into the order book—name, address and phone number of the customer, including the information that he has paid his deposit. When the record is delivered to the shop, he is telephoned, or contacted by post, and eventually arrives to collect his goods. He then pays the balance of his order, be it nineteen shillings and eleven pence or thirteen shillings and eleven pence.

So even though these odd sums are not the actual price of anything, they are not unusual amounts to be ringing up on the till.

My plan is simple to the point of idiocy. When a customer purchases an LP over the counter, he or she will usually proffer two pound notes. I take them, treat the transaction as if he were collecting and paying the balance of an order, pocket one of the notes, put the other in the till and hand the change to the customer. No-one ever asks for a receipt. The till is correct at the end of the day, and I have a pound in my pocket.

The book is always a mess, no-one really knows who has ordered what, or when, or who took the details, or how much was paid.

My fall-back plan, should I ever be challenged, is to say that I had made an over-ring of a pound earlier and am just correcting it—not the approved way to handle such an error, but hardly a crime.

It is amazing that I don't get caught. But during the entire remaining period of my employment there, I am never once queried. I am trusted, and Saturday afternoons are chaotic.

It is beyond easy.

Initially I am careful, and only go for two or maybe three pounds a day. Later, I will become greedier. My profits are carefully stashed away in a place that only I know.

By now, still trying desperately to keep all my spinning plates in the air, I am back on the scene again.

Among the many conjunctions that take place in our twilight world, there is the occasional commercial one. There are the one or two rough lads who hang around the station on their own, those who are what would now be referred to as 'rent-boys', I suppose. They sell their services fairly blatantly to the aged and desperate, and never mix at all with us, the in-crowd, the camp crowd, the queen-crowd. But there is, too, a limited market for my type, the fresh and youthful beauty. Inevitably there are a few gentlemen who want to indulge with a bright young thing, but can't do so easily, either because of their work or family situation, or their lack of attractive qualities. And whereas certain of we ladies of the town, as I have mentioned, profit indirectly from wealthy older gentlemen in goods and chattels, there are also opportunities for naked cash transactions.

The main 'fixer' for these events is a certain Patrick Calhoun, a short, balding individual (though Pat is only in his twenties) who seems to have this end of the market pretty much sewn up. His only business rival is a mysterious character we call The Bellboy—no-one seems to know his real name—who works at the Charing Cross Hotel, and pimps for their customers, whatever the requirements. He is less successful than Pat, mainly because his own urges get in the way of his business acumen, and if you are being conducted by him to an assignation, he will usually manage to manoeuvre you into a darkened doorway and have at least a little of his wicked way. Since he is young and not at all unattractive, no-one really minds too much, but it's hardly business-like. Angie, always reaching for *le mot juste*, describes him as 'taking a semi-liberty now and then', which covers his behaviour pretty well.

Pat, on the other hand, is a businessman. He is also a popular guy, well-liked by everyone. He has a permanent relationship with another friend of mine, Susan Strasberg, or Peter Grady, one of the nicest queens around. You might assume that two such delightful people were made for each other, to live together in peace and harmony, world without end.

Far from it. Their relationship is relentlessly stormy, and it is rare to see them without one or the other—often both—sporting the trophies of their latest domestic battle. And not just the occasional black eye. Cuts, bruises, scars, bandages, stitches. But it's clear that they are besotted with each other, mad about each other.

"*Aye, mad's the word,*" as Shirley remarked about them one evening long ago, before I knew her or them.

Neither Angie nor I is reluctant to exploit the commercial possibilities of our youth now and then, so the occasional venture into mild flesh-mongering does go on. It never takes more than half an hour or so, the work is light and undemanding, and it pays well.

Pat has a regular client known as 'The Priest', one who has enjoyed the attentions of almost everyone on the scene at one time or another. Certainly, I have obliged him now and then. The Priest is a weird-looking character, always dressed entirely in black. Perhaps fifty, he never speaks a word to anyone except Pat. If favoured, you are shown by the latter to a shabby bedroom in Morrison's Hotel, a cheap, low-class dive in Buchanan Street. You undress and simply stand there in silence, while The Priest sits in a chair nearby, gloomy, glowering, pleasuring himself. It's over in about ten minutes, and pays two pounds. No doubt Pat gets a gratuity as well.

Despite the name, I am pretty certain that this gentleman is no priest. It's just a nickname, surely, because of the way he dresses? But Angie insists that I am wrong.

"Oh yes, Audrey. Definitely. *Shaw-king*, really—I am told he's *ekchewly* a canon."

"A cannon? Then it's high time he was fired."

This conversation is taking place in the *Rapallo*, which is a *real* restaurant, not a snack bar. It's on the corner of Waterloo and Wellington Streets, and serves Italian cuisine (not Spanish, as some people claim to remember. Unless spaghetti bolognese and lasagne have Spanish roots, which I doubt.)

Angie and I have had a bolognese apiece, and she is knocking back a whisky while I am on coffee. We are just chatting fairly aimlessly about this and that. It's a Thursday evening, nothing much doing, pubs were dead, I imagine we'll be going soon.

Indeed, eventually, Angie looks at her watch and yawns.

"Think I'll head for home, Audrey. Had a heavy day at work today, need my beauty sleep. Hope you don't mind."

"Don't mind at all, Ange. I'm a bit tired myself, I'll be going across the road for my bus soon. Just going to have another coffee first."

She stands up and gathers her paraphernalia. Bag, scarf, gloves... She shrugs into her smart trench-coat.

"OK, give me a call at work. Maybe we'll go out for a drink or two on Saturday, if you fancy it."

"Yes, we'll do that. Hope things are a bit livelier at the weekend—there was eff-all doing tonight."

"As you say, Audrey. OK, talk to you soon."

She pats her hair into place, turns and is gone.

I consider leaving, too. I might as well.

"Did I hear you say you fancy another coffee?" comes a voice from behind me.

I turn round. I am sitting at the inside corner of a four-person table. The person who addressed me is in the adjacent row of tables, and our backs are diagonally opposite one another. He is alone.

Thrityish, maybe a little older. Not bad-looking, Thick dark hair, glasses, broad shoulders. That's about all I can register. I've certainly never seen him before; at least, as far as I can remember. And he's rather too old for me. But it's been a boring evening, anything to break the monotony.

"Yes, I wouldn't mind another one," I say.

"Milk, sugar,?" he says as he gets to his feet.

"Espresso, large, two sugars," I reply.

God, he's tall! I am no midget, but this guy must be about six foot three or four. Well built, not fat, bit of a thick neck from behind, but all in all quite presentable. Shame he's not a wee bit younger.

He returns with my coffee, along with one for himself, and sits down opposite me.

He's actually rather handsome, I realise.

"Sorry, I didn't mean to eavesdrop, but I heard you mention you were going to have another coffee. Hope you don't mind me horning in?"

I indicate that I don't. If he heard me say that, he probably overheard most of our earlier conversation too.

"Saw your friend had left and though you might not mind a bit of company. I'm on my own, too."

"I see. Well it's very kind of you, thanks. For the coffee, I mean."

"Oh? Not the company, then?"

"That, too, naturally."

There is a brief silence. I sugar my coffee, stir it, and raise it to my lips.

"Was that your boy-friend?" he says.

At that I narrowly avoid blowing my coffee across the table.

"Good God, no! That was my best friend, Gordon. He's no more than that."

The very idea!

"But… didn't I hear you call him 'Angie'? Isn't that right?"

"Yes," I nod. "He's Gordon, also know as 'Angie'. And I'm George, sometimes Audrey."

"Got it," he says. "Nice. So I suppose you two are—what?— sisters?"

"Oh no! We're not even religious!"

His smile is wide. "Funny. Very funny, Audrey."

"Thank you. Whatever your name is."

"I'm David."

I strongly suspect he is not.

He mentions that he lives in Cambuslang, and I confess to residing in Rutherglen—the two are only a couple of miles apart.

"Drop you off on my way home, if you like," he says "Save you getting the bus. The car's just round the corner."

I fake a frown. "How do I know you're not a sex maniac or a mass murderer?"

He grins. "And how do I know that you're not a mass murderer? If you're a sex maniac, on the other hand, I could probably deal with that!"

I think I blush a bit.

"So do you want that lift?" he says.

"Just a lift?"

"That will be up to you to decide."

"OK. Thanks."

"You'll have to direct me," he says as we arrive in Rutherglen Main Street.

"You can drop me off somewhere nearby. Not sure if I want you knowing where I live."

"Fair enough." He grins. "Being a bit cautious, eh? Don't blame you. Though I assure you, you've nothing to worry about."

"I'll be the judge of that, thanks."

I direct him up Stonelaw Road and get him to stop outside my old school, Rutherglen Academy. I live about five minutes brisk walk away.

He pulls over, but I make no move to get out. I have realised that I actually find him rather attractive.

"We can go on a bit, if you like," I say.

He raises his eyebrows.

"Oh? You know a little local bar that stays open late?"

"No. I was thinking... Maybe a little drive out into the country?"

"OK. Any suggestions?

"Cathkin, maybe?"

Only ten minutes drive, and deserted at this time of night. I have availed myself of its nocturnal tranquillity a time or two in the past.

"You'll have to direct me," he says.

"With pleasure."

When he removes his trousers and underpants I have to catch my breath.

He notices my reaction and grins.

"Brahma, eh?"

To the best of my knowledge, Brahma is the creator god of the Hindu pantheon. I don't remember ever reading that he was also remarkable for his endowment.

"Pardon?"

"A brammer, eh?"

I understand. A 'brammer' is 'a superior specimen of its type', according to the dictionary.

Yes, it's certainly that.

Later, just before he drops me back in Stonelaw Road, he takes two pound notes from his pockets and gives them to me.

"What's that for?" I ask.

He looks away.

"Oh, just a little thank you. You know..."

"It's not necessary."

I have had a good time, and discovered *en route* that he is actually a nice guy.

"Take it, please. I like to pay for my pleasure. And I'm sure you could use it."

Well, that's definitely true.

"OK, if you insist."

I pocket the money.

"Thanks."

"Welcome."

There's brief pause.

"Fancy meeting up again?" he says.

And why not? I have had fun, and made a bit of money into the bargain.

"Sure," I say.

We do, maybe three or four times. In the course of which he tells me that he is married, three children. Oh—and he's in the police force.

But likes to indulge his special tastes now and then. And likes to pay for the privilege. I suppose it makes him feel less guilty, and avoids him having to consider our encounters any kind of a relationship. Just a now-and-then treat that helps him relax. Like a cigarette.

Speaking of which…

I am in Central Station a few weeks later. I have run out of fags, and am essentially broke. And not very happy, as I am by now a confirmed smoker. I have bummed one from Connie, but don't want to get the same reputation as Maggie Wilde, and be despised as a chronic cigarette cadger.

Then I spot Derek crossing the station. Oh yes, he's 'Derek', not David, I know by now.

Saved!

"Hi Derek", I say, crossing his path.

"Oh, hello there. Nice to see you," he says.

And indeed, he seems to mean it.

"I was wondering… Fancy a little drive out somewhere?" I say.

He smiles and shrugs his shoulders.

"Love to. But sorry, can't. I've no money on me."

Damn and blast!

"None at all?"

He puts his hand in his pocket, and takes out some change.

He looks at it.

"Eight bob?" he laughs.

"That'll do," I say hurriedly.

Two packs of fags. And some fun. How bad can it be?

May 1963

I am having lunch with Nicky and Connie Stevens in *The Rainbow Room*, yet another of the cheap restaurants which proliferate in the town centre. Connie can't wait to share her latest news.

"Aye, it's a nice wee place, high time I moved oot the hoose. Me an' Wilma. Whit a laugh it's gonnae be—can ye imagine?—our ain flap!"

I look up from my soup, flavour indeterminate, tasteless but cheap. By now I am used to Connie's idiosyncratic vocabulary.

"I thought Wilma shared her flat with Bridget?"

Connie, also on the soup, bites into her roll, and speaks while she chews.

"Aye, she did, but Bridget's gone back tae London. So Wilma needs somebody tae spit the rent wi' her. Nice wee place in Anderston Cross, three quid a week. Ah'll move in in July, in a crupper o' months."

Nicky spreads some more of something claiming to be pâté on his piece of toast. It looks like meat paste to me. *The Rainbow Room* is not renowned for its cuisine.

"Nice, Connie," he says. "Yer too auld tae be livin' at home. It'll gie ye a chance tae spread yer wings."

"Aye, an' ma legs too," Connie adds indelicately, with a girlish *moue*. "Alec an' me'll be able tae spend some time thegither at last, in privet. It's aboot time, Ah've no' seen him at all for the last fortnight."

I happen to know that Mr Alec McGowan, Connie's 'husband', is currently enjoying two weeks holiday with his mistress, Big Olivia, in the latter's luxury caravan in Saltcoats. I realise this is probably not the best time to mention it.

Nicky puts his knife down. "Oh, Audrey—forgot tae mention it. Beanie's Easter party at the weekend. Saturday night. You're goin', of course, you and Miss Provine?"

"Oh, yes, we're going all right. We've got something planned, I told you," I say. "But I was wondering. Why is it an Easter party? Easter's past. Two weeks ago."

"Aye, but nae point in giving a party when everybody's away. You and Dorothy are both expected, ye know that, obviously. But Bill asked me just last week tae mention it tae ye, just tae be sure yiv no' forgot."

Connie is suddenly on the alert.

"Oh? A party at Beanie's? Ah didnae know—Ah suppose ma invitation's goat lost in the post?"

"Naw, Connie, hen," says Nicky, with a grin. "Sorry, ye're no' invited Ah'm afraid. Yer just too common."

Nicky is being facetious, but Connie is indignant.

"Oh, Ah see. Too commie, am Ah? Well don't be too sure Ah'll no' jist throw on a wee mink stove and turn up on the doorstep."

Nicky laughs again. "Ah widnae advise it Connie. There'll be bouncers on the door tae keep your sort out. Beanie disnae dae things by half."

Connie sniffs. "Well, Ah widnae go there if ye *paid* me, Nicky! Ah'm surprised *you're* goin', Audrey. Widnae huv thought it was your cup of tea at all."

I decide to leave it to Nicky to explain.

"Oh, Beanie widnae consider having a party these days wi'oot Audrey and Dorothy. Plays the piano, Audrey does, beautiful; an' Dorothy'll be entertaining, Ah hear."

Connie sniffs again. "Dorothy Provine? Entertaining? Aye, an' Ah can imagine how!"

But in fact, she can't.

Dorothy and I have been labouring in secret. We have been working on an 'act', and rehearsed it in a rented studio at the Royal College of Music. *Back to the Roaring Twenties*, we call it. Dorothy in full flapper attire, me on the piano. She is sure that, between us, we can do far better than the rather amateurish miming we saw at Beanie's last *soirée*. She has, I discover, an extremely good voice, and the ten minute act we have worked out is well prepared. We can't wait to astonish Beanie's guests, and become the toast of Queen's Park.

I try to explain some of this to Connie, but she is uninterested, and changes the subject.

"This is meant tae be a cheese an' ham omelette—but there's eff-all in it but cheese. It's a bloody library."

Nonetheless, she manages to engulf a large piece. "Anybody seen Shirley recently?" she asks between mouthfuls.

"Naw, no' for ages," replies Nicky. "Off on one of her jaunts, Ah suppose."

"No, I've not seen her for a good while," I say.

Connie examines her plate. "Oh look—a wee bit of ham. Anybody goat a magnetising glass?"

She spears it. "Ah hope she's aw right."

I push my soup aside, unfinished, and pull over the plate containing my salmon salad. Tinned, pink, not even the superior red variety.

"Oh, you know Shirley, Connie—always disappearing for a week or two, then shows up as right as rain."

"Aye," says Connie. "But it's been weeks now. They've goat Wilma up in the brothel these days lookin' after things."

As if conjured up, who comes through the door but the subject of our conversation.

Nicky stands up. "Shirley, good tae see ye. We were just talkin' aboot

199

ye, wonderin' where ye were. Sit down, have a bite tae eat, ma treat."

He resumes his seat. He has finished his pâté, and starts on his 'Vienna steak', otherwise known as a hamburger.

Shirley pulls out a chair, picks up a menu and joins us.

"OK, lassies, Nicky? Saw yiz through the windae. Aye, thanks, Nicky, Ah'll just have a sandwich or something."

Connie has finished her omelette and starts on her chips. "Where huv ye been, Miss Eaton, no' seen ye in ages? Was gettin' a bit worried."

"Aw, no need, no need. Just away on a wee bit of business."

She puts down the menu and looks up. "Aye, order me a ham and cheese sandwich, Nicky, wid ye?"

Nicky does so.

"Well Ah jist hope there's mair ham on it than there wis in ma amulet," carps Connie. "Anyway, nice tae see ye back, Shirley."

"Oh, Ah had tae get back for the weekend—Beanie's Easter party, wouldnae miss it for the world."

Connie looks up. "Ye mean, *you're* goin'?"

Shirley smiles. "Oh, aye, Nicky managed tae wangle me an invitation—never been tae one of Beanie's parties before, lookin' forward tae it."

She looks across the table. "What's the matter, Connie, were ye no' invited?"

She grins a little maliciously "Aw, shame, that…"

The Easter party is, if anything, even better than the New Year party. Many of the same guests, plus a sprinkling of new faces. A good mixture between the debutantes and the lower orders. Angie's invitation must have gone astray—at any rate, she is not there.

Shirley and I spend a lot of the evening together, and she introduces me to a couple of people I have not met. Bongo Betty and Big Anita are, in Shirley's words, '*London queens, these days…*'

"Aye, but we couldnae miss *this*, could we, Jim?" says Anita.

"No way, Joe," replies the other. "Aye, you can take the lassie out of Glasgow, but ye cannae take Glasgow out of the lassie. Jist got the coach up yesterday, back tae our roots, especially for Beanie's do. Shame Welsh Wanda couldnae get the time off work, but Ah'll tell her aw about it when we get back."

I am more than a little fascinated by these two. Though at heart pure Glasgow, they have a veneer of sophistication and worldliness that I admire. London… imagine.

"Have ye met Jungle, Audrey?" Betty asks.

Dorothy and I take to the floor quite late in the evening, and cause, in all modesty, a sensation. Dorothy is the wide-eyed flapper to the life in her beaded and fringed dress, singing her heart out—*Don't Bring Lulu*, her opening number; Charlestoning expertly to a medley of *Your Lips Tell Me No, No (But There's Yes, Yes In Your Eyes)*, *Baby Face*, *Back In Nagasaki*, and *Doin' The Raccoon*; and finishing with a show-stopper, *Hard-hearted Hannah*, during which she vamps outrageously, flirting with the guests, sitting on various knees and generally causing mayhem. She has to repeat the last number, such is the enthusiasm.

Miss Shushie Reid follows us with a repetition of her Marilyn mime, but tonight it sinks like a stone under barely polite applause.

"Fabulous, girls," says Beanie, "fabulous. You're like professionals, you two. Next party's not till New Year's Eve—I'm off tae Tangiers for the summer. So make sure you're there. I'll expect a whole new repertoire, mind..."

Dorothy and I don't for a moment doubt our ability to provide whatever is required.

"Do you not know Simon, Audrey?"

It is Elaine who is asking me.

We have been joined at our table in the *El Guero* by an elderly gentleman I have never seen before.

Elderly? Well, around fifty, I would guess. He is shabbily dressed. Nevertheless one can tell that his clothes were originally of good quality, and he exudes an air of old-world charm and a gentlemanly manner which are at odds with his rather shop-worn general appearance.

"No, I'm sure I would have remembered. Hello, Simon," I say, extending a hand.

He takes it and gently kisses it.

"This is Audrey, Simon."

The gentleman raises his eyebrows and smiles deferentially.

"Oh, Audrey? I see. Well, may I say what a pleasure it is to meet such a charming and lovely young creature."

At first I think this is a joke. Then realise he is perfectly serious.

"Why, thank you kind sir," I respond in kind.

Later, Elaine fills me in on Simon's background.

"Public school, all that, Audrey. He was a doctor or a surgeon when he was younger. In the navy, apparently. But a combined taste for illegal substances and lovely young bodies... Well, let's just say things aren't what they used to be for Simon."

"Shame, he seemed like a nice man, polite, and obviously well-educated. You should take a tip from him Elaine. See how you can end up with drink?"

Elaine frowns.

"Oh, Simon doesn't drink, Audrey. Well, apart from a wee beer now and then. No, it's not that. It was drugs. He used to rob the medicine cabinet on the ship where he worked, or so he told me. Got caught, and struck off, or whatever they call it."

"A dishonourable discharge," I say.

"Aye. Though that sounds more like some kind of a venereal disease."

We are enjoying a coffee in the *El Guero*. Though that statement could stand as a perfect example of the figure of speech known as an oxymoron.

"So what kind of drugs does he take? Morphine, I suppose? Opium?"

"No, no, not these days. He can't afford anything like that. No, what he does is bubble gas through a pint of milk and drinks it."

"Gas? What gas?"

This just seems to be too preposterous to be true.

"Aye, gas. From the gas tap. Ordinary gas, household gas."

"Surely not?"

I will later learn that this odd behaviour is not entirely unknown to a depressed Glaswegian in search of nirvana and short of funds.

"Oh aye, I've seen him do it."

Elaine takes out a double slice of bread and margarine that she has managed to pilfer while the assistant's back was turned.

"I stay round at his place now and then. He's happy to give me a pound for the temporary use of my body. Just once in a while, when he's in funds."

"No, Elaine! How could you? I'm shocked!"

I'm not, not really. As Elaine very well knows.

"Och, it's nothing. He doesn't want much. Just likes to press himself against me and rub away. Not even undressed. Takes about three minutes. I sometimes fall asleep in the middle of it."

Oh dear me, yes! I know this one of old. How well I remember Ginger Hastie's frantic frictions from my youth. Well, he *was* my youth. One of my youths, anyway.

I steal a bit of Elaine's sandwich.

"Frottage. That's what it's called," I say. "Frottage."

"I am perfectly well aware of what it's called Audrey, thank you."

I munch. The bread is stale and the margarine tastes like diesel, but I am hungry.

"But you said 'when he's in funds' Elaine. Poor old man doesn't look as if he as two pennies to rub together. And what about his gas bill?"

"Oh, he makes a wee bit of money now and then. From his medical background."

"Oh?"

"Aye, he helps lassies out if they get into trouble. If you know what I mean."

I do.

"An abortionist?"

"Aye, I suppose so, that's the word."

I swallow the last of the sandwich.

"Well, at least if he gets *you* in the family way, Elaine, you won't have to worry about the consequences."

Elaine smiles. "Oh there's no chance of that. It's true that once in a while he gets a little above himself, and makes a move to loosen my nether garments. But I know how to put a stop to that."

"Oh? How?"

"I put on a commanding tone of voice and call out *'Now now, sailor, you know the rules—no frigging in the rigging!'* And he jumps up and replies, *'Aye aye, captain'*, and salutes. After that he's as good as gold."

"No frigging in the rigging?"

"Old naval expression, Audrey. I doubt you would be familiar with it."

It's around this time that Elaine introduces me to Barry Nelson, brother of the famous Shug, of photo-booth fame.

They couldn't be more unalike. Barry is tall and good-looking, though he is more than a tad over-weight. Unlike the scowling but glamorous Shug—who continues to completely ignore me, despite our shared adventure with Suicide Sal—he is affable, sweet-natured, and, rumour has it, the regular lover of Charlie Sim, Scottish comedian and singer, star of STV's *The One o'Clock Gang*. Barry and I get along well; maybe because there is no sexual tension between us from either side. He's one of the good guys, unlike his devastating brother.

Barry has a small flat in Bonnar Street, just off Dalmarnock Road. He is rarely there, he says; more often, no doubt, he is in the company of his lover, who is a Big Name, and, I imagine, a Big Earner.

"Any time you need a place, for—well, for whatever, really—just ask. Ah'll give you the keys. Just leave them inside when you've done,

Ah've always got a spare set on me."

This is an incredibly useful offer. Having 'a place to go' is a kind of *passe-partout* when most of us live at home with our families. I foresee all sorts of exciting possibilities. Each, of course, contingent on being able to lay hands on Barry at the appropriate moment. I wonder briefly if he might consider letting me have a set of keys permanently, but realise that to ask would be pushing my luck, and might lead to the withdrawal of the original offer. Besides, I wouldn't want to blithely barge my way in and catch him and a friend in a compromising situation.

Barry's flat, and my access to it, will come to have a momentous impact in a few months' time, when my life will at last begin to settle into a pattern.

Less than a year from now it will shatter into fragments completely.

Exam time again. I pass without a problem both Music and Psychology, but fail English. Not good news. My tutor is beyond helpful, and tells me that, since I was obviously unwell at the time of the exam (I wasn't) and since I only failed by a small percentage, I will be allowed to re-sit before the end of June. General relief all round, particularly on the home front, where my lapse is viewed with considerable alarm.

June 1963.
Angie has a boyfriend! At last!

It's a curious thing that, in all the time I've known her, Angie has never, to my knowledge, had a regular man in her life. This is in spite of her constant yearning after this one or that one, her admiring glances and comments, her fantasy dates. I have begun to wonder if she has some problem with sex. Is she a kind of conflicted virgin? I even fixed her up one evening with good-looking Tam McLain, a here-today, gone-tomorrow petty criminal with whom I myself had shared the odd intimate moment. Tam had the hots for Angie, and since at this time I was experimenting briefly with independent living in the company of Mr George Cooper, decided to let them have the use of each other's bodies for an hour or two in my bed-sit. They certainly got as far as the bed—I was just downstairs—but whether they got as far as sitting, I don't know. Certainly Miss Dickinson emerged unconvincingly quickly from the fray—'*Have to catch my train*'—and left.

It was the very least I could do, indeed, it was my social responsibility, to ensure that Tam did not leave unsatisfied.

But Angie is full of news on the Saturday when I visit her place of work in my midday break to see if she wants to lunch with me. I have had a profitable morning at Caldwell's, and offer to treat her.

"Oh, I *cawn't* Audrey, love to, but I *cawn't*."

She takes a deep breath. "You see, I've got a lunch date with my new man. Chinese."

I am a little put out. Surely, if anyone is to be the trend-setter, the one to introduce an oriental flavour to our happy band, it should be me?

"You've got a Chinese boyfriend?"

"No, no, Audrey." She giggles; a little patronisingly, I feel. "Don't be *see-ly*. He's Canadian. The *restaurant* is Chinese."

'*Oh well,*' I think, '*That's all right. I've done Canadian.*'

We stroll along Gordon Street arm in arm.

"He's lovely, really, Audrey. Al, his name is, Al Fraser."

She pronounces his name 'Ell'. I have already noted that today she is in an ecstasy of upper class accent.

"Older gentleman, Audrey, about thirty, *claw-sy*. Canadian."

She is bubbling over with excitement and enthusiasm.

"Yes, you mentioned the 'Canadian' already."

"Well, he's good-looking, and he's *reech*. A big businessman. Everything a *gel* could want. Treats me all the time, anything I fancy."

She smiles smugly. "Even wants to fly me oot—out—to Canada to meet his *femmilee*."

Angie appears to have landed on her feet.

'*Oh God,*' I think, ungenerously, '*if this turns out to be long term, she's going to become unendurable.*'

But I expect that the odd, expenses-paid holiday in Canada could console me. I am already seeing Angie flying off (first class, naturally) to Toronto or Vancouver.

"So when do I get to meet him?" I encourage her, as we round the corner into Renfield Street.

"Oh, soon. *Naow*, if you want, Audrey. Come along. He'll be waiting for me outside the restaurant, just up the road here. Come and say *hello*."

She is in one of her most agreeable moods, smiling and laughing happily.

I am curious, so we continue up Renfield Street, chattering away.

A gentleman is indeed waiting, outside a restaurant called *The Wing Lu*.

"Ah, here you are at last, Gordon—was beginning to think you'd stood me up."

He smiles, bends down and kisses my sister on the cheek.

"As if I *woord*!" Angie shrieks coyly, simpering. "Sorry, Ell, I'm a working girl, remember. Now… I want you to meet my best friend. Audrey, this is Ell. Ell, Audrey."

It sounds as if she is introducing a matador. El Audrey, the toast of Madrid.

"Well, well, great. Hello, er—Audrey, is it? How-de-doo, nice to meet you. Any friend of my little flower, here…"

The little flower wilts becomingly. I get a handshake, not a kiss on the cheek.

"Hello, Al," I respond. "Call me 'George' if you prefer it, I answer to either."

"Just as you please. But I quite like 'Audrey', think it suits you."

Al is at least thirty. He could be forty. Certainly not bad-looking on the whole, he is tall and broad, with blond hair heading towards grey, a wide face and a firm handshake. Chunky, running a little to fat, I note, but, on the whole, quite presentable.

"It's hello and goodbye, I'm afraid," I say. "It's been nice meeting you, Al, but I really must be going, leave you two lovebirds to your lunch."

Angie smiles up at him like a schoolgirl in the throes of her first crush. As I turn to leave, she deigns to look over her shoulder.

"OK, Audrey," she dismisses me. "Call me later, at work."

But Al interposes, hand out.

"No, no, not at all, I wouldn't dream of it. Audrey, please say you'll join us for lunch, my treat. You two can catch up, I've got some paperwork to check over. Please, say you will."

He makes it sound as if a refusal might break his heart.

He looks down at her. "That's OK with you, honey, isn't it?"

"Well, of course, Ell, it's *fa-een* with me, it'll be fun."

Is that sunny smile genuine?

And it is fun. Between Angie's flirtatious giggles and glances, her demurely downcast eyes, her exaggeratedly rounded vowels, her occasional neigh of 'Oh? Did he *ray-ally*?' in response to some of my less edifying remarks, we pass an entertaining hour. I simply cannot resist aping her assumed posh accent, and we both get steadily more and more upper-class till we are well-nigh incomprehensible. I try to throw her by now and then dropping into broad Glaswegian, but she refuses to rise to the bait, and remains resolutely in the la-di-da stratosphere.

Throughout all this, Al continues to smile benignly, order wine for us (beer for him), and explain to us novices the intricacies of the menu.

And the food is delicious. This is my very first experience of Chinese cuisine, and I can't get enough of it. Chicken with *pineapple,* imagine; sweet and sour pork; fried rice. All, to me, wildly exotic. I resolve that, should I ever be lucky enough to meet a man with a few bob, this is where he will wine and dine me. Not that any one of my lovers up till now has ever had the inclination to go beyond fish and chips, let alone the means. But if Angie can find someone like this, anything's possible.

When we leave, both my sister and I are more than a little merry, but pleasantly so. Just as well, as we both have to go back to work.

Then, before we part, Al suddenly says, "Hang on, Gordon, just had a thought—what about that trip through to Edinburgh we talked about—next Saturday, remember?"

"Oh yes, our excursion. What about it, *dawling?*" brays Angie.

"Well, been thinking… Why doesn't George here come along too?"

"Oh, but Ell," Angie squeaks—she has by now attained a pitch which would allow her to communicate directly with bats—"I expect George is *beezee* next Saturday."

She turns on me a brilliant and fixed smile carrying a clear message. "Aren't you, Audrey?"

"No," I say bluntly, even though I know this is certainly not what Angie wants to hear. "Sounds lovely, Al. Thank you. What time?"

"Oh, seven, I think we said," says Al, looking down at her. "Did we say seven, honey?"

Honey thinks we said seven. Or rather, *say-ven.*

"Meet us by the Shell, in the station, George," says Al. "And bring a friend with you if you like. Make a foursome of it."

Angie decides to essay a little irony. "Oh yes, do, Audrey, do. One of your *chawming* boyfriends, perhaps?"

Her expression could ignite asbestos.

She turns to Al. "Audrey here is very popular with the working *clesses.* The funny thing is, not one of them *ekchewlee* work."

"Works," I correct her.

The subtext of all this goes right over Al's head.

"Up the workers, eh? Great people, great," he smiles. "See you both next week then?"

"It's a date," I say.

"*Sew* looking *faw-wird* to it," Angie trills through gritted teeth.

Is it just an innate mischievousness that makes me decide not to invite anyone to accompany me on the trip? Probably. I know Angie will not be happy, and will see me as attempting to compete for Al's attentions. But, though I have no current man in my life, I am not in the least interested in Al myself, and have no intention of trying to alienate his affections. Angie will just have to put up with my presence. Anyway, when we get to Edinburgh, I will leave the two of them alone, and have a scout round by myself. I am unknown in Auld Reekie, and may have an amazing adventure.

So I am on my own when I turn up at the agreed rendezvous at *sayven*, as arranged.

To find that Angie is way ahead of me.

"Audrey, darling, so glad you could make it," she says, kissing me on the cheek, obviously her latest stunt. I am pleased to note that, at least in the accent department, normal service has been resumed.

"Now, Audrey, I know you haven't got a man at the moment, dear, so sad, so I've invited someone along to keep you company. Al and I are going to want some time on our own, and the two of you can go off somewhere and have fun together. Do you know Juliet, by any chance."

I look at the person with Angie. Though we've never been introduced, and he is not a regular face from the town, I have seen this one a few times—this 'Juliet' is a conductor at the SMT garage, and is occasionally on duty on my bus home. Always outrageous, forward and bold, flirting with the passengers, the uniform's hat bent at the sides for a more stylish effect, the standard tie replaced with a thin ribbon knotted at the collar, the shirt clanking with badges and paraphernalia. The passengers are entranced, and 'Juliet' is full of wisecracks and one-liners. A real character, who brightens up everyone's journey. In person tall, well-built, twenties, and handsome. But the attractive man is all but submerged under the outrageous queen.

'*Hm—that's a pity*,' I think, on one level. But hey, to each his own.

We greet each other.

"Hi, Audrey," he says. "I'm Juliet Prowse. Whoever *she* was."

"*Is*, Juliet, whoever she *is*. She's a *star*, dear, as you should know," says an indignant Angie. "*Can-Can* with Sinatra, *G.I. Blues* with Elvis, what more do you want?"

"Disnae matter tae me. Ah never picked the name, you did." He turns towards me. "Ma real name's Steve Hudson—maybe ye should be callin' me 'Rock', eh?"

The accompanying wink confirms that this is blatantly said for comic effect.

"Rock Hudson? As if! Come on, Juliet, you're more outrageous than I am," says Angie, ruffled.

"Yes. And that's saying something," I contribute.

Of course, we know rather more about Mr Rock Hudson nowadays than we did in 1963.

"Right—all ready?" Al hurries over. "The car's parked in Bothwell Street. The sooner we get away, the sooner we get there."

And off we troop.

Naturally, Angie and Al are in front, and Juliet and I in the back. That's fine with me. It means these two can hold hands when Al is not changing gear, while Juliet and I can enjoy a gossip.

I like this new person a lot. He's warm, friendly and amusing. It looks as if we are going to be friends. As we make our way through the grey suburbs of Glasgow, we chatter away.

"I love that wee tie you wear with your uniform." I say. "Wish I could find something like it, something different to wear around the town."

"Ye want one? Ye can have as many as ye like, got hundreds. African Violet? Royal Blue? Scarlet O' Hara? Maureen O' Hara? Just ask, Ah'll get them for you."

"Well…" I ponder.

"OK—don't decide. One of each, consider it done."

I relax back in my seat, thinking, '*What a nice person. This should be a fun evening.*'

I am already seeing Juliet and I taking Edinburgh by storm.

However, I am a little surprised when I feel behind me a rather solid arm, tight round my shoulders. It feels a bit odd at first. But it also feels rather nice; companionable, cosy. We are going to be friends, it seems.

I snuggle in just a little bit.

The next moment, a mouth is on mine in a greedy kiss. My first reaction is to feel shocked and surprised. My second is to realise how good it feels. My third is to return the kiss with an equal fervour.

And this is no sisterly peck. I have never been kissed so well and so thoroughly in my life, and it is wonderful, wet, tongue-laden, exciting. It is not long before our arms are wrapped round each other and we are busy. It's what used to be called *heavy petting*; it never really becomes *sex*. Though where the one stops and the other starts might be a nice point to debate.

"*Tootsie-trade!*" I think.

I remember being warned about that despised commingling of the

209

pseudo-sexes, that crossing of barriers, that breaking of taboos.

'*Well, if this is what it's like, I'm all for it.*'

There is no question that this Juliet is entirely happy to be taking the active rôle; and taking it better and more effectively than most of the conquests I've made up till now. Juliet's Rock Hudson side is definitely to the fore. The passionate clinch goes on and on.

Opening my eyes for a second, I glimpse Angie's astonished expression in the mirror.

"Oh my God! Audrey, I'm *shawked*! You, my sister, locked in a lesbian embrace? And enjoying it! Oh, how can you, Audrey, before my very eyes!"

"Behind your very back, actually," I say, surfacing momentarily.

"Shut up, Angie," growls Juliet, by now unmistakeably Rock in every sense of the word.

The thought crosses my mind that this Juliet may just possibly be acting under orders, Angie safeguarding her property. Anyway, as my head swims, and I sink even deeper into that embrace, I realise that, either way, I don't really care. This goes on all the way to Edinburgh.

Once arrived there, we park in Rose Street, and then obediently start out on a round of the local gay hot spots. Throughout the evening Angie remains permanently attached to Al as if some bold Edinburgh bitch might be about to lassoo him and carry him off. The latter certainly doesn't seem to object to this possessive attitude, he remains as affable and good-natured as ever. Endearments are exchanged, little smiles and winks pass between them and there is a deal of discrete hand-holding going on. It's all fairly nauseating.

But in truth, to me their lovey-dovey antics are of secondary importance. It is the fourth member of our little troupe who has the bulk of my attention.

In Paddy's Bar, Juliet and I spend the entire time catching each other's eye, both of us trapped in urgent lust. Our knees press together under the table so hard that I am sure I will have a bruise tomorrow. It's a delightful torture to have to wait for the journey back to continue.

At some point, Angie returns to our table from the toilet. I notice she has been touching up her mascara, and deluging herself in *White Shoulders*, the perfume she is currently favouring.

As she squeezes in next to Al, she whispers, "Really, Audrey, I'm astonished at you. A woman of your quality and taste. You were saying to me only the other day that you wished you could meet a well-to-do fellow like my Al. Well, you're never going to get there like that, yielding to a common bus conductress."

As soon as we are inside the car for the journey home, we are climbing all over one another once again. Between our sounds of passion, we are made thoroughly aware of Angie's heartfelt disapproval.

"Really!" she intones regularly. "Tut-tut!" now and then. Even, "Disgusting!" on one occasion. We have to stop for a second or two each time to stifle our giggles.

With immaculate timing, just as we reach George Square, Glasgow, matters come to a head, and things finally spill over the edge. And, oh dear me, we are both in a bit of a mess, and are going to need an intimate freshen-up as soon as possible.

And that's it. We do run into one another occasionally, Juliet and I, and I get the ties I had asked for. But it never happens again.

And neither it should. It was just one of fate's little gifts, a mad moment, a consolation prize for all the shit and rubbish life usually throws at you.

At the end of June, I re-sit my English exam, and wonder of wonders, manage to pass. I scrape through, just. Never mind. A pass is a pass.So all is well, for now, in that quarter. And the summer stretches ahead of me, endless. I am full-time at the record shop for two months, so my secret nest egg will increase by leaps and bounds. Things at home are a little less troubled.

The real, the famous, Summer of Love will not take place until 1967. I don't know it yet, but 1963 is going to be *my* summer of love. But there will be a month or two of showers and cloud before the sun comes out.

12. Dreamin'

Dreamin' I'm always dreamin'.
Dreamin' love will be mine.
Searchin', I'm always searchin'.
Hopin' some day I'll find...
Johnny Burnette, 1960

July 1963.

Why can't I find a man? Where's my dream lover?

I can't believe it. Not only does Angie continue to bask in the attentions of Mr Al Fraser (although there is as yet no sign of the promised airline ticket, tee-hee), but Elaine has a new boyfriend. What's the matter with me? How come I am still single? I've just celebrated my nineteenth birthday, but for all the difference it has made, it might as well have been my ninth.

I'm at the Modern Homes Exhibition in the Kelvin Hall—Caldwell's has a stand there, and I am earning some overtime, Thursday evening, six till nine. In the background, Carole King is singing *It Might As Well Rain Until September*.

'*Yes, Carole,*' I think as I listen, '*it might as well.*'

The record comes to an end. I'm in the mood for oldies, so I put on Brian Hyland singing *Don't Dilly Dally, Sally*. A little lump comes to my throat as I remember the last time I heard it. Months ago, at the Kelvin Hall, on the Waltzer with Angie.

I wonder how Billy is faring in London? I wonder, not for the first time, if I should write to Brian in prison? That business now seems so long ago. But it is in fact just a few months since I had every eligible bachelor in Glasgow at my feet.

What went wrong? Why can't I get a man? The world is rotten.

I decide to revenge myself on the rotten world by plundering Caldwell's takings even more vigorously.

Yes, Elaine is now part of a couple. Little Joe is the man in question. Elaine seems to have an endless supply of acquaintances with whom she has shared prison lodgings in the past, and Joe is the latest in this long line.

And Joe is a darling. Nothing special to look at, short and skinny, with a bit of fluff on his upper lip pretending to be a moustache, he is about twenty-three. But he has a handsome face, and the sweetest nature

212

imaginable. He is the most tractable of people, and Elaine rules him with a rod of iron, which seems to suit him.

And he is 'Little Joe' because he is on the small side, about five feet six.

"Well, Audrey," Elaine confides, "he'll never replace Donnie in my heart..."

She pauses, lost in reminiscence. Donnie is a figure from Elaine's distant past, one she still carries a torch for. Specifically because, in her own words, he is the owner and proprietor of '*a chopper tae his knees*'.

"But Joe's good tae me," she goes on. "Looks after me, so—why not? And it gets Tony the Geek off ma back, me bein' a married woman these days."

She casts a sidelong glance in the direction of a small figure over by the bookstall.

"He's been pestering me for ages, Tony, dying to get his leg over. And believe it or not, I was just on the point of giving in to him, in desperation—Ah mean it's been a while since Ah had a bit of excitement in that department myself, and a woman has her needs. Then, hallelujah, Joe showed up."

She shudders.

"Aye, Tony the Geek. Thank God I waited. Just imagine—a woman's most precious gift thrown away on that one."

Poor Tony the Geek is permanently doomed to celibacy, it seems. Like Mental Gillian, forever waiting for the date who never shows up, Tony is a quasi-permanent habitué of the station. No more than five feet four, stocky build, round face, with the strongest glasses I've ever seen on anyone. He is forever trying to score with one queen or another. As far as I know, unsuccessfully. Harmless enough; in fact quite agreeable to chat to. But not a young girl's idea of romance.

Elaine takes a half-smoked dog-end from her pocket.

"Mind, Audrey, they *do* say he's hung like a donkey, that wee Tony. Maybe so. But if he wis offering me a ride on the beach, I think I'd settle for the donkey."

Elaine and Little Joe are both residents of *The Popular Hotel*. Little Joe is as unemployed as Elaine, and, I would imagine, about as unemployable.

"Oh aye, Audrey, and on weekends we take the Bridal Suite, Joe and me. Have to pay a wee bit more, but it's worth every penny."

For a moment I am taken in. "What? The Bridal Suite? In *The Pop*?"

Elaine laughs. "No, no, come on, Miss Hepburn, are you daft? It's just a double room, that's all. They only have half a dozen. Joe and me have one reserved for Friday and Saturday. Take in a bottle or two."

She lights up her cigarette. "Oh—another thing. Did Ah tell you? Ah've got a job!"

Truly, this is a day of wonders.

"A job? You?"

This is about the last thing I ever expected to hear.

"Aye. Don't look so surprised, Miss Hepburn—I *have* worked, now and then. Never for very long, sure, but the dole office gets the hump if ye don't manage tae find something once in a while."

"I see—so what is this job?"

"Well—dae ye know Mary Pickford?"

"Oh, yes."

Indeed I do. Mary Pickford is a wizened little queen well into her sixties, who only occasionally shows her face around the town. She is a foul-mouthed, bad-tempered and ill-natured old harridan, and nobody's favourite. I seem to recall that she works in the Central Hotel kitchens.

"Well, she's taken me on, Mary has. Ah'll be a kind of assistant."

"Assistant what? Cook?"

I can't somehow see Elaine as the Glaswegian Fanny Craddock.

"No, no, pearl-diving. Tae start with, anyway."

"Pearl-diving?"

"You know—washing up. Horrible job, Ah hope they supply Marigolds. But maybe I can move on tae something a wee bit more glamorous before too long. Then I can ask Mary tae get Joe a job there too. And when we've got some money saved up, we'll look for a wee room, or even a flat thegither."

I am so pleased that Elaine seems to be on the point of getting her life in order at last.

"Well, I wish you luck, good for you. Hope it all works out. And mind you stay off the drink—well, as much as you can, you hear me?"

She laughs. "Well, Ah'll dae ma best, but ye know Miss Stewart, Audrey. Me getting a job at all is a miracle on its own, ye mustn't expect too much."

"Come in, Audrey, come in! Great tae see you. Nothing much going on right now, afternoon is the quiet time. But—ye never know. The unpredictable thing aboot this business is—well—that it's unpredictable. Cup of tea?"

Shirley ushers me through the front door of the famous brothel, her place of employment since we first met. It's on two floors of a building on the corner of Elmbank Street and Sauchiehall Street, over the ultra-respectable Lyon's Book Shop. I have had an open invitation for a long time but am only now taking advantage of it.

"Yes, love a cup, Shirley, thanks."

"Coming right up. Milk and sugar? Fine. Now—come in and meet the girls. The customers' saloon is just this way."

I follow her into a large, shabbily decorated room, and take in the picture.

I have been expecting a scene straight from the harem, envisioning negligée-clad odalisques reclining voluptuously on divans and *chaises longues*, flimsily attired houris flaunting décolletage in every direction. I have anticipated the tinkling of rose-water fountains, and imagined the air blue with the redolence of scented cigarettes. But apart from the fug of stale smoke, the reality is very different.

Four girls are sitting around on the down-at-heel sofas and worn armchairs. One is painting her nails; one is reading a magazine; one is screwing rollers into her hair; a fourth appears to be asleep, mouth agape, snoring gently.

I am somewhat disappointed when I realise that this is not the oriental fantasy of *Scheherazade*, it's the gritty reality of *The Threepenny Opera*.

"Right, lassies," Shirley enthuses. "Ah want ye tae meet Audrey, a good friend of mine, and a lovely Glasgow actress. Ah don't know if you've met her before?"

I smile, and say, "Hello, girls."

The nail stylist and the hair-dresser return my salutation languidly.

"Now," continues Shirley, "these are Linda and Margaret."

Linda is small and pretty with short dark hair, while Margaret is a taller redhead, who looks rather as Shirley herself might look if she were in drag.

"That's Big Marion over on the couch there…"

I recognise this last—she was Wilma's dance partner when Angie and I made our one and only visit to *Betty's Bar*.

Marion looks up from her magazine, smiles warmly and says, "Hi Audrey, nice tae see ye again."

Shirley completes the introductions by kicking the somnolent one none too gently on the leg.

"And sleeping beauty here,"—the eyes fly open—"this is Jessie, the lazy hoor."

Jessie shakes her head vigorously from side to side, presumably to clear it.

"Jessie—meet Audrey, Audrey Hepburn, that is."

"Oh, sorry, Shirley, Ah must hiv nodded off, had a few drinks last night. Is it a punter? Is it ma turn?"

This Jessie has just about the deepest voice I have ever heard, male or female. For a second I wonder… But no, Jessie certainly appears to be the genuine article, though she does look a little like Mick Jagger.

"Naw, naw, ye daft cow. Naw, this is ma friend Audrey, she's come for a wee visit tae see how the other half lives."

Jessie looks up at me, yawns indelicately, and stretches out a hand.

"Oh, hello, Audrey," she growls, *basso profundo*. I shake her hand, feeling slightly awkward.

Suddenly, there is a ring at the doorbell, and it is action stations.

"OK, now quick, lassies, quick, big smiles, pose—oh fer fuck's sake, Linda, ye could *try* tae look just a *wee* bit interested, couldn't you? Get these nails dried, and you, Margaret, put that hair-dryer away. And fer Christ's sake, stop *yawning*, Jessie."

And Shirley heads off into the hall.

The girls, side by side, assume what I take to be their professional postures, which, even to my inexperienced eye, look something less than alluring. I wonder if I should make myself scarce?

I look at Marion interrogatively. "Should I…?"

"No, no need, Audrey. The way business has been goin' the day, it'll probably be *you* the guy chooses, no' one of us. Ah just hope yer up for it."

And all four laugh appreciatively.

We hear Shirley chattering away as she heads back through the hall with the visitor. Anticipation rises.

And is dashed to the floor when we realise that the new arrival is not some dollar-laden sheik. No, it's only Wilma, in female, or at least, highly ambiguous, attire.

We pass a pleasant hour or two, and it is gradually borne in on me that these are really just a group of very ordinary girls in a rather extraordinary profession. They certainly don't in any way match up to my expectations of how business ladies should look or behave.

A few seedy looking gentlemen come and go—one for Linda and one for Marion, regulars apparently. And two others who specifically ask for Jessie.

"Well," I say to Shirley quietly, as Jessie slouches gracelessly out of the room for the second time, "despite appearances, that Jessie must have something a bit special."

Shirley agrees. "Aye, she's very popular. Ah don't understand it at all, masel'. Unless it's just that some men have a fascination wi' the retarded."

Margaret scoffs. "Naw, it's no' that. They know she's that stupit she sometimes forgets tae ask fer the money."

None of these encounters takes more than fifteen minutes. Wilma recounts a story of a client she has entertained from time to time, one whose particular obsession is to slice off her stockings and suspenders with a razor blade. This sounds rather risky to me, although Wilma speaks of the matter with total unconcern. She is, it appears, in some demand among customers whose requirements are a little specialised.

Later, Marion offers to back-comb my hair, which is fairly long by now, and fashions it into a heavily lacquered helmet.

"Lovely hair ye have, Audrey, and that style really suits you."

I look in the mirror, and realise that, were the opportunity to masquerade *en travesti* once again to arise, I would not have to concern myself with headscarves. Maybe I'll do some shopping, just in case. I can certainly afford it these days.

"Fabulous, Audrey," both Wilma and Shirley agree. But I don't quite have the courage to leave the premises thus coiffed, and, slightly regretfully, I brush the back-combing and spray out of my hair.

"Oh afore ye go, Audrey," says Wilma, "let me write doon ma address for ye. Come round an' see the flat sometime—Connie's due tae move in with me in a week or two, so pop round and we'll have a girly afternoon."

I remember Connie mentioning that she was hoping to share Wilma's flat at some stage, and while the latter writes down the address, I make my farewells to these unlikely ladies of the night.

As Shirley sees me to the door, the bell rings yet again.

"There you are, Shirley, another client. Not been a bad afternoon, all in all, has it?"

"No, no, okay for a Wednesday."

She opens the door, and I see a rather nice-looking young man on the step.

'*Gosh*,' I think, '*Why would this guy have to pay someone for sex? Lucky girl, whoever gets him.*'

I hope it's not yawning Jessie, this one deserves better. I mutter my opinion to Shirley.

She laughs. "Oh no, Audrey, this is not a client. This is Rob, my new boyfriend, he's from Auchtertool, don't ye love it? Wis over there on a wee bit of business last week and picked him up at a cattle show."

Shirley's leisure activities are obviously even more varied than I had suspected.

She pulls the door wide.

"Come in, Rob—Audrey here is just leaving. Go in and sit down and I'll put the kettle on."

Her boyfriend?

In all the time I've known her, I have *never* known Shirley to have a boy-friend. I had assumed that she simply wasn't particularly interested in that side of things. But it seems I was wrong.

Another happy couple.

What's wrong with me? It's so unfair!

I walk down Sauchiehall Street in a decidedly piqued mood.

And it gets worse.

Angie is bursting with news when we meet up in the *Strand* at the weekend.

"Well—it's sorted at last, Audrey. I've been pestering and pestering him about it, and now it's all organised. Tickets bought, flights booked, the lot. Just have to dig out my *pessport*."

It's been a long day at Caldwell's. I yawn. "What are you talking about, Ange?"

"Oh come on, Audrey, wake up. The trip—the trip to Canada, me and Ell. It's finally *heppening*. We fly out on the twenty-sixth, a Friday, from Prestwick to Toronto, to spend some time with his *femmilee*. Then on to Vancouver for the second week—Ell has relatives there too—and then back here. Isn't it exciting?"

I should be pleased for her. I *am* pleased for her. But I'm also jealous. Oh, not of Al—he doesn't interest me in the least. But my single state is beginning to really irk me, especially with all this conjugal bliss in the air. Angie and Al—Shirley and Rob—Elaine and Joe.

All I need to hear is that Connie has finally ensnared Alec McGowan.

Angie however, is completely unaware of my thoughts.

"Oh dear—I'm going to need some new clothes. But I can probably help myself to a couple of shirts from the shop, if I'm careful."

Angie has much the same cavalier attitude to her employers as do I.

She suddenly remembers something, and digs in her pocket.

"Oh, by the way Audrey, I got these for you; consider them a birthday present, since I forgot your birthday. Emerald, they are, just your colour."

I take the little box from her and open it. They are huge green glass carbuncles, and I *never* wear cufflinks, but it's the thought, I suppose.

"Thanks, Angie, they're super."

"Thought you'd like them—you should wear green more often with your red hair."

"Auburn hair."

"Yes, sorry. Now," she goes on, irrepressible, "*say* you'll come shopping with me next week and help me choose a couple of items."

I really can't be bothered, but I suppose…

"Please, Audrey, I value your opinion," she wheedles.

"Of course I will, Angie."

I hope I sound more enthusiastic than I feel.

I am sitting in the *El Guero* on a wet afternoon, alone, bored, making a coffee last as long as I can, when a troupe of my friends makes an entrance. Along with long-faced Kay Starr and bespectacled Vivien Leigh is Lena Horne, a queen I know only slightly, and another one I don't recognise at all. Behind these four trails Vivien's boyfriend—oh yes, yet another happy couple. I can't for the moment remember the guy's name.

"Audrey!" cries Vivien, waving, "We'll come over and sit with you, dear, keep the seats."

Since I am currently the only customer in the restaurant, it seems unlikely that they will have to compete for my company. But I am pleased to see them—although Kay Starr is a dispiriting companion, always complaining about something or other, Vivien is gentle and kind-natured, and the other one, Lena, is good fun, always full of wit and wisecracks. The fourth of this merry throng is a mystery. Tall, young and notably good-looking, he is at first very quiet and restrained.

'*A new face on the scene,*' I think to myself.

Vivien's rather unprepossessing boyfriend, whose name continues to elude me, pays for their teas and coffees—Glasgow queens always seem to be permanently broke—and they head towards my table.

"You remember Russ, Audrey? My other half?" says Vivien, pulling out the chair opposite mine.

Of course. Russell, known as Russ. A pleasant enough guy, although on the beefy side, maybe thirty, he sits down next to me, with Lena facing him. Poor Kay Starr has to sit at an adjoining table, along with the unknown one, which naturally evokes a flood of complaints delivered in her customary whining tones.

"Have you met Jackie Kennedy, Audrey?" asks Vivien. "Sitting with Kay there—she's a new face in town."

Ah, yes, as I suspected. I reach over and shake hands with the newcomer, who seems pleasant enough on the surface.

"This is Audrey Hepburn, Jackie, a big Glasgow star. Come on, make your curtsey."

Unexpectedly, that's exactly what she does, getting up and sweeping a reverence to the floor with considerable aplomb.

"You can't start training these new girls too soon, I always find, don't you agree, Audrey?"

I say nothing, somewhat taken aback by the extravagant gesture.

"Mind you," Jackie says, sitting down, "it should really be you who curtseys tae *me*, Audrey. Yer a big Hollywood star, sure, but Ah'm the First Lady of the USA, the president's wife."

I am not too sure whether this is meant to be funny or not. She certainly sounds deadly serious, but that of itself doesn't mean anything. I decide to let it pass for the moment.

"Christ, this coffee is stone cold, and as for the sandwich—it must have been made a week ago," complains Kay. "And how come it's always *me* who gets left out of the table, and has tae sit wi' this yin?"

"Ye should consider yersel' honoured, Kay," says Jackie with a sniff and a tight little smile. "Ah'm the next thing tae Royalty in this toon."

There are a few queens around who appear to take their *noms de guerre* totally seriously. That is to say that they adopt their given rôle in a realistic way, living the part in their conversation and their behaviour. All slightly mental, in my opinion.

But this one definitely needs putting down a bit. She has altogether too much to say for a new face.

"Royalty, Jackie? Hardly that," I say, after taking a sip of my coffee. "I suppose you've yet to meet The Queen Mother, or the Duchess of York?"

"Well…"

I don't let her finish. She is beginning to irritate me.

"And the Kennedys and the Bouviers—your own family, Jackie— are *nouveaux riches* parvenus, not an ounce of real class among them. American pseudo-aristocracy, that's all."

"Well," she says, after a moment, "yer entitled to your opinion, but it's money that counts these days, no' class, as you call it."

"Yes, money, as you say. There you are, condemned in your own words, Miss Kennedy. And…"

"It's *Mrs* Kennedy, actually."

"…just like your namesake, you give your origins away every time you open your mouth."

What is threatening to escalate into a full-scale bitch-fest is interrupted hastily by Vivien.

"You'll not have heard the news, Audrey. You know Miss Horne here, of course, Lena Horne? Well, it's her mother."

I turn my back on the Kennedy creature. "Oh?"

Vivien pulls a folded newspaper from her pocket and turns to an inside page. "Here—have a look at that."

She passes it across, and I take the paper. I examine the headline. *Meet Mabel The Miracle Maker*, it reads.

I learn that a certain Mrs Mabel Dryesdale was one day carrying a bag of rubbish to the communal midden when an astonishing revelation occurred. Peering into the half-full bin, she was apparently able to make out the face and figure of the Virgin Mary, formed by the decomposing rubbish already in the receptacle. According to the article, a lengthy conversation ensued between the Virgin and the widow, and finally the Blessed Mother graciously suggested that Mrs Dryesdale might like to take a quick photograph of her before getting on with her household chores. Mabel obediently rushed off to get the family Box Brownie, stopping for a moment *en route* to telephone the local newspaper, and the resulting snap forms the centrepiece of the article.

Try as I may, turning the page this way and that way, I am quite unable to force the image to resemble anything except a bin-load of wet and soggy debris. But the article reports that good Catholic God-botherers now regularly flock to Anniesland Cross to bow their heads at the midden cum shrine.

Unfortunately, between the original sighting and the arrival of the newspaper people, the bin men had called, and, despite Mabel's protests, and threats to throw herself under the wheels of their lorry, they had consigned the Queen of Heaven to oblivion and the local tip. So this bizarre photograph remains the only evidence. Not that the believers who throng Mabel's flat apparently require any stringent proof to support their convictions.

I pass the paper back, and look across the table.

"So, what do *you* make of this, Lena?"

Lena stirs her tea, puts down her spoon and give a non-committal shrug.

"She's half-mental, ma maw. She's already seen Christ in the bedroom wallpaper and Saint Michael in the lavvy window. Long chats wi' both of them, apparently. She's what you might call religiously challenged, Mabel."

She sips the tea, and adds, "Mind you, mebbe she's no' that daft. Since this came out, she's giving readings and messages from the saints and the Virgin and the whole gang of heaven. A pound a time, she gets."

She winks. "Maybe she's just got an eye for a racket, ma maw, what dae ye think?"

I think that that is very probable. I also think that the way this Russell is pressing his knee hard against mine is unlikely to be accidental.

After they leave, taking the objectionable Jackie Kennedy with them, I am putting my jacket on when I suddenly espy a piece of green paper peeping out from under my saucer. At first I think it is a pound note, but when I pick it up and unfold it, it is not. No—it says, '*Please call me, any evening after seven. I think you're sexy. Love, Russell.*' Followed by a phone number.

I am amazed at his boldness, this note-passing taking place quite blatantly in front of his established girl-friend, Vivien. What if I had spotted it earlier and read it out?

I certainly won't be calling him—Vivien is a good friend, and I wouldn't be that disloyal. It was she, with her nursing background, who was able to tell me that, for the eradication of crabs, it is not actually necessary to apply the dreaded blue ointment for three consecutive days.

"No," she said, "a single dousing with Lorexane shampoo for nits, well rubbed in, a half-hour wait and a hot bath. That should do the trick."

And it did.

And, apart from any question of sisterly solidarity, the pleasant but overweight Russell doesn't appeal to me in the slightest.

So I tear up the note and throw the pieces in the bin.

'*Still,*' I think, '*it's nice to know I've still got it.*'

Wilma's flat is in rather a rough area, near Anderston Cross, a stone's throw from the docks, her regular hangout. I am admitted by a slatternly woman, hair in rollers, who, it appears, occupies the ground floor flat, while Wilma's bijou residence is on the first floor.

"Ur you fae the council? It's aboot time. Two weeks ago Ah rang aboot the rats," she says when she opens the door, a snotty-nosed infant of one sex or the other clutching her grubby apron.

"Er, no, I'm not—I'm looking for a Mr Mitchell, William Mitchell."

"Oh ur ye? Aye, OK."

She twists her head round and calls up the stairs in a raucous tone. "Wilma—Connie—there's somebody here tae see ye."

She turns back to me. "Up the stairs, first on the right."

"Thank you." I head towards the stairway.

As I look up, Wilma cranes her head, also full of rollers, over the banisters and calls down.

"Yes—who is it?" Rather correct for Wilma. Maybe she too is awaiting a visit from the council about the rats.

"It's me, Audrey," I call back.

"Oh, that's nice. Come up, Audrey, come up."

She shouts over her shoulder, "Connie, it's Audrey, she's come tae visit. Pit the kettle on."

Wilma's flat, consisting of a bedroom, a lounge, and a small kitchen and bathroom, is, to put it no more strongly, a mess. It's not that it's dirty, in fact the little one can see of it appears clean enough. But it is impossible to form any sensible opinion, as every chair, table, bed, in fact every piece of furniture, every corner of carpet, has disappeared under piles of clothing, male and female, make-up, underwear, hair-rollers, toiletries and other less identifiable articles.

"Excuse the mess, Audrey, there's still a load of Bridget's stuff here, nae idea if she wants it back or not."

Wilma clears a space at the table for me by the simple expedient of hurling a bundle of assorted summer wear into a corner. Connie brings in three mugs of tea, and we settle ourselves for a catch-up. I haven't seen Connie for quite some time, and remark that she is looking particularly smart.

"So, Connie," I say, as I settle myself and light up a cigarette, "You've moved in, have you?"

"No, no' yet, Audrey. It'll be in the next couple of weeks, though. Jist here the day tae gie Wilma a haun' tae get the place straight."

Looking round, I can appreciate that Wilma is going to need all the help she can get.

"But," I go on, "I see you've moved your things in already?"

'Surely,' I think, *'this mountain of clothes can't all belong to Wilma?'*

"No, no. Next week all ma stuff will be arriving. Ma husband's bringing it over, ye know, Alec. He offered tae help—goin' tae borrow a wee van, he says. 'Cos Ah've a lot of gear, this an' that, bits of furniture, good quarterly."

'*Furniture? Good God,*' I wonder. '*Where is it all going to go?*'

But Wilma has other things on her mind. She sniffs disparagingly.

"Yer husband? Alec McGowan? Aw c'moan Connie, gie it a rest, how long has this been going on for now? Years. Face it, Alec's nae mair your husband than he's mine."

"Aw, don't start aw that again, Wilma,"

Connie has no doubt heard it all before. But Wilma's not going to leave the subject alone.

"Naw, naw, Connie, Ah'm sick of hearing aw this. Enough's enough. '*Ma husband this, ma husband that.*'"

She bangs down her mug on the table. "C'moan Connie, tell the truth. Yiv never even had Alec in bed, have you? He's Big Olivia's man, no' yours. Face facts, fer Christ's sake. Ah'm no' havin' this day in an' day oot when yer livin' here."

I'm a bit surprised at Wilma. She's usually placid and calm, but today she sounds really pissed off.

Connie's face reddens, and she buries her head in her hands.

Wilma shrugs, and gets to her feet with a heavy sigh.

"More tea, Audrey?"

She turns to her flatmate. "Connie, have a fag, yil feel better. He's no' worth the trouble, Ah'm tellin' ye. Ah had Alec years ago, an' yer missin' nothing."

She picks up our mugs.

"And don't you start greetin', or yil have me at it too. Ah've goat ma ain problems."

She heads off in the direction of the kitchen.

"See whit ye can dae, Audrey, will ye?"

Eventually Connie raises her head and lights the cigarette that Wilma has left on the table next to her.

"What's the matter with Wilma?" I ask, looking after her. "Seems in a bit of a mood, not like her."

"Och, it's the tabloids. She's up one minute, doon the next."

"The tabloids?" Is Wilma being hounded by the press?

Connie flicks her ash on the floor.

"Aye, the pills. She's on these tablets, hormone things, gets them fae somewhere or other. Thon Bridget used tae take them for her tits, tae make them grow."

Yes, I remember now that Wilma had mentioned that she was planning on taking some kind of pills.

"But—OK, it may be a silly question, but—why does Wilma want, er, breasts?"

A bit more cigarette debris drops. Connie looks round for an ashtray.

"She's thinkin' of getting a sex-chair."

"A sex-chair?"

"Oh aye, as soon as she can. But don't say anything tae her, she wants tae keep it quiet for the moment. But she's made her mind up. She's goin' tae become a woman."

Oh. Not a sex-chair, then, but a sex-change. I recently read in the papers about April Ashley, the model and socialite. Her originally male gender was revealed in a detailed article in *The Sunday People*. Speaking of the tabloids.

"Wow," I say, inadequately.

"An' it makes her a bit moody and bad-tempered. Always havin' a go at me for one thing an' another. Ah should know better than tae mention Alec."

"That must be tough, Connie."

She sighs. "Aye, it is, Audrey; got tae watch everything Ah say."

She finally manages to locate an ashtray.

"Mind you, she's right aboot him, Wilma is," she says. "Ah've tried everythin', so Ah have, everything tae get him interested. But nothing works."

She takes a draw on the cigarette. "And Ah love Alec, Ah really do."

And I realise that this is simply the truth. I have always seen the Connie and Alec business, and her fixed obsession with him, as something of a joke, but now realise that to Connie it is far from that.

I remember my own passion for Nicky, equally unrequited, and feel a pang of sympathy. I put my arm round her shoulder as Wilma returns with our tea and joins us at the table.

A youthful voice floats up from outside.

"Wilma, Aunty Wilma? Can ye get us a jeely piece? Ma maw's goat nae bread."

Wilma tuts. "Och, my God, that Betty Boker an' that wean…"

She rises and heads to the window, raises the sash and shouts down. "Awright, Johnny, hang oan a wee minute."

"Whit can Ah dae, Audrey?" Connie asks me. "Whit can Ah dae?"

I take a deep breath.

"OK. Here's what you do. He's helping you move in, you said?"

"Aye."

"Well, when he arrives here with your stuff, make sure you're on your own—Wilma can be out, surely?"

I look at Wilma, who is spreading some jam on a slice of bread. She shrugs, disinterested.

"Offer him a drink, or something. Get a bottle in, get him a bit mellow. Then—just make your move," I finish.

Connie sniffs and raises her eyebrows. "Make ma move? No' very ladylike, that."

If this weren't all so pathetic, I could collapse on the floor at her delicate scruples.

Wilma continues to spread vigorously.

"The hell wi' *ladylike*, Connie," she says. "Jist go for it, don't gie him a chance tae refuse. "

Wilma wraps the slice of bread and jam in a sheet of newspaper, goes to the window, and throws it down into the abyss.

"There ye are, Johnny," she calls.

"Thanks, Aunty Wilma," the little voice floats back.

Wilma slams the window closed and returns to the table shaking her head.

"That Betty Boker—she's nae idea how tae look after her weans. Jist as well Ah'm here tae keep an eye oan them."

She sits down, and gets back to the matter in hand.

"Aye, that's the answer, Connie, smash and grab. Smash him across the mouth and grab his cock. Use yer womanly wiles. He'll be flattered, won't he? We all know whit men are like."

And the three of us bob our heads sagely. Of course we do.

But Connie is still a little unsure. "Dae ye mean Ah should—well—jump on him?"

Wilma smiles nastily. "Well, if that's what it takes, Connie. Anything, so long as it shuts ye up."

She becomes suddenly brisk. "Anyway, he can always say *no*."

"OK." Connie hesitates. "But—if he *does* say *no*, he'll have the story all over the town in nae time. People will talk, Ah'll become the subject of gusset. Whit aboot ma reputation?"

God, she's hard work.

Wilma's smile turns grim. "If Alec objects, ye can tell him that that's fine, end of story. But warn him that if he says a word aboot it tae anyone in the toon an' it gets back tae me, Ah'll batter him senseless masel'. An' so Ah will."

Good for Wilma. The prospect of getting battered by all six foot two of her is, I think, enough to choke off even the most juicy gusset at its source.

Connie is almost back to her usual self. She smiles and blows her nose.

◆

Later, they both come downstairs to see me off. The woman who let me in is standing in the street by the close mouth, smoking, staring into space, the toddler holding her hand.

"Awright, Betty?" says Wilma. "How's the weans?"

"Aw, no' too bad, Wilma. Johnny's givin' me problems as usual, but that's nothing new, is it?"

She takes a draw on her cigarette, and turns to us, shaking her head. "Ah mean, nae herm tae youse queers, Wilma, but if it was wan of ma ain…"

Just at that moment a little figure appears at the far end of the entryway.

"Mammy, look at me, look at me, am Ah pretty?"

Betty turns—indeed, we all do.

"John—Jesus, fer Christ's sake, will ye get that fuckin' dress *aff*," she screeches.

She races towards him, and makes a lunge as he darts back inside the house.

'*Another couple of quid and I'll stop for the day,*' I think, as I take a pound note from the latest customer and ring up the sale on the till.

Caldwell's is busy, and the basement record department is sweltering in the summer heat. A couple of fans behind the counter try their best to create a mild breeze, but with six of us on duty, and probably twenty customers in the shop—some browsing, some listening in the booths and some queuing to be served—their effect is barely noticeable. I give the lady her change, and pass her the bag containing her purchase.

"OK, who's next, please?" I ask. And look up into Angie's tearstained face. Her eyes are bloodshot, and her expression utterly miserable.

"Angie!" I yelp, completely forgetting discretion. "What on earth's the matter? What's happened? Yesterday, wasn't it? You're supposed to be in Canada. Don't tell me you missed the flight?"

"No, nothing like that, George. Listen, can you take a break? I need to talk to you. Please."

The shop is rammed. There is no way I am going to be allowed to disappear just like that for a while, not on a Saturday afternoon, it's out of the question.

Unless I have a very good reason.

Time, then, for a little inventiveness.

I move to the far end of the counter, where Iris, the manageress, is filling in some paperwork.

"Iris," I say, as I reach her, "listen. My friend over there, Gordon, has just heard that his mother has been rushed into hospital. Seems it's serious, she's desperately ill, and he doesn't know what to do. You can see the state of him. Is there any chance—any chance at all—that I could take fifteen minutes just to help him sort things out?"

She's only half-listening, and looks at her watch with a sigh.

"Aye, OK, George, take an early break if you like. Just a quarter of an hour, mind, it's mad in here the day. But, OK, off ye go."

She shouts across, "Marlyse, never mind the racks for now, come and help out on the till."

She follows me back to the counter, and turns to Angie. Her puffy, powdered face assumes a solemn and funereal expression.

"Ah'm sorry for your loss, Gordon," she says as she moves away.

Angie looks after her. "Eh? What is she talking about? Who died? How did she know my name?"

"Never mind that, Ange. Look, head over to the *Renfrew*, the fish and chip shop. I'll be there in a couple of minutes."

I have seven pounds stuffed down my sock and need to relocate it before I venture out on the street. It has been a profitable day.

"OK, thanks. Don't be long now, will you?"

The whole sad story comes out over a coffee. Angie went to the airport, she tells me, and waited for Al to arrive with the tickets. And he didn't turn up.

It's just as simple as that.

I am baffled. "Did you wait—I mean, did you hang around? Maybe he got held up?"

Angie is calmer by now.

"I waited for two hours, Audrey. Till the flight had left. No sign of him. I got a bus back to Glasgow. Had to lie to my people that the flight had been cancelled, you can imagine how embarrassing it would have been to explain the truth. Naturally I hadn't told them the real situation, just that a friend was treating me to the trip."

The ghost of a smile plays on her lips. "Told them my friend was disabled and needed help getting around."

Her expression hardens. "And he *will* be disabled once I get my hands on him."

'*There must be an explanation*,' I think.

"And he's not been in touch?"

She shakes her head.

"But—can't you phone him? Get hold of him somehow? Find out what happened?"

She sips her coffee. "No. I don't have a number for him. He never gave me one, said it was difficult in his position to take calls. He always called *me*, at the shop or at home."

"Where does he work? Maybe you could contact him there? What's his second name, anyway?" I know I've heard it, but can't bring it to mind.

"Fraser. Al Fraser. Of The House of Fraser, you know, the department store chain. Nephew of the big boss, apparently, according to him. Or so he said. I'm beginning to wonder, myself."

"Did you try ringing them, their offices?"

"Yes, of course I did. They've never heard of him."

This is all very mysterious. Can it be that this Al is some kind of weird con man? But if so, what's his game? He spent money freely, treated Angie well, bought her gifts, took her out, even paid for me from time to time when we were together.

It is perhaps a little uncharitable, but I find it hard to believe that all this romancing, all this spending, which has been going on for months now, was done just to allow him to get inside Angie's knickers. Anyway, he could have got there for a couple of quid on a quiet day.

On this subject, one thing is bothering me.

"Angie, sorry, this is a bit personal," I say, "but—did you ever sleep with him, with Al? Ever have sex with him, I mean?"

"Ssh—not so *loud*, Audrey, please."

She looks around and lowers her voice. "Not really. We kissed and cuddled a bit, that was it, and maybe a *leetle* exploration. He said he was old-fashioned, and wanted to save full *een-tee-mee-see* for when we were away together. I wasn't that surprised, to tell you the truth. You know how difficult it can be, getting together privately, when you're living at home."

God, she's naïve. No, stupid. This just doesn't make sense. This man spends money like water—couldn't he have paid for a hotel?

I decide not to broach this with Angie, not for now, as I am relieved to see that she appears to be feeling a little better. The same question obviously hasn't occurred to her, which in itself is strange. All in all this is a very odd situation indeed.

I wonder how I can cheer her up? Maybe a bit of gossip might do the trick?

"Oh, Ange, before I forget, got some interesting news. Wilma is going to be having a sex-change."

Her lip curls. "Oh—turning into a man, is she?"

"No, I meant…"

She looks completely uninterested.

"Oh well, never mind."

That was a waste of time. And anyway, I have to get back to work.

"So—what will you do now, Ange?" I say as I get up.

She shrugs. "What can I do? I've booked two weeks off work, so I won't be going in there. Just stay at home, I suppose. Haven't got the courage to face the world right now."

"Oh, come on—why don't you come out for a drink with me later? Get pissed, maybe, have a laugh, that usually works for you."

She gives a watery smile as she stands up. "A drink? That's about the last thing I need—I would just end up in tears. No, I won't Audrey, thanks. I'm just not up to it at the moment. Maybe I'll pop into your shop one day next week and we can have lunch. I'll call you."

"OK, Ange, if you're sure."

We move towards the door together. Just before we reach it, she stops.

"Thanks, Audrey, I don't know what I would have done if you weren't here."

I put my arm round her shoulders and give her a quick squeeze. Then I head back to work.

Distress and disappointment seem to be par for the course right now. I am passing through Central Station a few days later, when I see Elaine standing with Little Joe by the buffet. Astonishingly, Elaine is in floods of tears. I hurry over.

"What on earth's wrong, Elaine? What's happened? Why are you crying?"

Elaine is too distressed to speak. Her shoulders shake and she is racked with sobs.

"It's that Mary Pickford, the cunt," says Little Joe. "She's been makin' Michael's life hell for the last two weeks while he was workin' over there. Naggin' him, criticisin' him, callin' him all sorts of names. An' Ah only just found out, he never mentioned it till now."

I have never seen Joe look even slightly annoyed before. He's usually equable and smiling. But right now he is furiously angry.

"No!—really? Elaine, I'm so sorry…"

Elaine finally manages to speak. "Oh, Audrey, she was *h-h-horrible.*

I've never really liked her much, but I'd nae idea she could be so horrible. Ah mean, Ah would do a load of the washing up—and *that's* horrible too, Ah can tell you, but I did as Ah was told. Then she would complain that the stuff wasn't washed properly, wasn't clean enough, and make me do it all again. '*Maybe that's the standard* you're *used to, Miss Stewart, but it's certainly not up to mine!*'"

"Cunt!" mutters Joe, looking away.

Elaine stops for a moment to wipe her eyes.

"And Ah had no drink all the time Ah was there, none at all. Ah don't know how I managed to stick it for two weeks. But after today Ah just can't face any more. She told all the other staff Ah was a layabout, naebody wanted me, that Ah was an alcoholic, a scrounger and a waste of space…"

And once more she bursts out in tears. Little Joe puts his arm round her and she buries her face in his shoulder.

His jaw is set.

"That auld bastard, that *bastard*…" he mutters between clenched teeth. "Ah'll *kill* her when Ah see her, so Ah will."

Now Miss Pickford is getting well on in years, and is hardly robust, but Little Joe looks as if he has the punching power of a wet Woodbine.

However he is fiercely angry, and I have to admire his loyalty and determination.

He takes Elaine by the shoulders and holds her at arms' length.

"Why did ye no' tell me, Michael? Why did ye stick it for as long as ye did? Ye should huv walked oot on the first day."

Elaine has managed to regain a bit of control. "Ah did it for you an' me, Joe, tae try tae make things a bit better for the two of us. You know that."

"Aye, but even so—naebody should have tae pit up wi' that kind of thing. Ah wish ye'd said."

Elaine takes out a handkerchief and blows her nose loudly. She seems to have cheered up a little.

"Well, Ah didn't want to give in to her. Anyway, Ah gave it a go, that's all Ah could do. Ah'm just glad to be out of there. Better luck next time, eh?"

She gives a little smile.

"Aye, let's hope so," says Joe.

He smiles back at her. "Anyway, yiv still got me, haven't you? And that's enough for anybody tae cope with. C'moan, let's get a coffee, eh? See ye later, Audrey, OK?"

"Yes, see you soon, Audrey, sorry tae leave ye, but we need a bit of time on our own, it's been a helluva day."

And they head off together, his arm still tight around her shoulder.

I feel more than a little twinge of envy. They are so obviously a couple, and, despite their lack of means, happy together.

Why can't I be that lucky?

I look round. The only other person in the station is Mental Gillian, still waiting for her non-existent knight to arrive and carry her off on his white horse.

'*Well*,' I think, as I look at her, '*things could be worse, I suppose. At least I'm better off than Gillian, poor soul. I mean, I've had my moments, even if the last one was some time ago.*'

I go over to her. "All right, Gillian? No sign of your date yet?"

She looks at me a little confusedly. "No, he's not here yet. He's a bit late, that's all. It's Audrey, isn't it?"

"Yes, that's right."

I prepare to leave. "Anyway, good luck. I'm sure he'll turn up soon, keep your chin up."

As I turn to go, I think I hear her say, "*Oh, it's OK—here he is now. And about time, too.*"

What?

I turn back, to see Tony the Geek bouncing up the Union Street stairs, a small bunch of flowers in his hand.

I have never seen him so smart—his hair is combed, his glasses are clean, he has on a pair of jeans which look new, and he sports a jacket that is verging on trendy.

Surely there is some mistake? Has he ram-raided Angie's window while she's still in purdah?

Gillian calls out girlishly, "So *there* you are, you—what kept you? Ah've been here *hours*."

She is suddenly flirtatious and animated, where she's usually listless and apathetic.

Tony rushes over. "Sorry, Gillian, sorry—got a wee bit held up."

He takes a deep breath, and with all the polish and elegance of the Old South, presents his tribute to his lady. "These are for you."

He hands her the bouquet and Gillian blushes like the virgin she may well be.

And if so, I remember, she's not the only one. Technically, at least.

"Aw, thanks, Tony."

She buries her nose in the flowers, in an ecstasy of adolescent, first-date happiness.

"Awright, Audrey?" Tony asks, looking up. "Don't mind us leavin' you like this, but we've got plans, Gillian and me. We're off tae the pictures. An' Ah'm a bit late, so we've got tae make up for lost time, isn't that right?"

She blushes again. "Aye, that's right Tony."

And off they trot, arm in arm, obviously just as happy as two pigs in a poke.

Everybody is at it, it seems. Everybody except Audrey.

Is there, I wonder, something *wrong* with her?

What will Audrey do next?

The story continues in

ALL ABOUT AUDREY II

'WHAT AUDREY DID NEXT'

ISBN: 9798690274504

Available on Amazon

Players in the Drama

'**AUDREY HEPBURN**' (George Logan), me, the protagonist

The Stars, Boys Who Are Sometimes Girls

'**Angie Dickinson**' (Gordon Curran), my best friend, a conflicted virgin
'**Elaine Stewart**' (Michael Feeley), my dearest friend, a 'devil woman'

'**Shirley Eaton**' (Archie Dunlop), a friend who bears watching
'**Connie Stevens**' (Jim Stephenson), a friend with a speech problem
'**Wilma Flintstone**' (William Mitchell), a friend with an adventurous dress sense
'**Dorothy Provine**' (David Wallace), a friend with an eye for the main chance

'**Sandra Dee**' (Donald Matthews), a friend who is often a girl, but prefers being a boy.
'**Juliet Prowse**' (Steven Hudson), a friend, similarly ambiguous
'**Susan Strasberg**' (Peter Grady), a friend and a sweet-natured person
'**Jackie Kennedy**'(Jack Kennedy), a young person, a bit of an idiot
'**Dame Margot Fonteyn**'(Alan Fountain), a cunning *prima ballerina*
'**Agnes of God**'(Angus Todd), a gravely unbalanced individual, religiously inclined
'**Olivia de Havilland**' (Oliver Havelock), a jolly person, and a dangerous one
'**Mental Gillian**' (Martin Mercado), a simple soul
'**Bridget**' (Cliff Watts), a person of extraordinary boldness

In Supporting Rôles

Maggie Wilde, Brenda Lee, Vivien Leigh, Kay Starr
Ava Gardner, Lana Turner, Vikki Lester, The Duchess of York
The Divine Sarah, The Queen Mother, Lena Horne, Shirley Temple
Julie London, Judy Garland, Mary Pickford, Vera Ellen
Petula Clark, Kay Kendall, Bridie Gallacher, Susan Hayward
Gina Lollobrigida

The Co-Stars, Boys Who Are Always Boys

Andy X, a troubled boyfriend
George Cooper, a temporary boyfriend
Billy Donaldson, barely a boyfriend
Brian Campbell, a significant boyfriend
Bobby Savage, an insignificant boyfriend
Tam McLain, more than a friend, less than a boyfriend
'Nicky' Adam, a close friend, but never, sadly, a boyfriend

Alec McGowan, initially Olivia's boyfriend, later Connie's, a man in some demand
Little Joe, Elaine's boyfriend, a good guy
Pat Calhoun, Susan's boyfriend, a procurer, but another good guy
Al Fraser, Angie's boyfriend, a bad guy
Jake Quinn, nobody's boyfriend, a very bad guy indeed

Barry Nelson, a good man with a useful flat
Shug Nelson, his brother, a bad man with an unusual hobby
Ernest, aka Dirty Mary, a pimp and a black person
Tony the Geek, initially a neglected man, later Mental Gillian's boyfriend

Printed in Great Britain
by Amazon

22861570R00136